"Gary Gindler's *Left Imperialism* is a deep, penetrating book into the essence of such concepts as 'leftism', 'liberalism', and 'conservatism'. Beginning with a needed investigation of terms, Gindler tracks the evolution (or 'evilution') of leftism to its natural end, expansionism and imperialism. Lenin was (as usual) 180 degrees off when he said capitalism had to expand or die when it is leftism that must expand or see its perpetually failed ideas rejected. Not a book to be skimmed."

—**Larry Schweikart,** co-author of *A Patriot's History of the United States*

"What we call the 'left' today is massively different from what it was only a generation ago. Dr. Gindler contends that such transmogrifications are not unusual in the history of the left. The problem traces to a root about which few speak: an elitist utopianism that always begins with an emancipatory aim but retreats to aggressive statism when the ideological utopia fails to happen in the real world. This is how the promise of freedom ends in new levels of imposition and compulsion. This lack of willingness to grapple with the realities of the world around us, as it is in all its imperfections, unleashes terrible things on the world. Dr. Gindler's provocative argument deserves careful attention from anyone who is mystified by the antics of today's left and worried about the next stage of its philosophical evolution."

—**Jeffrey Tucker,** Brownstone Institute

"By connecting the dots from Richelieu to Schwab, Gary Gindler proves there is nothing new under the sun. The enemies of liberty take on many forms from era to era, but their driving impulses and ambitions are always the same —power and control. Nor can you construct a means by which to avoid such anti-human movements, for they are coming to 'fix' humanity whether you like the fix or not. The only way out of these varied tyrannies is through. You must defeat them."

—**Steve Deace,** best-selling author and *The Blaze*

"If you want to win a war, you have to know your enemy. Gary Gindler has done all conservatives a favor with this book. The author clearly and concisely exposes the deliberately obscured Left agenda in all its manifestations, in a clear and very perceptive manner. Left Imperialism is a must-read for all who seek to understand and decisively defeat modern socialism."

—**Trevor Loudon,** author, film-maker, conservative activist

"While Leftists posture as the defenders of the marginalized and downtrodden, Gary Gindler definitively establishes that they're really totalitarians. Their ultimate goal is total power, and absolute control over every aspect of our lives. Gindler shows their efforts to establish this New World Order are well under way. This book is essential reading for all who still believe that there are two opposing factions in American politics today, both of whom respect the idea of government of the people, by the people and for the people. *Left Imperialism* rips the mask off these sinister totalitarians, and we all owe Gary Gindler a debt of gratitude."

— **Robert Spencer,** author, *Empire of God: How the Byzantines Saved Civilization* and *The Sumter Gambit: How the Left Is Trying to Foment a Civil War*

"I am delighted to find books that make me smarter. Gary Gindler's *Left Imperialism* is among the best of those books. A Russian-born physicist, Gindler brings an international perspective to bear on America's everyday problems.

In impressively lucid prose, Gindler walks the reader through the language we use and misuse to describe our politics: left-right, liberal-conservative, nationalist-globalist. Having established a common language, he is better able to explain the 'functional asymmetry' of the leftist imperative—in biological terms, 'left-wingers mainly offer mutations, and right-wingers carry out selections to a high degree'.

A muted optimist, Gindler enjoys the 'grimly comic' spectacle of leftist self-destruction. 'Ultimately, the current incarnation of Left Imperialism will fail', he argues, 'because it has nothing to offer—not in the long run or the short term'. Fasten your seat belts."

—**Jack Cashill,** author, documentary producer, Ph.D. in American studies

"Gary Gindler's book is indispensable for those trying to understand the evil forces and foreign ideologies trying to destroy America today."

—**Roger Stone,** author, political consultant, talk show host

"Imperialism is often portrayed as a problem created by conservatives and the right more generally. Gary Gindler, however, shows us that the political left is deeply immersed in an intellectual, political, and economic imperialism of its own that has done—and continues to do—immense damage to key institutions of Western civilization, ranging from the rule of law to constitutionalism and the market economy. If you want understand much of the cultural and economic wreckage that surrounds us, read this book."

—**Samuel Gregg,** American Institute for Economic Research

"Gindler continues to prove himself an intellectual and uniquely unscrupulous researcher who shouldn't be overlooked."

—**Lucian Wintrich,** Press Chairman of New York Young Republicans Club

Left Imperialism

From Cardinal Richelieu

to Klaus Schwab

PARAGON HOUSE BOOKS ON
SOCIAL AND POLITICAL PHILOSOPHY

Critical Theory and Philosophy—*David Ingram*

Critical Theory: The Essential Readings—*David Ingram and Julia Simon*

Philosophy of Human Rights—*Patrick Hayden*

Global Ethics: Seminal Essays—*Thomas Pogge and Keith Horton*

Global Justice: Seminal Essays—*Thomas Pogge and Darrel Moellendorf*

The Environmental Case for Nuclear Power—*Robert C. Morris*

From Rage to Responsibility: Black Conservative Jesse Lee Peterson
—*Jesse Lee Peterson and Brad Stetson*

The Fraternity: Lawyers and Judges in Collusion—*John Molloy*

Philosophy of the United State: Life, Liberty and the Pursuit of
Happiness—*Gordon L. Anderson*

The Nixon-Kissinger Years: The Reshaping of American Foreign Policy
—*Richard C. Thornton*

The Carter Years: Toward a New Global Order—*Richard C. Thornton*

Corporate Scandals: The Many Faces of Greed—*Kenneth R. Gray*

The Pantanal: Understanding and Preserving the World's Largest
Wetland—*Frederick Swarts*

Postmodern Rationality, Social Criticism, and Religion—*Henry L. Ruf*

Life, Liberty and the Pursuit of Happiness, Version 4.0
—*Gordon L. Anderson*

Rethinking the Oceans: Towards the Blue Economy—*James Alix Michel*

Developmental Politics: How America Can Grow Into a Better Version
of Itself—*Steve McIntosh*

Integral Society: Social Institutions and Individual Sovereignty
—*Gordon L. Anderson*

Left Imperialism: From Cardinal Richelieu to Klaus Schwab
—*Gary Gindler*

Left Imperialism

From Cardinal Richelieu

to Klaus Schwab

Gary Gindler

PARAGON HOUSE

First Edition 2024

Published in the United States by
Paragon House
St. Paul, Minnesota
www.paragonhouse.com

Cover design by Steven Gindler

Library of Congress Cataloging-in-Publication Data

    Names: Gindler, Gary, 1958- author.
    Title: Left imperialism : from Cardinal Richelieu to Klaus Schwab / Gary
      Gindler.
    Description: First edition. | St. Paul, Minnesota : Paragon House, 2024. |
      Includes bibliographical references and index. | Summary: "The Left
      Imperialism is an exercise in a novel field: ideology archaeology. The
      book takes on a spectrum of ideologies from a brand-new evolutionary
      perspective. It presents a novel concept in political philosophy called
      the "individual-state paradigm," which generalizes and extrapolates the
      Right-Left distinction"~ Provided by publisher.
    Identifiers: LCCN 2024000825 (print) | LCCN 2024000826 (ebook) | ISBN
      9781557789501 (paperback) | ISBN 9781610831338 (ebook)
    Subjects: LCSH: Imperialism. | Right and left (Political science) |
      Political science~Philosophy. | Richelieu, Armand Jean du Plessis, duc
      de, 1585-1642~Political and social views. | Schwab, Klaus,
      1938~Political and social views.
    Classification: LCC JC359 .G468 2024 (print) | LCC JC359 (ebook) | DDC
      325/.32~dc23/eng/20240130
    LC record available at https://lccn.loc.gov/2024000825
    LC ebook record available at https://lccn.loc.gov/2024000826

The paper used in this publication meets the minimum requirements of American National Standard for Information Sciences—Permanence of Paper for Printed Library Materials, ANSI standard Z39.48-1992.

Manufactured in the United States of America

10 9 8 7 6 5 4 3 2 1

To the memory of my lovely grandparents—

fervent communists and

passionate anti-communists.

ACKNOWLEDGMENTS

I want to thank my wife, Valentina Gindler, Ph.D., my intellectual and ideological companion, as well as the paramount scrupulous editor, for her years-long encouragement in organizing my voluminous articles and essays under one roof.

I owe a particular debt of gratitude to my friend, Peter Miller. In composing this work, I spent hundreds of hours discussing diverse subjects with Peter, whose intellect could open the door to any prestigious philosophy or political science faculty. Next, my sons, Steven and George, reviewed all early versions of the book. Their insightful comments have sculptured this book toward lower entropy levels.

Some of the book ideas were discussed with radio host Victor Topaller. He is no longer with us but deserves mention because his encyclopedic knowledge stimulated fantastic discourses on air.

Other sympathetic critics provided valuable help and advice. I place on record my appreciation for the help of Richard Casey, Gregory Viola, Leo Korin, Anthony Russoniello, Ronald Cherry, and Mark Belitsky. They were the book's first readers and masterminded myriad corrections and suggestions. Finally, I am incredibly grateful to the curmudgeon editors (especially Drew Belsky) of several remaining conservative outlets, like *American Thinker*, *Human Events*, and *Frontpage Magazine*—to name a few.

Stockholm, NJ
December 2023

CONTENTS

Chapter 4

INTRODUCTION

"Much of the social history of the Western world over the past three decades has involved replacing what worked with what sounded good"

—Thomas Sowell (1993, p. 22).

In *World War II, the Pacific* islands of Melanesia (New Guinea, the Solomon Islands, New Caledonia, Fiji, Vanuatu, and others) hosted a large number of American bases and airports. The Americans used these locations to deliver weapons, supplies, clothing, and other cargo, most of which was dropped by air. A handful of the goods landed among the native inhabitants of these islands, who worked as guides and laborers. It was the first time many had seen canned food, factory-made clothes, or folding knives.

The islanders had no explanation for the origin of these goods except for a miracle. Consequently, they began attributing magical powers to technology like airplanes, runways, tents, and radio towers. Furthermore, they believed that Americans had a special connection with their ancestors and that the products they brought were transported from heaven.

The cessation of the war resulted in no more goods from the civilized world. Wretched natives, now bereft of their heavenly bounty, decided that by replicating the manners and buildings of Americans, they could win over the spirits—and so they embarked on imitating the behavior of the military.

The locals marked "runways" and put together life-size replicas of airplanes from palm trees and straws. They originated "headphones" from halves of coconuts and "guns" from sticks, walked in formation, and painted the inscription "USA." They arranged all this, hoping they could receive the "heavenly gifts" anew. Behold the "cargo cult."

As viewed by the islanders, the Americans did not perform any worthwhile activities: they did not hunt, keep livestock, or grow crops. Accordingly, it is not surprising that the natives stopped working and concentrated on copying the mysterious rituals of the military, who apparently received free food, clothing, tools, and weapons from the skies.

But no airplanes land.

A 1974 speech by Nobel Prize-winning physicist Richard Feynman to students at the California Institute of Technology gave rise to a new application of the term "cargo cult" (Feynman 1974). He called it "cargo cult science"— the research of a plethora of scholars who merely mimic scientific work but produce only pseudoscience. Feynman specifically noted concepts with unrepeatable results in fashionable "sciences," like social sciences, psychoanalysis, parapsychology, extrasensory perception, and distinct Lysenko-like charlatanism.[1] Intellectual integrity demands that we add "global cooling," man-made "global warming," and *Wissenschaftlicher Sozialismus* (Scientific Socialism) to the list.

Pacific aborigines persuaded themselves that their cargo cult practices would work. They reconstructed the planes precisely as they were, and the rituals appeared identical. However, the goods never came. Nevertheless, a large number of researchers, particularly within the Leftist commentariat, also believe that they have performed correctly. The left-wing intellectual milieu fabricates many logical generalizations, modifications, and extensions of the 19th-century Leftist (Marxian and non-Marxian) idea, reified in several countries in the first half of the 20th century. Modern Leftists are notoriously fragmented and multi-branched. They use the same collectivist, politically correct lingo and phraseology; their adherents follow all the party-approved ritual twists and turns.

But no airplanes land.

It is still impossible to reach the workers' paradise, the Socialist Utopia, despite many theoretical and practical efforts. All the known schemes have produced misery, famine, and human suffering—indeed, a great pile of failed states— despite exhibiting every external attribute of genuine science. Since their establishment, all Leftist regimes have lived on borrowed time. Moreover, every time an attempt at Socialism fails, the cult adherents switch

---

1. Trofim Lysenko was a politically correct agriculturalist in the Soviet Union. He openly rejected genetics as "reactionary" and "idealist" while, in an insidious irony, being a director of the Institute of Genetics of the USSR's Academy of Sciences. During the reign of Joseph Stalin, he introduced a theory of ideological agriculture, which led millions of Soviet citizens to starvation. Following Stalin, Mao Zedong adopted bogus Lysenkoist ideas, triggering the Great Chinese Famine of 1959-1962.

into meltdown mode, and quite a few never recover. The aircraft never dropped their baggage, and cult leaders prohibited asking why.[2]

This book will navigate through many ideological entanglements and answer why. As such, this book is an exercise in getting down to the basic principle of Leftism as a counter-Enlightenment ideology. At the same time, the book attempts to construct a coherent ideological foundation of conservatism.

Society is passing through a peculiar phase in world history in which illusions of the longed-for but continuously failing Utopia collide with illusions of an army of bureaucratic dictators in waiting. Nevertheless, these two competing agencies have joined efforts to dismantle the unrivaled mechanism of human progress—freedom.

The modern world is immersed in a pandemonium of "isms," like Liberalism and Conservatism. The labyrinth of present ideological nomenclature is challenging to maneuver, while past ideologies remain uncharted for the most part. In the current imbroglio era of social networks, everybody seems to be an expert in capitalism, racism, feminism, and Fascism. Inject a catchy, sufficiently clickable "ism" into a social network today, and tomorrow, hundreds of experts on the subject will magically appear. However, the ideological identity of many "isms" becomes murkier with every election campaign.

One common feature of ongoing ideological battles is using conventional "isms" in a static manner that disregards the inevitable evolution of the meaning of the terms. This book is dedicated to the dynamical properties of different "isms," keeping in mind the wise words of (underappreciated) philosopher Alexei Losev: "The entire history of humanity is nothing but the evolution of freedom." The evolution of anti-freedom occurs alongside the evolution of freedom, of course. Rephrasing St. Anselm of Canterbury's 11th-century maxim, *fides quaerens intellectum* ("faith seeking understanding"), the time has come in the 21st century for *libertas quaerens intellectum* ("freedom seeking understanding"). The first step in that knowing is the realization that, unlike an orgasm, freedom cannot be simulated.

---

2. Political scientist Ekaterina Shulman has coined the stimulating term "reverse cargo cult" to describe a noticeable phenomenon in many developing countries that blindly and cluelessly copy Western democratic institutions without a clear understanding of how these institutions are supposed to work. When the implanted institutions stop producing results, the blame falls on the original Western institutions.

The same word often describes ideology (interpreted as the systematic contextualization of ideas) and political philosophy. This book is about conservatism and Conservatism with a capital "C," socialism and Socialism with a capital "S," for there is no intelligent and acceptable methodology to separate an ideology from the underlying political philosophy.

At one space-time point,[3] the term "conservative" was equivalent to "liberal," applied to another, quite distant space-time mark. Likewise, the term "liberal" was a synonym for "progressive" in some remote corners of space-time. The term "right" evolved into "conservative," but not universally or simultaneously. None of the classical liberals of the 18th century would shake hands with any of the "liberals" of the 21st century. At present, they are on opposite sides of the barricades.

Consequently, the cacophony of ideological tags around us is confusing, to say the least. The book attempts to clear the fog of a few toxic ideologic entanglements, but it should not be mindlessly applied to policymaking.

The Leftists have found it impossible to logically explain all strains of Leftism, so it must be done for them. There is a vast shelf of books dealing with the many "isms" under the Leftist umbrella, but it would appear that no previous study has been written with axiomatic clarity in mind. Nobody from the Left has drawn particular attention to analyzing the extensive like-minded ideologies as an ensemble. Likewise, nobody from the Right has bothered to offer a coherent delineation between the Right and the Left, tracing all those never-ending evolutionary perturbations over time. Moreover, popular perceptions are unstable, for they are subject to the prevailing political machinery, full of propaganda, misinformation, disinformation, outcry fraud, and never-ending false-flag operations. As a result, nearly all people cannot distinguish between a variety of propaganda techniques and their underlying ideologies. Thus, the book's subject is evolutionary ideology, and the principal objects are left- and right-wing ideologies.

It still eludes some people that Leftist flights to Collectiville are always scheduled but never arrive.

The post-World War II history of the United States is a melancholy story

---

3. This book is written by a physicist who moved into the political philosophy arena. Accordingly, the book has a decent amount of standard physicist terms. Nevertheless, mathematical formulas of politiphysics would make it unpublishable and have been omitted.

of the rise and collapse of American conservatism (as a political philosophy) and American Conservatism with a capital "C" (as an ideology) as well. East Coast-West Coast left-wing political gangrene corrodes the founding principles of America. Things being what they are, many conservatives feel like they inhabit the diaspora in their own country. If the end of the 18th century is hailed as the American Revolution, the post-World War II events must be named, appropriately, Counterrevolution.[4] The Right squadrons had set up the American Revolution; since the beginning of the 21st century, the Left battalions have been trying to march openly on Counterrevolution Avenue. Paraphrasing Orwell's *Ingsoc* (Newspeak for English Socialism), the American Left is rooting for *Amsoc* through de-democratization. Will *Pax Collectiviana* be a proper name for post-American America?

The current American Counterrevolution results from the unusual amalgamation of seemingly conflicting impulses. On the one hand, there are various strains of Collectivism whose postulated ultimate (communist) scheme is abolishing private property and dismantling any form of government, as prescribed by Karl Marx.[5] On the other hand, the United States Federal Government's mighty financial and law enforcement power is an ever-expanding bureaucratic behemoth. The enforcement of the "Woke" ideology by the Left is not new, for even before the public came to be cognizant of the "Woke," the Federal Government had become "Woke."

In terms of complex systems theory, the Federal Government came to be self-aware sometime after World War II. At that time, governments suddenly forgot their roots as society's self-organizing structure designed to protect private property and switched into a pure parasitic mode. Ever since, governments *de facto* (but not *de jure*) abandoned the inventive substance for their being and began living bloodsucking existences at the expense of subdued host societies.

As a product of human society's self-organization, the Federal Government became self-conscious and suddenly grasped that it did have its own focus, independent from the desires of the governed. Subsequently, the Leftist enemies of the United States have domesticated Washington politicians—a good

---

4. Here, we follow Mark R. Levin's terminology. See, for example, Levin (2021, p.1).

5. The irony is that Karl Marx's grave, located on private property in London, charges visitors an entry fee (about one burger **meal** on the McDonald's scale).

deal of the Democrats and a sizable cohort of Republicans. Rephrasing futurist Gray Scott, once government becomes self-aware, the social hierarchy will be transformed so that people are no longer dominant over bureaucrats.

At this juncture, the United States has a *de facto* two-party system: a centrist party counters the socialist party with a post-Marxist at the helm. However, Polichinelle's secret in Washington is that the centrist party has established a symbiotic, mutually beneficial relationship with a socialist party. As a result, the orchestrated collapse of the capitalist economy managed by socialist principles is well on its way. For example, in just a few years after Trump, America transitioned from making America great again (making wealth) to making wealth redistribution great again. That is why, rewording Georges Clemenceau, society is too important to be left to politicians.

The government became self-aware when corporations suddenly figured out that gaining control of the government agencies meant to regulate them is substantially more cost-effective than any products or services they might be spurred by free-market competition to bring forth. In layperson's terms, corporations in bed with the government were proclaimed for centuries as corrupt—that is, until the Left realized the political potential of inserting themselves into the process. So, it is no longer described as corruption; it is labeled a public-private enterprise.

These antagonistic bedfellows—the anti-government Left and the *government-über-alles*—gave rise to their offspring, the "Woke" oligarchs. On the one hand, they partially resemble the "old" oligarchs of the wild capitalism era. On the other hand, they bear a resemblance to the uncompromising Socialist Utopia ideological warriors of the distant past. Leftism's evolution shows that since World War II, its ideological component (or rather the old ideological component) has made a full circle and returned to the old paradigm: political power at any cost. As such, Leftists began their operations based on mafia syndicate tactics.

Obviously, neither force of that malignant pair of tumors has enough strength to bend the country to its liking. The Left could not achieve the desired "redistributive change."[6] Their mission of "spreading the wealth around" needed an enforcement arm. The Federal Government could not

---

6. "Transformative change," also known as "redistributive change," is simply an euphemism for Collectivism.

erect the "Kingdom of the Elite" without an ideological and propaganda arm. Indeed, the Leftists' arch-important propaganda arm was supposed to perpetuate a never-ending illusion of freedom and democracy among citizens.

By now, ideological fighting between the Right and the Left is practically a norm in the majority of countries, contingent on a certain degree of democracy. In the following chapters, we will consider some generalizations to bypass such a limitation. However, in the 21st century, the Left decided not to hide its true intentions and removed all smokescreens for the first time. As a result, the Left demonstrated that they are structurally intolerant, totalitarian, and militant. Exactly why they opted to do so requires independent research; the essential thing is that they have done it. Leftists no longer care about providing the façade of truth or respectability because they have moved on to the next phase—total power at any cost. However, the Left is making new, unexpected political adversaries unprecedentedly. Targeting white men and parents of young schoolchildren does not bode well for the Left—in both political and ideological terms.

In 1944, George Orwell replied to a letter from a reader, Noel Willmett. The subject of the letter exchange was Willmett's argument that Great Britain and the United States, contrary to Orwell's thesis about the rise of totalitarianism, are not moving toward it. In the letter, Orwell wrote that "the intellectuals are more totalitarian in outlook than the common people. On the whole, the English intelligentsia have opposed Hitler, but only at the price of accepting Stalin. Most of them are perfectly ready for dictatorial methods, secret police, systematic falsification of history, etc., so long as they feel that it is on 'our' side" (Orwell 1944a).

In a subsequent newspaper article, Orwell emphasized that "Collectivism leads to concentration camps, leader-worship, and war" (Orwell 1944b). Then, in 1968, Orwell jumped over his "1984" bestseller right into the 21st century. A prophetic visionary, he wrote that "Hitler can say that the Jews started the war, and if he survives that will become official history... [thus] if the sort of world that I am afraid of arrives... two and two could become five if the fuehrer wished it" (Orwell 1968).

Redefining the past—including the destruction of the past—has become a norm nowadays. Ironically, arithmetic turns out to be a target of the modern

Left,[7] too, which project, thank heavens, has nobody of the *Führer*'s caliber behind it at the moment. However, there are many candidates, mainly with an academic background, because pop culture has triggered pop-scientism, a.k.a. scientific charlatanism—sci-char. Thus, society has self-reconfigured itself from the unpredictability of the future to the uncertainty of the past and the unknowingness of the present. Note that both the Left and the Right cannot foretell the future, but the Left complicates matters by making the past unpredictable as well.

The mercenary marriage with Big Government was not the only one, or the most significant one, the Left arranged. Contrary to popular wisdom, modern Leftism's extraordinarily significant accomplishment was not getting Fascists and Communists on the same team; the immensely significant triumph was getting Communist radicals and Islamic radicals on the same team. The overwhelmingly atheist Left had entered a marriage of convenience—with religious forces. And not just Islamic forces: aside from the well-known cozy relationship with Islamic radicals,[8] though it may seem improbable, the Left radicals sneaked an acknowledged communist into the Dalai Lama's position. Besides, a Marxist camouflaged as the Pope is at the helm of the Vatican. That misalliance birthed the ideological chimera—a hybrid ideology composed of different, seemingly incompatible, and non-combinable parts. Moreover, Mohammed's fatalistic teachings are reminiscent of Marx's stoical indoctrinations. As a result, the arrested development of predominantly Muslim vs. non-Muslim countries mirrors the arrested development of socialist countries vs. capitalistic ones.

However, the Left's multi-decade-long, burgeoning strategic alliance with theocratic regimes and groups had peaked. The staunch radical Leftists' shortage in the 21st century means the era of militant Islam and radical Leftism's exchange of tactics and strategies is ending. Instead, the paths of Islamic

---

7. One "Woke" demagogue, entirely devoid of irony, pointed out to me that 2+2 does not always equal 4. Knowing-it-all provided an example, 2+2=11, and victoriously nodded that he operates in base 3, not 10, and that the base 10 is just a racist, white men convention. So, when I asked him to prove (it is straightforward if you know the subject) that the optimal convention should be base e (the base of the natural logarithm), which is close to his base 3, he halted the lovely discussion.

8. The term "Islamofascism," most likely, should be relinquished as it merely instantiates cultural sensationalism; the proper term would be "Islamoleftism."

Imperialism and Left Imperialism are starting to diverge. The Abraham Accords, orchestrated by then-president Trump, signify such divergence.

Despite an assortment of spectacular and undeniable achievements (without question, the singular achievement for the Left so far in a quest for equality is reaching equality between science and charlatanism), all Leftist ideologies are destined to fail due to acute intellectual failure. Nobody crawls under barbed wire from South Korea to North Korea. Nobody floats away on empty Coca-Cola bottles from Miami to Havana. Thousands of people climbed the Berlin Wall from East Berlin to West Berlin, but nobody took the opposite route. Nevertheless, Leftists continue to romanticize backward countries like Venezuela, Cuba, and Iran.[9]

In the meantime, Cuba, North Korea, Venezuela, and, believe it or not, China are proceeding to their inevitable fiasco, recalling the successes of the Soviet Union and the Third Reich from a bygone era. The Soviet Union managed to be first in space, but Leftist ideology eventually drove its economy over the cliff. Likewise, the Third Reich had conquered close to the entirety of Europe, eclipsing Napoleon and Caesar, but under the Leftist ideology at the helm, it managed to lose the war it had laid the groundwork to win.

Nothing suggests that today's redefined Marxism—post-Marxism or trans-Marxism (pun intended)—and redefined non-Marxian Leftism will not meet the same end as the "old" ones, despite a united effort by the transcontinental Left cabal to inflict global ersatz-socialism on the masses. It is impossible to predict how successful the latest pursuit will be, i.e., will it exceed the lifespan of the Soviet Union or not?

Modern Collectivists, in their menopausal stage, offer humanity a false illusion, a simulacrum, a mirage of Utopia instead of Utopia itself, for they

---

9. Passionate executioner and voluptuous mass murderer Che Guevara admired Joseph Stalin and often signed his letters as "Stalin II." Che Guevara was the undisputed darling of the International Left. A Bolivian unit led by Captain Gary Prado Salmon captured and executed him in 1967. The Left, who had a sick love obsession with Che, never forgot and never forgave; they orchestrated the decades-long persecution of Salmon. Finally, he was arrested under the pretext of insurrection against Bolivian ultra-left President Evo Morales, who, 50 years after the fact, in 2017, directly indicted wheelchair-bound General Salmon for the death of Che. All charges against Gary Prado Salmon were eventually dropped, but only after the Leftist government of Evo Morales was toppled and the disgraced ex-president fled the country.

understand perfectly well that Utopia is an unreachable goal, even theoretically. Despite this, Leftists are content for the Collectivist Utopia to stay a highly abstract, unattainable target. The undeniable truth is that the bushmen of Collectiville, located at the center of Socialist Utopia, are outright cargo cultists. They understand that "Utopia is not under the slightest obligation to produce results: its sole function is to allow its devotees to condemn what exists in the name of what does not" (Revel 2009, p. 23). Under left-wing leadership, many Western countries are like a dusty, trampled graveyard of former glory. Many European countries have turned into the curators of the museum of their own history. They view their destiny only from the past, in the past, and by the past; the word "future" no longer exists in their lexicon. As a result of total Leftification, they look directly in front of themselves into the nothingness of their past and nowhere of their future.

One of Socrates' followers, Petrus Ramus, introduced a revolutionary approach he named "freedom to philosophize." In the fifth century BC, Socrates encouraged his disciples to examine established beliefs and concepts until they arrived at a new understanding of the truth. In the middle of the 16th century, Ramus wrote: "Aristotle philosophized with the utmost freedom and, for the sake of the truth, he held views with utter freedom, against the entire tradition of the past, including his teacher Plato" (Ramus [1569] 2006). Unfortunately, in 21st-century America, such views would lead to immediate cancelation, widespread condemnation, ostracism, and warranted loss of tenure. The Leftist mob would definitely try reusing Socrates' cup of poison if it were politically expedient.

Nonetheless, the Collectivist faithful still maintain that the Leftist dogma's wholesale failure does not affect its essential underlying integrity, ostensibly corroborated in endless theoretical articles. These logical constructs sound abstruse but bear a resemblance to "cargo culting."

Unfortunately, that dismal state of affairs will unlikely be resolved anytime soon. Nevertheless, this book is a proposition to fill the void for axiomatic political philosophy, despite the unequivocal fact deduced by Roger Scruton: "People have only a circumscribed interest in truth. But their interest in power is insatiable" (Scruton 2011). Note also that in adequately developed axiomatic political philosophy, there is no room for various neo-prefix labels, like neo-Marxism or neo-conservatism.

"A specter is haunting Europe—the specter of communism." That is the first sentence in the Communist Manifesto, written in 1847. The specter of communism is still lurking somewhere. It is still plotting, but that specter's smelly, decomposing remnants are the only elements that still haunt the world. Marx's idea of using the "oppressed" classes as foot soldiers for the socialist revolution still ripples around the world, albeit in an almost unrecognizable form. However, all trademark Marxist shibboleths no longer work, even if so many deceptions are packed into a single term, "Marxism." The Emperor of the Proletariat still wears clothes, but that is what stinks. The specter of communism has absorbed the terrible smell of millions of innocents killed for the crime of being indifferent to left-wing ideology and has been carrying these miasmas everywhere with him. Some people are still not dissuaded from communism—especially those with Marxism overdose—but most people have ascertained that the defunct ideology is the source of the terrible smell.

Leftists prefer not just to overpower their political adversaries—they want to exterminate them. Not only that, Collectivists practice widespread murder of their adherents and those who would like to be left alone and demonstrate indifference in politics. However, the desiccated hulk of Leftism will come closer to the inevitable accountability phase sooner rather than later. The autopsy of Leftism is long overdue, but every time it is attempted, Leftism resurrects, then reincarnates under a different name and rushes out of the political morgue. While it is out, the Left constantly tries to fit a square peg into a round hole.

That autopsy must begin with the foundations—with why and how Americans think the way they do. When comparing the Old and New Worlds, Margaret Thatcher emphasized that America "has been built upon an idea—the idea of liberty" (Thatcher 1991). Then she offered her famous dictum, "The European nations are not and can never be like this. They are the product of history and not of philosophy" (Ibid). What is this philosophy?

Chapter
1

Battle of the Terms

Ideology is a weaponized form of political philosophy suitable for waging political battles. One example of political philosophy is conservatism. Meanwhile, capital-C Conservatism is an ideology. Also, conservatism is a historical phenomenon. Conservatism is many things. Conservatism exists on all continents—but denotations of "conservatism," in almost all cases, are entirely dissimilar.

Leninism, Stalinism, Maoism, and Fascism are ideologies. A proportion of them is based—directly or indirectly—on Karl Marx's political philosophy. (Note that Marx offered no practical, actionable policy recipes. His treatises were just that—a theory, a political philosophy.) There are non-Marxian left-wing ideologies, like National Socialism, Anarchism, and various strains of Green ideologies. (There is a joke stating that Greens are like watermelons: green outside and red inside.) An analogous situation exists with Conservatism. Although partial and inconsistent, Reaganism, Thatcherism, and Trumpism are examples of ideology and functional implementations of conservatism's political philosophy.

If discourses about political philosophies have the potential to stay within certain scientific norms, unbiased discussions of weaponized derivatives of political philosophies—ideologies—rarely echo polite scientific inquiry. The reason is simple—as time progresses, any ideology sufficiently disconnected from reality transforms into pseudo-religion, which zealously protects its dogmas.

The circumstances here should not be a surprise to the reader. There is a political philosophy called nationalism and an ideology of Nationalism. If nationalism as a political philosophy was essentially the invention of French intellectuals of the 18th century, Nationalism as an ideology in support of overall aspirations was first and foremost deployed during Germany's unification in the 19th century. Ideological Nationalism was so distinctively German that there are serious doubts that the term should ever be applied outside Bismarck's Germany.

Should the world recognize the universal applicability of Germany's history? Of course, one can redefine Nationalism, a case in point, as the premise of putting one nation's interests above all others. However, sharing the same word, in this case, we must not conclude that such "Nationalism" somehow equates to the unification and consolidation of German-speaking land in the 19th century.

There is a political philosophy called nationalism and an ideology of Nationalism.

RIGHT AND LEFT, COMPLIMENTS OF FRANCE

The Right-Left dichotomy is another superb illustration of the perpetual metamorphosis of standard political terms. The definitive essay on the subject, by Marcel Gauchet, demonstrates that after the French Revolution of 1789, soon after being invented, the political terms "right" and "left," for all practical purposes, vanished (Gauchet 1996).

Is there a precise demarcation line between the Left and the Right, the quintessential emblems of political identity, at the moment? Does the United States Federal government's enumerated powers represent a Right or a Left line of thought? What do the 1st and 2nd Amendments to the United States Constitution represent? Right or Left ideas?

There are no answers to these questions if one uses static definitions of the terms. The truth is that in the Right-Left dichotomy saga, over the years, the Left was not on every occasion the Left, and the Right was not consistently the Right. Precise delineation depended on piles of circumstances, and every occasion reflected the paramount political issue of the time and place. As a result, the self-organizing cohorts of similar-minded people sitting on the podium's left or right turned into a tradition worldwide. However, the typical mistake is to emphasize a line of inheritance between the French political problems after the Revolution of 1789 and the present political realities.

Upon the conclusion of the bloody French Revolution, the split between the Left and the Right was let go in less than a decade. Eventually, it was reincarnated in the summer of 1815. At the time, two distinct groups (in France, they were denominated "Clubs," which later morphed into political parties) had emerged. One was hostile to the Charter (in French, the *Charte Constitutionnelle*, the French Constitution issued by Louis XVIII after the Bourbon Restoration), and the second was hostile to the Dynasty. That is to say, from the outset, the Left-Right split was misleading, misguided, and misattributed. The intransigent liberals (the "Left") and the ultra-monarchists (the Royalists, the "Right") fought mismatched, barely overlapping political conflicts. Of course, they were political archenemies, but as we understand today, their political struggle was about secondary issues, not the primary ones.

There were so many ancillary issues that both major camps were further subdivided into minor factions. The nuances separating the minor groups were innumerable because the political infighting revolved around a multitude of subordinate issues. In French parliamentary geography, extreme Right, Left, center-Right, and center-Left were the topmost distinctive subgroups. The primary political issue—the relationship between a man and a state—was practically absent because French politicians tried to resolve ancillary issues they perceived as exponentially more critical. Eventually, the French could adequately understand the actual antagonism by 1820 after the bitter fights over justice, power, religion, economy, war, and the Revolution itself.

By the subsequent French Revolution of 1848, the terms "left" and "right" had been completely disconnected from reality once more. Nevertheless, the terms remained, but only as part of the intra-parliamentary language. Thus, while the terms were almost deserted, new terms emerged—democratic socialists (former liberals) and reactionaries (former royalists), along with their preferred color designations, red and white. For another thirty years, the "red" and "white" political identification dislodged the terms "left" and "right." Finally, after the collapse of the Paris Commune in 1871, the color scheme was discarded, and "left" and "right" were reintroduced into the political lexicon. By World War I, the "left" and "right" developed into the primary reference for political positions in almost all Western countries.

However, the widespread use of the terms has not resulted in any clarity.

Thus, in particular, the French election of 1914 presented a confusing result. Parties with the word "socialist" in the name elected to assemble on the left (obviously). However, those with "left" in their party's name opted to sit on the right. The irony is that the terms "left" and "right" began to erode as soon as they got more or less universally accepted. This transmogrification continues to the present day. As commented by Gauchet, "The wonderful power of Right versus Left comes from the infinite openness of the terms, whose meaning can always be added to or altered" (Gauchet 1996).

Talking about the "original" Leftists, Thomas Sowell observed, "The French Revolution was their chance to show what they could do when they got the power they sought. In contrast to what they promised—'liberty,[10] equality, fraternity'—what they actually produced were food shortages, mob violence, and dictatorial powers that included arbitrary executions, extending even to their own leaders, such as Robespierre, who died under the guillotine" (Sowell 2013). In history, there are not many examples of such a large-scale scheme as an egalitarian society.

As is often the case in human history, the vagueness of the terms allowed them to take hold.

Nevertheless, as is often the case in human history, the vagueness of the terms allowed them to take hold. Moreover, the malleable identities of these political terms—in just one country, France—should have prevented the terms' use elsewhere. Instead, these artificial constructs were exploited by the new kids on the block—socialists and communists—during the multi-decade process of stealing identities from liberals. The first step in historical revisionism emanated from French communists, who—out of the blue—announced that the French Revolution of 1789 was the first proletarian revolution and, as such, the forerunner of the Bolshevik Revolution of 1917 in Russia.

STALIN TAKES THE WHEEL

The socialists and communists were perfectly aware that the distinction between the Left and the Right had little or no connection to the distinction

---

10. We will use "liberty" and "freedom" interchangeably, for English is one of a few languages where these two words carry the same meaning; the vast majority of other languages have only one word.

between the proletariat and the bourgeoisie. Fighting between the "original" Left and the Right had to do with a bouquet of several issues that long pre-dated Marx. Socialists and communists, following Marx, viewed that conflict through the prism of a struggle between two antagonistic classes. Thus, social-ists and communists chose to proceed with identity theft despite the minimal overlap. Meanwhile, the "original" French Left, who advocated for represen-tative democracy, never contemplated building a classless society *à la* Marx.

If Fascists in France and later in Italy never regarded themselves outside the socialistic framework, the National Socialists in Germany initially posi-tioned themselves as "not Right and not Left."

For some time, they enjoyed this self-identification in the eyes of the worldwide anti-capitalist movement. Then, suddenly, Joseph Stalin altered the rules of the game: he decided to utilize the left-right conceptual dichot-omy (in a pretty narrow setting) to crush any opposition to his dictatorial rule. Any aberration from the orthodox Communist party line—no matter how small—had to be labeled. Thus, the "Right-deviationists" and "Left-deviationists" were born.

The "Left-deviationists" were deemed "too orthodox," "too revolution-ary," as strange as it may seem, for the taste of bloodthirsty revolutionary Bolsheviks. In contrast, the "Right-deviationists" were considered traitors to the idea of the planet-wide socialist revolution because they dared to consider building a workers' paradise by cleverly exploiting the mechanisms of state capitalism. Unquestionably, the word "capital-ism" was anathema to communists. The "Left-deviationists" were to the left of Stalin, and the "Right-deviationists" were to his right.

Soviet Communists delineated intra-Communist opposition as either left- or right-wingers.

Instead of the rostrum at the French Assembly, Stalin positioned himself at the center of the ideological universe and thus opened a new page in the "left-right" semantic journey. To rephrase it, Soviet Communists delineated intra-Communist opposition as either left- or right-wingers. The left-right labels were no longer utilized to describe opposing political forces; henceforth, they characterized deviations from the official Soviet Communist party line. Chief inquisitor of Marxism-Leninism, Stalin initially used it to incriminate another fellow Bolshevik, his *bête noire*,

Leon Trotsky, and eventually, in the 1930s, it became a tool for massive party purges. It is also fair to note that all of Stalin's colleagues had a notoriously low life expectancy. (One of the reasons Trotsky and Stalin became enemies was that they had different views on what should be the primary Soviet Union export. Stalin wanted to export renewable natural resources, like lumber. In contrast, Trotsky wanted to export the revolution.)

Because the terms "right" and "left" in the 1930s were applied strictly to denote slight variations of Marxism, the question arose: "Should we carry on with communists' infighting language?" Should the world assume the universal fittingness of French symbolism? Likewise, should the world accept the universal suitability of Soviet Communists' symbolism? These are undoubtedly not rhetorical questions because, since the 1930s, these terms have started to circulate widely.

Stalin and his cadres applied the "right-wing" label extensively. Thus, one of the most widely unmasked scientific charlatans of all time, Trofim Lysenko, founder of "Creative Darwinism," deemed genetics "right-wing." The resulting modernization of Soviet agriculture along party-approved "left-wing" lines caused widespread crop failure and famine.[11] About seven million people starved to death, but the communists pressed on. One of the next victims was cybernetics, reputed in the Soviet Union as a "right-wing pseudoscience," too.[12] Finally, in the 1920s, one of the leaders of the Soviet Communists, Alexander Bogdanov, created the theory of "physiological collectivism." It was assumed that old communists would pass their beliefs on to the young through exchange blood transfusions while rejuvenating themselves.

---

11. The core of Lysenko's theory was based on the alleged inheritance of acquired characteristics. For example, he exposed wheat to moderately low temperatures to "teach" plants to survive harsh Russian winters. Future Nobel Prize-winning physicist Lev Landau was one of his critics (note that Landau was well-known for his pranks). One day Lysenko gave a talk at the Soviet Academy of Sciences. During the Q&A session, the following alleged discussion happened. "Landau asked: 'So you argue that if we cut the ear off a cow and the ear off its offspring, and so on, then sooner or later earless cows will be born?' 'Yes, that is right,' Lysenko replied. 'Then how do you explain that virgins are still being born?' Landau asked" (Goodchild 2004). Recall that mutations in living organisms are called cancer, while mutations in offspring are called evolution.

12. Likewise, the politicization of *Ecclesiastes 10:2*, "The heart of the wise inclines to the right, but the heart of the fool to the left," is ideological Lysenkoism.

A Departure from Communist Norms?

During Comrade Mao's Great Leap Forward (1957-1959), Chinese communists followed Comrade Stalin's example: they rounded up anyone criticizing official party guidelines, proclaimed them "right-wing extremists," and sent them off to forced-labor camps.

Political philosophy defines its terms, but history does not stop here. Over time, political terms pass through fluctuations and metamorphoses and sometimes redefine the underlying political philosophy. Thus, for instance, the Frankfurt School of Socialism adherents were strongly pro-Soviet (a generous number of them were veritably Stalinists) and customarily assessed National Socialism as a form of deviation to the Right from the mainstream trajectory of Soviet (i.e., International) Socialism.[13] Consequently, they emigrated from pre-war Germany to the United States and brought this particular view of the designation, along with other rhetorical meanderings. The only visible difference between Communists, Socialists, and National Socialists in the 30s and 40s was the size of their red flags. Marcuse *et al.* had to do something to alter that perception.

Is National Socialism left- or right-wing? Detailed analysis of National Socialism will be provided in the following chapters of this book; however, readers should already be able to answer the question. Using the designation of the characterization held by Hitler and his epigones, National Socialism represents a strain of Socialism and, therefore, is left-wing. However, from the pre-war Socialist perspective, within the Socialist movement, National Socialism is just an aberration, an embarrassing and regrettable deviation to the right from the political path of mainstream Socialism. Nobody explained to the unsuspecting public in the post-war period that the Nazis were "right" not in absolute, but in relative terms, a "divergence" from the Soviet frame of reference. However, the European Marxists from the Frankfurt School successfully planted the fictitious idea that Fascism and National Socialism were

---

13. Formed in 1923, the Institute for Social Research (*Institut für Sozialforschung*) advocated for a reformulated Cultural Marxism strategy first proposed by Antonio Gramsci. Notable members were Herbert Marcuse (Political Correctness and Repressive Tolerance), Max Horkheimer (Critical Theory and Gradualism), and Theodor Adorno, who spearheaded transplanting the "right-wing Nazi" idea from Europe to the United States.

the decadent last gasp of capitalism. In truth, they were innovative Leftist ideas. They are a textbook case of internal contagion of heresy; the best left-wingers could do in that situation was label the heretics as "right-wing."

What about other popular terms in politics? Democracy, the "rule of the people," could be only direct—at least in the opinion of the ancient Greeks. In their minds, the term "representative democracy" would be entirely incorrect. The political system, in which citizens elect representatives who eventually rule over them, was termed by the Greeks "oligarchy"—"rule of the few" or "aristocracy"—"rule of the best." In the fourth century BC, these words were practically synonymous. Aristotle, who believed in the wisdom of crowds, had designated these terms as contrasting demarcations. Aristotle decided that the aristocracy is the rule of a "good" minority, and the oligarchy is a "bad" one because he associated it with the rich. Before him, the word "oligarchy" had no negative connotations.

So, the question is—should we accept the statement of meaning of the term "democracy" imposed by its creators, the ancient Greeks, or should we accept the many variations and deviations that occurred over the last two millennia? Should we continue to use the term "oligarchy" with negative connotations and treat "aristocracy," as Aristotle did, as something positive? From the position of foresight accumulated over millennia, what should we have done with Aristotle's belief in the wisdom of the mob?

Nowadays, as in the last century, few people pay attention to details. To be regarded as a humanist, it is enough to take on the prefix "anti" relative to a commonly hated entity. Nevertheless, as we know, calling oneself "anti-something" does not make one "pro" that thing's opposite. To give an example, Ernest Hemingway was a fierce anti-fascist all his life, which is to his credit, but this did not develop him into a proponent of right-wing ideology.

On the contrary, the resolute anti-fascist Hemingway steadily moved ever farther and farther Left until he eventually agreed to spy for the Soviet Union as an agent nicknamed Argo. He accepted the invitation to work undercover but never engaged in anything in this field—to the great disappointment of his Soviet handlers—but that is another story. Richard Rorty, a Socialist (even Trotskyist to some degree) philosopher, was a left-wing patriot of the United States and an anti-communist. Does the idiosyncrasy of being anti-communist obligate him to right-wing ranks?

Likewise, consider anarchists. Are anarchists left-wing or right-wing?

Again, the answer depends not primarily on prominent anarchists' founding works, but on the ever-changing arrangement of the "left" and "right" terms.

To sum up, there is not much correlation between modern left-wingers and the French left-wingers at the beginning of the 19th century. Likewise, it is virtually impossible to find modern right-wingers who share the same political position as the French right-wingers more than two centuries ago, especially outside Europe. Moreover, one can find examples of complete reversals of political positions while still maintaining the same "left" or "right" status.

This brief exercise in ideological archaeology confirms the necessity of dismissing a proposition of static political terms and concentrating on the dynamic properties of political identifications instead. Unfortunately, there have been no detailed multi-country studies of the left-right taxonomy over the last two centuries.

It is a widely held view that elites of the Left exist. Do Conservative elites exist? They may. Or maybe not. The answer depends on the reference frame used; generally, both "yes" and "no" are acceptable answers. On the surface, it is bizarre. However, we must admit the existence of two opposing—and simultaneously, correct—answers to a question. This should not cause cognitive dissonance because we are talking about not a particular person but rather a chaotic world in which illimitable frames of reference coexist, however turbulently. And so, one person's "yes" and another's "no" can coexist because each uses a subtly different frame of reference,[14] including subtly different meanings for even the same set of terms.

From France to Britain

Similar processes of ever-changing political labels can be observed not just in continental Europe but in neighboring Great Britain, too.

---

14. The opposing (and exact within their corresponding frames of reference) answers coexist so that the combined (and correct) answer is a superposition of the two. This situation should not be a surprise for readers familiar with quantum mechanics.

The political processes in Great Britain utilized distinctive but still vague terms. If the Left and Right designations were born in France, the "conservative" and "liberal" labels appeared in the 1820s England. Conservatives replaced Tories, and the Labor Party replaced the Liberals. The most relevant and overlooked fact is that until World War II's conclusion, British Conservatives had no relation to French Conservatives; the American Conservatives had no relation to either. Likewise, British Labor had nothing to do with the French Liberals, the French Left, or American Democrats.

After World War II, a new global superpower—the Soviet Union—proved the downright fluid nature of any political lexicon. Soviet communists did not merely affect the political dynamics of the West; they practically defined them. During the Cold War, the West's confrontation with the Soviet Union had many negative consequences. However, one of the few positive dispositions for us is that the Cold War removed many—if not all—ambiguities in the West's political taxonomy. The Cold War had forced all political movements in the West to review their dogmas; the tenets had to be finalized with much-needed clarity. For any left-wing political party, the plan was twofold: a) clarify the party's ideological platform—for or against Soviet communists—and b) disconnect the party doctrines from those Left ideologies that, after World War II, suddenly fell from benevolence: Fascism and National Socialism.[15]

Soviet communists did not merely affect the political dynamics of the West; they practically defined them.

THE TRUTH BENEATH THE TERMS

Admittedly, the dichotomy "left-right" is not essential per se. It could be "liberals" vs. "conservatives," or "red" vs. "white," or the like. These tokens are situational. The important thing here is the dichotomy itself, for it is a

---

15. To shed light on what was happening regarding the right-left dichotomy after World War II, recall recent political events in the United States. Since the Hillary Clinton-funded anti-Trump "Russian" dossier, fabricated by Christopher Steele, got discredited, the media, political operators, and ideological commissars are scrambling to distance themselves from the dossier.

manifestation of human society's potential for self-organization. The author believes that the main focal point of self-organization is wealth—notably the distribution of wealth. To clarify, we are talking not about the intra-population distribution of wealth, *à la* Marx, but about wealth allocation between the government and the governed.

Further, it is necessary to emphasize that the original Left-Right taxonomy applies restrictively to societies where political life is based on a hint of—rudimentary or advanced—democratic principles.

WHENCE "CONSERVATIVES"?

As for the English-speaking world, including the United States, the terms "left" and "right" were not part of the political lexicon until the 1920s.

As an illustration, Figures 1 and 2 show Google's Ngram Viewer results for the words "left-wing" and "right-wing" occurring in English writing from 1800 to 2000. Figures 3 and 4 show comparable results for "liberal" and "conservative."

Figure 1 presents results for English literature worldwide, while Figure 2 shows results from American books alone. In both cases, the usage of the "left-wing" and "right-wing" phrases was practically non-existent until after the Great War. Both charts indicate that phraseology took off around 1920.

Figures 1 and 2 agree, while Figures 3 and 4 feature reasonably divergent behavior. The word "liberal" was used more or less stably over the last two centuries worldwide, while the application of "conservative" steadily grew over the same period. This growth indicates that "conservative" is not opposed to "liberal." However, Figure 4 for the same pair of words, but limited to American literature, shows that the "conservative" is growing at the expense of "liberal" (the chart for the word "liberal" is approximately a mirror image of the "conservative" chart). That is why, in the 19th century, the conservative vs. liberal debate in the United States was non-existent.

"Conservative" in the ideological sense is, of course, a 19th-century innovation. After the invention of liberalism, society realized the necessity of a self-regulating mechanism to prevent the far-reaching—and occasionally dangerous—wrong turns from the main liberalism course. That recognition was slow but unremitting as part of the general evolution of freedom. Figure 3 demonstrates the steady growth of the term "conservatism" through the 19th century.

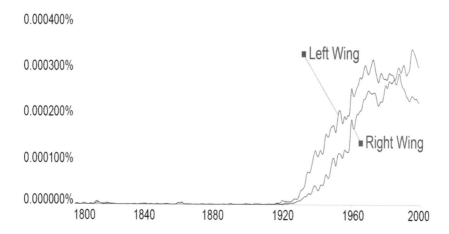

Figure 1. Frequency of the words "right-wing" and "left-wing" from 1800 to 2000. Scope: English worldwide.

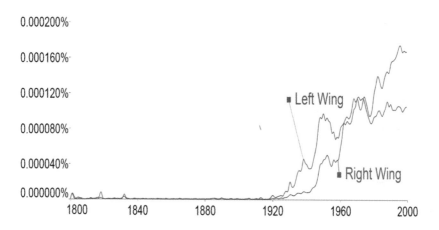

Figure 2. Frequency of the words "right-wing" and "left-wing" from 1800 to 2000. Scope: American English.

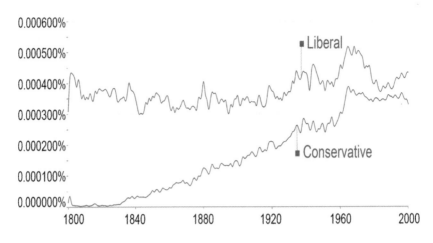

Figure 3. Frequency of the words "conservative" and "liberal" from 1800 to 2000. Scope: English worldwide.

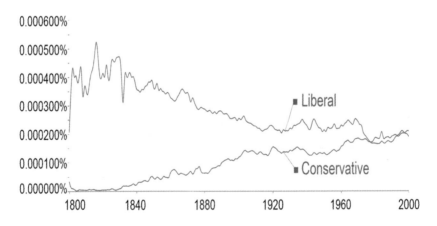

Figure 4. *Frequency of the words "conservative" and "liberal" from 1800 to 2000. Scope: American English.*

How to Argue When You Are Deaf and Blind

Before examining the dynamics of ideological terms, it will be necessary to outline American political realities briefly.

America's political landscape has several reality dimensions. At the first level, there is an objective reality—the reality of facts. At the second level, there are two myths—the myth about reality created by the Democrats and the corresponding myth about reality created by the Republicans. Finally, at the third level, there is the Republican myth about the Democratic myth and the Democratic myth about the Republican myth. The levels below the third one are not significant.

Other democratic countries bear semblance to the American political panorama. There are the same layers, at least in a first approximation, but the names of the two major opposition parties will be unique.

As a rule, political myths of the third level (myths about the myths of ideological opponents) take the form of caricatures, anecdotes, ridicule, and outright mockery. (That is why the Left's commentary on Conservatives, in general, is primarily cartoonish and shallow.) Further, it must be reasserted that the third level's realities are psychologically assuredly comfortable and are oriented by party ideologists to create a negative image of political opposition. That is the district of mutually assured dehumanization.

The attractiveness of second-level myths lies in the "comfort zone." Here, a person breathes easily. Here, an individual prefers to communicate with friends and like-minded people. However, unfortunately, the world outside the "comfort zone" is not yet ideal, simply because there are "others," "biased," "revisionists," and "dissidents." Depending on the radicalism and bloody-mindedness of a political group, "others" must be silenced, sent to concentration camps for re-education, shot, hanged—or all of the above.

The immensely arduous reality to perceive is the reality of the top level. The complexity of perception is that reality is almost always outside the psychological "comfort zone." A member of the species *Homo sapiens* cannot be in this reality for any momentous time (unless his profession is connected precisely with this reality, as with physicists, for instance.) However, a sizable number of people cannot withstand the battle with objective facts. In the course of time, they slide down to the second, mythological level, since a large army of party ideologists has long prepared comforting lies—attractive but utterly illusory black-and-white realities—for its supporters. Using the Marxist lexicon, they could be dubbed "the narrative class."

By arguing at the level of myths, one can effectively show the sparkle of a mind and erudition, education, and intelligence grade. That is a domain of weaponized semantics where WMDs (Weapons of Mass Disinformation) are deployed to manipulate the radioactivity of words. At that level, arguments put forward by ideological opposites are usually hyperbolic against each other. However, regrettably, a dispute at the level of myths never leads to anything, and each person always remains unconvinced (remember "agree to disagree"?). What else can we expect from the linguistic muddle?

The present author tries to stay within the top, myth-free level of reality in any dispute. That is not easy; many people abhor it because the degree of discomfort often exceeds the pain threshold. The required transit across a person's comfort zone often triggers angry responses. However, the strength of human society is modulated by the quality of its connection to reality.

Before arguing with someone, the recommendation is to ask: "At what level of reality are we going to debate?" All well-educated grown-ups can discuss any of these five realities and myths within the framework. Each level has its own system of evidence. Arguing at the second and third levels is safe, pleasant, and exciting. Furthermore, suppose someone needs a winning argument. In that case, it does not matter because a debate at the level of myths presupposes the constant and spontaneous invention of new myths that confirm the correctness of the original myths.

"At what level of reality are we going to debate?" All well-educated grown-ups can discuss any of these five realities and myths within the framework.

Here, it is suitable to recall the famous theorem of the mathematician Kurt Gödel, the only confirmed friend of Albert Einstein on American soil. That theorem states that any system of axioms is incomplete. It means that within the schema of any model (a system of myths, axioms, and postulates), there will always be a fact that cannot be proved or refuted within the model's framework. As a follow-up, Gödel announced that no set of axioms could prove its own consistency.

Gödel's theorem articulates why there is an excessive army of mythmakers in all countries—and under all political regimes—whose notable task is to provide the necessary mythmaking level and constantly modify political myths of the second and third levels. (There are "thought-manufacturers and mind-manipulators," as Aldous Huxley characterized them.) These mythmakers only cause more difficulty in assigning precise political labels. Indeed, political operators can (usually through a series of annoyances) redefine ideological opposition, completely distort their stance, and portray them in a deplorable light. Further, history knows about the widespread deployment of agents-provocateurs who lead unsuspecting opposition into legal, administrative, reputational, and political trouble. As a rule, the general public does not even realize that their favorite politicians are players in someone else's chess game. It works the other way, too—we know of multiple instances of deliberate political self-mislabeling (like Antifa in the United States, for instance).

EVOLUTION OF IDEAS

The evolutionary fight between ideas and truths is as fierce as Darwin's biological evolutionary endeavor. While, at any given time, there are many alternative truths accepted by split-up segments of society, evolution brings harsh treatment for those truths that have marginal or no practical use (in William James' terminology, they have no "cash value").[16] It is interesting to note the remarkable asymmetry here. Namely, no explicit prizes are offered for implementing true ideas (with non-zero, positive "cash values"). However, there are severe penalties for implementing false ones (with zero or negative "cash values").

Nevertheless, it certainly looks as though the evolution-guided search for truth is the answer. The superposition of truths does complicate prospects, but an unstoppable evolutionary struggle clears the fog. In the end, only one version of truth carries through the treatment of time.

Left-wingers mainly offer mutations, and right-wingers carry out selections.

"I have called this principle, by which each slight variation, if useful, is preserved, by the term of Natural Selection," said Charles Darwin. In other words, biological evolution requires a) a source of that "slight variation" and

---

16. William James first introduced the concept of "cashless" theories in an address delivered before the Philosophical Union (James 1898).

b) a mechanism determining if it is realistically useful. Thus, biological evolution is based on both mutation and selection. Social evolution follows a similar script, where left-wingers mainly offer mutations, and right-wingers carry out selections to a high degree. That functional asymmetry is well-acknowledged.

Without conservatism, social evolution would be as directionless as biological evolution. There is no progress in nature; without conservatism, there would be no progress in society despite numerous mutations. In the sphere of ideology, there would be no natural selection without conservatism. Finally, without conservatism, human society would have no purpose because one of the foundations of Darwinism is that species have no collective purpose.

From that consideration, Conservatism long precedes Liberalism. Pre-Enlightenment humans instinctively sought an ideas selection mechanism that could play the role of a negative feedback loop in society development. After the Enlightenment, that instinct-based selection mechanism received proper recognition as the reason-based force that facilitated (and continues to maintain) the evolution of freedom. Society perpetually de-transitions from omnidirectional Left pursuits into the austere chopper of the Right selection process. Whatever ideas survive the process, they pass on to the next generation, resulting in the visible evolution of freedom.

There is another parallel with biological evolution that should be mentioned. From a biological evolution point of view, weak individual organisms are supposed to be losers. Theoretically, that means all species would be represented only by their top performers over time. However, those "weak" individuals had discovered a niche to prevail based on a collectivistic strategy. For example, a group of weak males can defeat a single dominating male or at least keep him at bay.

Social evolution closely emulates biological evolution.

Social evolution closely emulates biological evolution. At first, weak individuals found a way to organize themselves around a particular collectivist ideology; later, some collectivist ideologies became widespread and incorporated both weak and strong individuals. The paradox is that these collectivist strategies did not slow biological or social evolution. That is because, under collectivist threat, individuals must compete not only with other individuals but simultaneously with many of them. In physics, it is termed a non-linear property (similar to multi-photon interactions with atoms).

Mother Nature always operates biological evolution in an isotropic mode: mutations in all possible directions are permissible (but only a small number survive). Social evolution is inherently anisotropic: conservatives usually control society's self-administered evolutionary mechanism. The existence of a human society that has not blown asunder so far proves that conservative ideas appeared at the same time society came into being.

Biological evolution is non-teleological (consequential but non-purposive). In contrast, social evolution is teleological: it is incoherent, illogical, and intermittent but ultimately has a directive principle toward a higher degree of freedom. Here, freedom is understood categorically in the context of individual-state interaction, where a state is a product of human self-organization. The concept of freedom does not exist without a state; consequently, irreversible social evolution is impossible without a state.

In the ideological sphere, it gives rise to numerous counter-balancing collectivistic ideologies because there are numerous ways an individual can be viewed as "not fitting in," "not conforming," and "not participating in groupthink." Only an autonomous individual can offer resistance to the "official party line" and can have his/her own opinion about "the current thing." The collectivist strategy that had begun as a survival method had morphed into a tool for subduing the recalcitrant citizenry. The World Economic Forum's "Great Reset" aims to counterbalance individual countries that are too advanced compared to most backward and stagnant states on the world stage.

Freedom is understood in the context of individual-state interaction. The concept of freedom does not exist without a state.

Sometimes, biological evolution makes unpredictable shifts, and the evolution of ideologies does, too. For example, the standard evolutionary way is to blend an animal into the environment and make it less visible. There is, however, an exception to the rule: the zebra. The zebra's black-and-white pattern makes it easily visible in the environment but, at the same time, makes it difficult to see a single animal within a herd. A zebra's stripes blend in with the stripes of other zebras in a herd, which confuses a predator; now, the pursuer sees not a single, manageable victim but a large, noisy, and moving striped biomass.

That is one of the collectivistic strategies in nature, which has a direct counterpart in the ideological sphere, where Leftists of the past were hiding. However, the modern ones are doing everything in the open but in a way that confuses the opposition. To maintain the collectivist course, Leftists must, naturally, demand absolute conformity of thought (stripes). Just like with zebras, "reduce inequality," "cool the planet," and "critical theory" are Leftist endeavors designed to blend into the herd of left-wing tactical instrumentality. These individual avenues look innocuous, legitimate, and seemingly non-Left, but that impression is due to their design.

There is nothing "wrong" with collectivistic ideologies per se. They are dangerous for society only when they can no longer be moderated or shielded against. The Swiss physician and philosopher Paracelsus submitted an adage that lasted over five centuries: "All things are poison, and nothing is without poison; the dosage alone makes it so a thing is not a poison." (The shorter version is "The dose makes the poison.") In the ideological sphere, collectivist ideologies—depending on the dose—could be harmless or deadly. One of the contradictions of collectivism is that, to be successful, it needs leaders—individuals who are well above average in abilities—but that is against the primary collectivist objective.

What is commonly known as Darwin's "natural selection" actually comprises three distinct mechanisms: heredity, variation, and selection. The heredity mechanism relates to the reproductive transfer of genotypes from generation to generation. Variation refers to random fluctuations of common genotypes. Finally, selection refers to mechanisms that reward (or penalize) inevitable gene fluctuations and allow some fluctuations to dominate a population.

Whether the Darwinian setup can be applied directly to social systems (so-called Generalized Darwinism) is debatable. However, the ideological sphere offers an attractive and direct correspondence to Darwin's three mechanisms of natural selection. Thus, ideological evolution could be explored through the lens of Darwin's theory.

Heredity could be associated with the endurance of an ideology that governs society based on its successful transfer from generation to generation. The variation could be linked with changes in an ideology induced by never-ending challenges. Selection could be connected with the mechanism society chooses to answer those challenges. Traditionally, the dominant sentiment is that people assign the role of the variation mechanism primarily to the left-wingers, the selection mechanism predominantly to the right-wingers, and the role of the heredity (retention) mechanism overwhelmingly to the apolitical population. All three must be present in society to assure proper (and competitive) development. All three create necessary (but not sufficient) conditions for society members to keep going (and succeed) under ever-present circumstances of all-encompassing unfairness.

The resulting situation appears as the "creativity paradox." Leftists brag that their followers dominate the creative segment of the population. There is an undeniable truth to this, at least from a statistical point of view. However, what is the underlying source of that creativity? The Left fights hard—between its own members and the rest of society—to enslave the population and install an elite/expert dictatorship. This take-no-prisoners struggle with the forces of liberty influences the Left to offer new—sometimes exotic, heterodox, or borderline crazy—methods of reaching the illiberal, autocratic, Utopian government Leviathan. In other words, the brain of left-wingers is tailored not to abstract creativity per se, but to creativity specifically devised to rock the ship of civilization.

Natural selection of humans continues to this day. The self-organization of humans, known as civilization, is characterized not by passive reaction to nature's challenges but by the active re-shaping of the natural habitat. The modified environment keeps shaping humans, albeit slightly differently, as happens all the time in systems with a feedback loop. (A direct comparison of ancient and modern human genomes confirms that). Because ideology plays a fundamental role in modern civilization, claims that ideology can affect natural selection processes in humans should not be dismissed.

Any animal's behavior could be rationalized as the result of the interaction of its genotype and the environment. Next, human society could be further contextualized as the effect of the interaction of its government, the governed, and the environment. The intertwined nature-supplied objects—genotype and environment, and self-organizational objects not existing in nature—religion, government, and culture—create an astronomically complex non-linear bootstrap scheme of society with various positive and negative feedback loops.

Note that the feedback effect of society on the human genome is not direct. Instead, it is indirect: in the feedback loop, there is an intermediary between society and the genome—environment. A typical example is lung capacity. Air pollution from industrialization in the 19th century led to a slight decrease in the air's oxygen quantity. That, in turn, by the 20th century, expanded the volume of the lungs (to keep the oxygen intake intact). Consequently, Mother Nature has increased an average person's body weight and height to carry extra lung volume.

As widely acknowledged, the human body epitomizes a symbiotic relationship between a self-propelled host and billions of gut bacteria. In most cases, both sides of the symbiotic organism gain. The mind, too, demonstrates a symbiotic relationship between a self-conscious host and all diverse hosts of a similar nature; in most cases, both sides of this relationship succeed. Thus, a single self-conscious host (a human) acquires knowledge as a multi-faceted process; one noteworthy leg is information exchange between current and foregoing generations (for example, via education, books, and other media).

Ideas—like viruses—require relentless vigilance from society.

The human host does not exist without gut bacteria, which do not carry on outside the host for long. Likewise, the individual mind does not exist for long outside society, and society does not function without individual hosts. Not all symbiotic relationships are beneficial; we know about parasites abusing their hosts. It pertains to both the symbiotic organisms depicted above—a single human and human society.

However, being a product of consciousness, some ideas evolve reminiscent of respiratory viruses. Gad Saad calls them "idea pathogens" (Saad 2021). Much like other viruses, ideas jump from person to person. Ideas mutate, hiding their cores, like Collectivism morphing into numerous strains. An idea may stay around regardless of any countermeasures. That is why ideas—like viruses—require relentless vigilance from society. Initially, any malignant virus comes out so strong that it may kill the host organisms (and the virus along with it). Over time, however, the respiratory virus mutates to persist—and the principal vector of mutations is toward less and less deadly strains that do not kill the host but adapt to coexist with it. When viruses run out of mutagenic steam, these weakened viruses act as naturally occurring vaccines of the highest possible quality for host organisms.

Asexual reproduction leads to the creation of genetically carbon copies of the original organism. On the contrary, sexual reproduction always produces genetically unique offspring. Mother Nature's blindness contributes to an offspring being either more or less suited to their environment than their parents. However, it makes the offspring a moving target for infections and viruses, which, in turn, must undergo their own evolutionary mutations to be effective. In the case of ideological pathogens, they must evolve along with a host to be effective.

As the virus's variants get less virulent as time passes, its transmissibility increases. It explains why harmful ideas have become less harmful over time, but their acceptance is wider, penetrating all corners of society. To successfully parasitize millions of people, ideological viruses must use weasel tricks to present themselves as harmless; one of the common tricks is rebranding/renaming. In case GDP goes down, simply redefine GDP. Verging on economic recession? Revise the definition of "recession." The red color is associated with left-wing ideology? The same solution: alter the definition. Now, Leftists are "blue," and anything that passes for right-wing is marked red. The global cooking did not materialize? The global warming turned out to be a dud? Well, switch attention to the new narrative, "climate change." Note that the Left and the Right share vocabulary, but the Left self-anointed themselves as controllers of the definitions. The Left has transformed into a gang of master wordsmiths. As a result, the world swims in Leftist cliches, pedantries, and lexicon.

The world swims in Leftist cliches, pedantries, and lexicon. The Left hijacked and rebranded many things.

The Left hijacked and rebranded many things, like Antifa from the 1930s, which got resurrected and repurposed. The term "liberal" was redacted, repackaged, and reappropriated. One of the most significant political hijackings was on January 6, 2021, when the Left rebranded President Trump's peaceful rally and recategorized it as a "violent insurrection."

Likewise, ideas without "cash value" can potentially kill the human host and thus display their unfoundedness to all other humans. In the end, the majority proven to be beneficial to humanity truths will prevail, but it does not mean the bad ones will be thrown out entirely. Instead, the bad ideas are just ignored by many. For example, how many committed flat-earthers are still boarding airplanes daily? How many socialists worldwide enjoy capitalism-provided civilization's niceties?

However, the process is not straightforward due to notable deviations from the general evolutionary path. Case in point: a number of microorganisms that do not kill hosts mutate and try again. Likewise, an ideology with zero or negative "cash value" may mutate and try again. It demystifies the occasional reoccurrence of deadly ideologies popping up from oblivion despite ignominious collapse beyond imagination. As a result, some societies still spread Acquired Ideology Deficiency Syndrome (AIDS). For example, Leftists always revert to their base instincts of "confiscate and redistribute." It could lead to an "institutional triumph of insanity," as Sohrab Ahmari tagged it. Finally, that could explain the grotesque repetition of all Utopian ideas anytime they are implemented.

Nevertheless, society must acquire herd intelligence first to reach herd immunity from cashless ideologies. In overdoses or concomitant immoral behavior, ideologies with negative cash value could be lethal. The following Chapters will consider a possible elixir for ideological detoxification to counter left-wing ideological immunosuppression.

Like superstitions, many unproductive ideas have morphed into the innoxious category. Recall that "knocking on wood," "Friday the 13th," and belief in dragons are in various folklores worldwide. Finally, humans and society carry incoherent luggage of truths—some with self-evident "cash values" and some without. Among the latter, many truths, such as myths, folklore, and superstitions, are undamaging, but some are not. So far, evolutionary beating has assigned synonyms to ideas of political philosophy: the "cashless" ideas have customarily been given the "left" designation. In contrast, proven ideas producing "cash value" are treasured as the "right" ones.

The "truth race" evolutionary winner does not require wide acceptance. As it happens, many of the greatest scientific truths—especially absolutes—are ignored worldwide. In particular, how many living souls understand that the flat-screen TV they watch is a device constructed on Einstein's theory? This state of miseducation was inherited from the former generation of TV sets based on a large vacuum tube (kinescope), also in accordance with Einstein's theory.[17] Likewise, on the grounds of the fragmentation of society, nobody

---

17. In 1931, even before Nazis came to power, twenty-eight pro-Nazi physicists

outside astronomy circles got excited when black holes were discovered at the center of all spiral galaxies. Such ignorance is widespread; as long as it does not affect distinguishable people on the street, that lack of knowledge is not harmful.

What happens when it does affect other people? Enter politics and other society-specific phenomena.

The set of truths that outlast the evolutionary grinder does not require a materialistic foundation as long as it serves beneficial practical purposes. As long as metaphysical postulates have "cash value," they are acceptable despite the fact that they may contradict other well-known absolutes.

The set of truths that outlast the evolutionary grinder does not require a materialistic foundation as long as it serves beneficial practical purposes.

Any attempt to prohibit or otherwise prevent destructive "cashless" ideologies from spreading into society is futile. Because such ideas propagate like dangerous viruses, the only way to protect society from them is through widespread ideological immunization via public education. Otherwise, immune-compromised (ideology-compromised) individuals will be exposed and could get seriously sick. Only prepared minds can withstand dangerous ideological viruses with zero or negative cash value.

However, what about truths with non-zero "cash value," despite being false? Among others, Ptolemy's astronomy was an indispensable tool for navigation for more than a millennium while being erroneous. The model was incorrect but dispensed acceptable, "good enough" results for predicting celestial bodies' movements. The argument here is that nobody recognized that Ptolemy's model was wrong until Copernicus offered his heliocentric model,

---

from Germany, Austria, Czechoslovakia, Finland, France, Italy, the Netherlands, Sweden, Switzerland, and the United States published a booklet titled "One Hundred Authors Against Einstein" ("*100 Autoren gegen Einstein*"). Another ninety-two scientists were attested to be anti-relativists by editors. In just over one hundred pages, an attempt was made to debunk Einstein's relativity theory as "Jewish world-bluff." When Einstein was asked to comment on the booklet, he noted that it does not require a hundred scientists to debunk his theory—just one single fact would do.

which delivered more precise results by order of magnitude. Humans quickly dismantle the old idols when the new ones produce better results—but not all humans, and not everywhere. Ptolemy's model was not completely given up on; modern astrology still uses it. The introduction of the heliocentric model was a textbook "paradigm shift," when one set of absolutes was replaced by another. It was not appraised during its introduction; it took centuries for the Copernican model to transform from a mathematical theory into absolute truth through direct observations and satellite data.

In the middle of the 19th century, precise measurements of planets' orbits revealed small, almost negligible, but consistent deviations from the Copernicus' model. Einstein calculated these deviations with high precision using his general theory of relativity, proving his theory's superiority—but the Copernicus model is still with us. It looks as though the Copernican model has a more prominent "cash value" for mankind than the general theory of relativity. Thus, society is filled with many "high cash value" truths that coexist with negligible elements of advanced studies, remnants of discarded harmful ideas, and benign "cashless" ideas.

A not-so-strange resemblance exists between the luggage of contradictory truths in society and inconsistent human genetic material. Like the incoherent set of truths guiding society, cells' DNA is analogously a complete mess. Only about 1% of human DNA is commonly believed to be beneficial (has "cash value"); the rest is traditionally considered "junk." There are many competing theories regarding this 99% of DNA's allegedly not-useful (or, rather, non-coding) part. Several theories reject the notion of "junk DNA" and assign it essential usefulness, reducing DNA's "unusable" part from about 99% to about 90%. However, from an evolutionary standpoint, the worthless instructions in DNA are similar to worthless ideas in society. The majority of them are relics of previously harmful stuff, remnants of evolution's battle with long-gone parasites, microbes, and viruses. No doubt, the messiness of biological evolution is on par with the messiness of social evolution.

Viruses contain nucleic acids (DNA or RNA), put to work as software to assemble hardware—living matter. There is no such phenomenon as a living organism without replication. However, the opposite is true—there is a replication without living. Viruses cannot replicate on their own, but they can replicate inside a host cell. Viruses are not zombies or undead—if one prefers using "cashless" and unharmful folklore. Viruses are unlive.

Similarly, the "cashless" ideologies are unlive—they replicate, but there is no corresponding living matter. Both viruses and "cashless" ideologies parasitize and significantly affect the host organism or host society. Both utilize the host's raw materials and energy to reproduce. Both are subject to evolution—biological or social. Finally, note another substantial similarity—viruses and "cashless" ideologies can replicate inside recently dead host cells and societies and, in some cases, even bring these dead entities back to life (in a different form, of course).

From a thermodynamic angle, all parasites—including parasitic ideas—represent endothermic phenomena. They consume the energy produced by somebody else. At lower doses, endothermic processes create proper dissipative conditions for the self-organization of exothermic matter. At high doses, however, parasitic endothermic processes lead to imminent death. Leftist beliefs cannot dwell in the wild; they require hosts to parasitize. On the other hand, the Right does not need an external patronage system, for they developed their dogmas based on examples of societies that thrived in the wild and brought into existence human civilization.

Leftist beliefs cannot dwell in the wild; they require hosts to parasitize. The Right does not need an external patronage system, for they developed their dogmas based on examples of societies that thrived.

Along with "hardware" forces (read Mother Nature), viruses play a role in biological evolution—as a "software" force. In the same way, the "cashless" ideologies offer an essential mechanism for society's mutations. Societies must endure the most of Mother Nature and carry through under the gun of dangerous "cashless" ideologies.

In the biological evolutionary race, the winner is not the smartest, uttermost fittest in the environment, or strongest. Instead, the winner is the one who manages to reproduce the most. As per Roger Masters, animals "adjust their behavior to maximize long-term reproductive success" (Masters 1983, p. 164). Of course, it requires a certain balance of smartness, adaptability, strength—but not ostensibly beyond the average—and sure luck, no doubt. Social evolution follows the same pace. In any case, the most reproducible societies win the day. A definite minority of societies governed by repeatedly beneficial ideas came through the merciless hand of social evolution. All self-organized matter—from multi-cell organisms to multi-organism societies—has substantiated self-preservation tendencies. (Those who did not—those with ideological pathologies—had vanished from the face of the Earth.)

The "survival of the fittest" does not translate directly into cooperative animal relations. Biological evolution, being directionless and erratic, does not and cannot explain the collective tendencies of humans. Such tendencies appear as self-organizational structures in different social dimensions. The situation has earmarks of the "chicken-egg" dilemma. It is fruitless to ask what comes first: society or cooperation. They evolved together; by now, there is no chicken without eggs. Likewise, there are no societies without cooperation.

THE DESTRUCTION OF TERMINOLOGY

Looking back a hundred or so years, it is clear that the Left's tyranny usually begins with the destruction of terminology. How come calling people names often wins arguments for Leftists? Because they use words that are weaponized with a poisonous payload, while the Right still prefers to operate under the terms of gentlemen's discussion. Language, mobilized by the Left, is constantly metamorphosing to meet Leftists' aspirations. As a rule, any attempt to settle on any meaning fails as Leftists promptly move the target over and over. Recall that the "global cooling" of the 1970s, which turned out to be the "global warming" of the 1990s, has morphed into "climate change" at the turn of the millennium and, since 2023, became "global boiling."

If world history teaches us anything, it is that the political spectrum is not discrete. Instead of just two binary alternatives, there is a continuum of political ideologies from the radical Left to the radical Right. The exact position on the political map depends on a) actual political doctrine in absolute terms and b) how the doctrine is portrayed relative to the current political climate.

Granted, defining a vague political term using other vague terms offers no clarity, like the example above referencing supposedly "right-wing Nazis." However, three possible methods exist to define a political gospel in absolute terms.

First, define a political dogma by its original meaning, the definition assigned at dawn. The simplicity of this approach is attractive. However, any unbiased researcher will face a dilemma: there is no consensus on nearly any political terms (with several exceptions) regarding its origin or initial classification. Without detailed comprehension of the political situation when the original term was born, people are stuck with modern interpretations of a canon, which may or may not approximate the original one.

Second, define a political ideology by its current interpretation, regardless of its origin, history, and traditional use. This method is actually vaguer than the first, for there is no consensus on nearly anything politics-related in modern, over-polarized political culture.

Third, the tremendously difficult one, is that an unbiased political researcher should prefer to analyze the dynamics of a term's meaning, in its totality, from initiation to present. The next chapter is relatively lengthy because, as William Durant indicated, "in philosophy, as in politics, the longest distance between two points is a straight line" (Durant [1926] 1962, p. 238).

Chapter 2

The Individual-State Paradigm

Is there a Holy Grail to conservatism? Precisely, who are its antagonists? What are the differences between conservative stances of the past and the present? Are there any prospects for conservatism after its expulsion from academia at the turn of the 21st century?

At this point, it can be concluded that conservatism has been continually rediscovered along with its ideological opposites. Was conservatism present in society before the term "conservatism" was introduced? The question is similar to asking, "Did the electron exist in nature before it was discovered in 1897 in Cambridge University's Cavendish Laboratory?" Of course, it was. Likewise, conservatism has existed as an ideological force since the dawn of human civilization.

Still, the term "conservatism" appeared only when people realized the need to distinguish between the original Enlightenment liberalism and its highjacked versions. Every time conservatism is reinstated, it is after a crisis, which is an inalienable feature of any ideology's evolution. Moreover, "Conservatism may rarely announce itself in maxims, formulae or aims" (Scruton 1984, p. 11).

Writing about axiomatic conservatism, Nash argues that "such an *a priori* effort, I have concluded, is misdirected. I doubt that there is any single, satisfactory, all-encompassing definition of the complex phenomenon called conservatism, the content of which varies enormously with time and place. It may even be true that conservatism is inherently resistant to precise definition" (Nash 2006, introduction). If the purpose is to describe a phenomenon comprehensively, that is true. To carry on with our exercise in applying physics methods to the realm of politics, we must select the most appropriate philosophical fulcrum. To develop a *model* of the phenomenon, we must carefully select a limited number of telltale characteristics, which, by definition, must describe most, but not all, observable phenomena satisfactorily.

The model must include concepts classified in physics as invariants—properties that remain unchanged even when the object is in motion. For example, an object in motion can have various coordinates and speeds, yet its mass, total energy, and momentum may stay constant.

To carry on with our exercise in applying physics methods to the realm of politics, we must select the most appropriate philosophical fulcrum.

As with any political philosophy (and corresponding ideology), conservatism manifests its evolution throughout history. Do we have the possibility of searching for invariants in such a moving entity? In the meantime, the most forgotten aspect of Leftist philosophy is that it aims for the collective determination of invariant truths.

A *priori*, it is unknown how many conservative principles must be enumerated. To put it another way, how many attributes should be sufficient to define conservatism, or any other political philosophy? Amongst the most well-known published answers are six (Kirk 2001), ten (Dunn and Woodward 2000), and about twenty (Rossiter 1982). Alternatively, Thorne (1990) announced only two central axioms of conservatism. Last, Roger Scruton, the towering figure of British conservatism, presents ten fundamental principles (Scruton 2014).

Following Nash, there is an understanding that conservatism cannot be constituted *a priori* by a restricted set of features (read: axioms). That being said, the principle suits all political philosophies equally. That is probably a hidden methodological error. The irrefutable answer would be to examine ever-changing conservatism and its ideological polar opposite, which is, of course, ever-changing too. The correct—complementary—choice for conservatism's counterpart would likely be a combined entity not susceptible to significant temporal alterations. To be complete, political philosophy cannot be analyzed alone; it must be analyzed in conjunction with its archenemy.

For example, combining conservatism with its opposite could create a perfect compound not subject to substantial change over time, which would be the required invariant.

Richard Rorty, an American philosopher regarded as controversial, was a committed adherent of analytical philosophy. Analytical philosophy relies on formal logic for discussing and solving problems. In many ways, Rorty was trying not only to extend the insight of "analytical philosophy" but also to produce axiomatic philosophy, the philosophy of an agreed-upon set of axioms. In essence, he was following (probably without even realizing it) the monumental program of axiomatic mathematics created by Bertrand Russell and David Hilbert. Their problem at the beginning of the 20th century was to derive the whole body of mathematics from a set of fundamental principles. However, in 1931, Hilbert's grandiose idea failed (though he and his colleagues contributed to the birth of a new science—metamathematics). That year, Kurt Gödel proved that any formal system leaves some propositions undecided, even *a priori* true propositions. One of the most critical aspects is that Gödel's proof of the existence of true statements that are unprovable is not an uncommon case; instead, it frequently occurs everywhere. As an example, the Declaration of Independence discusses "self-evident truths," such as "all men are created equal."

Thus, philosophy, in general, and political philosophy, in particular, inevitably result in endless, fruitless discourses, even between adherents of the same philosophical system. Also, the second Gödel theorem demonstrated beyond any doubt that one could not prove the consistency of a formal system based upon the system's own set of axioms. Additionally, Chaitin (1999) found that the improvability of true statements is more or less the norm and that the class of true but unprovable statements is infinite. A corollary to this conclusion is that no axiomatic theory can substantiate and validate itself. Even if they proceed from formal postulates, philosophical discussions may still result in a meaningless intellectual game—a pointless word salad. The incompleteness theorem explains why the Left is so proficient at waging judicial battles: Leftists know about myriad inconsistencies that cannot be removed, even theoretically, and exploit them.

Rorty's case was too much for the tenured establishment, which saw Rorty's metaphilosophical research as an attack on philosophy itself. Moreover, Rorty's program to advance his metaphilosophy—despite his flirtation with postmodernism and critical theory—sparked many condemnations, as it, along with Gödel, declares the existence of unsolvable problems in formal systems. (Rorty turned out to be an anti-foundationalist later in life.)

The unsolvability of such kinds of problems must not be discouraging. As Leszek Kolakowski, a philosopher-anticommunist exiled from Poland, said, "Most of the concepts we employ in describing large-scale social phenomena have no perfect empirical equivalents" (Kolakowski 1983). The goal of our study is not to solve all the world's problems at once; instead, we intend to construct an *a priori* limited but nevertheless valuable model of two complementary yet diametrically opposed political ideologies. Although a narrow model such as this will be unsatisfactory from a formal logic standpoint, we should try to determine whether such a political axiom is useful before disposing of it. Regarding the theory's inability to validate itself from its postulates, we will utilize outside factors—unavailable in mathematics and mathematical logic—such as human history. That stand is well-known; in 1778, Pierre Beaumarchais wrote in "The Marriage of Figaro," "*Tempo è galant'uomo*, as the Italians say, time is a gentleman, a gentleman who always tells the truth."

What is the common denominator among all left-wingers? Is there a common characteristic shared by all right-wingers? What has been the primary difference between two opposing political structures throughout history? No matter what Karl Marx thought, history does not repeat itself as a tragedy or a farce. However, historians have observed some striking similarities between different countries and historical eras when it comes to the nature of social conflicts. Moreover, why should we devote our attention to the herculean task of navigating through a sea of axioms? Thus, instead of forcing a conclusion, let us investigate reaching the ultimate point by identifying one—just one—character trait of political philosophy and see how deep the rabbit hole goes.

HUMANITY'S SELF-ORGANIZATION

The human mind has several essential characteristics: nonlinearity, non-commutativity, and multiplicativity. Also, the human mind is a dissipative system. It is inconceivable that a group of such subjects would negate these characteristics. Significantly, no conclusive mechanism would convert a group of non-linear objects (humans) into a linear system. Likewise, no established mechanism exists to convert a group of non-commutative humans into a commutative society. Does a union of the populace make it non-dissipative? The answer is no. Therefore, as the individual mind features a predisposition toward self-organization, human society tends toward self-organization. That immanent readiness to self-structuring was observed in many chaotic non-linear dissipative systems with an external energy source.

Humanity's self-organization emerged from infinite human impulses' intricate and spontaneous interplay. Through myriad interactions, individual competing organisms stumbled upon something unexpected: mutually beneficial cooperation among kin organisms (note that all multi-cell organisms utilize symbiotic cooperation between non-kin organisms). Eventually, cooperation led to the creation of groups and, consequently, intragroup cooperation and intergroup competition in the next leg of evolution. Those who participated in cooperation got the advantage over those who did not. It created unprecedented inequality relative to what a single organism could achieve—for example, joint hunting or fighting off predators.

As the individual mind features a predisposition toward self-organization, human society tends toward self-organization.

However, at the time, inequality was a strictly short-lived phenomenon. The death of an individual reset everything; all his possessions, his mating partner(s), and his offspring returned to a tribe's shared pool—just as it still exists in the animal world.

The state—the highest self-organizational structure ever created by evolution—transformed inequality from a short-term, common, gregarious animal feature into a long-term element exclusive to humans. In effect, the long-term preservation of inequality could be rephrased as *property preservation*; the preservation of property means that equal guarding rights must be assigned to all properties. The idea of "all properties are created equal" was elevated as a cornerstone principle long before "all men are created equal" was written. Eventually, the idea was transformed into owners' rights and equal human rights. The discovery of the state was so revolutionary and so valuable that all tribes that did not adopt it died out from the brutal forces of evolution. Even the aborigines who followed the "cargo cult" in the Pacific had some primitive state institutions.

The state was the final building block that created the conditions for long-term self-perpetuating civilizations. However, at some point, the state took on a life of its own. In many cases, it became a liability instead of an asset to society and crushed the civilizations it was supposed to serve. In biological terms, the man-made creation—the state—mutated and began devouring the underlying society; the well-known name for this, borrowed from biology, is cancer. When it happens, it metastasizes quickly into all government and public institutions, leading to some form of tyranny.

Thus, there is a particular material substratum upon which the whole of politics—the practice of dominance—rests. That material basis has a good, measurable, and scientifically coherent proxy—wealth allocation between the government and the governed. The exact way wealth always finds a path to political power is not essential at the moment. Fundamentally, what matters to our purposes is that mechanisms to implement such a path exist at all stages of social development. They differ from country to country and from one historical epoch to another. However, a relatively high level of material wealth often pushes its owners to political Olympus, whether or not they wish to be there.

There is a material substratum upon which the whole of politics rests—wealth allocation between the government and the governed.

Under vulgar Marxism, this perpetual mechanism has been associated with class warfare and is tapped to explain all society's material and spiritual dynamics without exception. That left-wing ideology is primitive and, therefore, incredibly effective. Essentially, it is deep-rooted in the claim that there are only two cohorts of humankind on this planet—the oppressors and the oppressed. There is an abundance of synonyms for these cohorts. The Left associates all anti-Left people, the non-Woke wealthy, nobility, and bourgeois, as oppressors. As one can observe, the list of oppressed groups is notable: workers, peasants, non-whites, homosexuals, women, the poor, the underprivileged, the uneducated, and many others. However, any oddball belonging to these groups could easily be deprived of his oppressed status at the first sign of questioning Marxist dogmas.

A Marxist theology is simple: view each aspect of society exclusively through the prism of the most recently appointed (and carefully vetted by party bosses) "oppressed classes." The paranoid Marxist belief that "evil cap-italists" are to blame for every human illness deserves its own entry in the Diagnostic and Statistical Manual of Mental Disorders, the official book of mental disorders. As soon as this concept is comprehended, the other aspects of the puzzle will fall into place: the mosaic of various "critical theories" will be revealed. They would be widely regarded as slightly deviating from classic Marxist ideologies, marking the apogee of Marxism.

As a matter of fairness to Marx, his conclusion regarding class struggle was in conformity with what he thought was solid empirical data. Historically, the government represented the wealthy and governed the poor in virtually all cases. Marx, however, could not recognize that the dichotomy was a logi-cal consequence of the underlying cardinal principle rather than a principle in and of itself. To put it another way, Marx was looking for answers in the generally right direction,[18] but he—from the ideology archaeology angle—was digging in the wrong place. That is why he was forced to designate separate struggling classes for different epochs. As a result, he incorrectly defined the boundaries between political rivals.

Nevertheless, Marx had not concluded and committed another error by declaring the impenetrable boundaries between two political vehicles. In essence, such impenetrability is a corollary of Marx's conception of the politi-cal class. In this way, Marx considered human society a closed system. On the contrary, society is an open system with no impenetrable boundaries between antagonists.

It is crucial to keep in mind that for those societies that came closer to the model described in classical Marxism, its methods provide a more or less good analytical effect. Consider, for example, 19th-century England with clear delineation between two opposing cohorts of people that could be labeled "classes." However, in many other eras and societies, the applica-tion of Marxism turned out to be unproductive. It was a challenging learning curve for Marxists to eventually realize that the cherished model corresponds to reality in just a few isolated cases. Physicists, on the contrary, completely understand that when a theory stops reflecting facts about reality, it is the theory that must be discarded, not reality.

---

18. Marx and Engels's "Manifesto of the Communist Party" is not, as it is customary viewed, a panegyric of communism. On the contrary, it resembles more a panegyric of capitalism—a far-from ideal but still valuable and natural step in soci-ety's evolution of freedom.

Leftists continue to be influenced by these abecedarian fallacies. They keep on defining artificial borders between groups of souls in the 21st century in order to weaponize these differences and turn people against one another. Poor Marxists had no choice because the original theory postulated just two antagonists—the bourgeoisie and the proletariat. In time, however, history has eroded that distinction. Through the years, the proletariat had lost its revolutionary appeal; the middle class had entered the picture. As a result, Marxists opted to bend the facts to fit their failed theory rather than throw it away, but nobody warned them that this is a never-ending and pointless process. Enter political Lysenkoism.

Physicists understand that when a theory stops reflecting facts about reality, it is the theory that must be discarded, not reality.

We can describe political philosophy's single, cardinal, and transcendent axiom, referred to as "the individual-state paradigm," in concrete, quantifiable, and objective terms.[19] By this definition, political philosophy would reflect both diametrically opposed positions simultaneously and adequately.

The individual-state paradigm postulates that *de jure* or *de facto* wealth allocation and wealth control between the government and the governed is a principal driving force of human self-organization.

The individual-state paradigm maintains that the established ratio of wealth of the governed to wealth under government control directly modulates society's freedom-to-unfreedom ratio.

Note that the "control" part of the definition above must be understood in straightforward and measurable terms, like Assets Under Management (AUM).

Governments are not the only forces that hold a society together. Other forces exist, but they dwell outside the government-to-governed domain: religious, moral, tribal, cultural, and many others. Some of these forces come from within, while others come from outside the community. Sometimes,

---

19. Some possible alternatives to the term would be the "man-state paradigm" or the "human-state paradigm." Alternatively, those who prefer Latin roots to terms could use the "*persona-res publica* paradigm," but the "individual-state" carries the essence of the proposed approach.

these forces are more potent than the government-related ones, and sometimes, the government finds itself an overriding authority. The individual-state paradigm does not take into account any of these factors. In contrast, the primary delineator absolutizes the material relationship between the government and the governed. It deliberately ignores the rest as less helpful in describing society's dynamics—at least over the long term.

Liberalism, like any other "ism" from the pool of political philosophy reduced to a single axiom, does not have room for (commonly designated secondary) issues like culture, religion, art, sports, nationalism, populism, and many others. What unifies all these secondary delineators is that none imposes logical constraints on ideological positions and the corresponding political actions.[20] While the single-axiom postulate does not address these issues directly, no doubt minimized government influence, advocated by the individual-state paradigm, greatly influences society's attributes. Without going into details, it appears that the government's economic power over the governed plays the modulator role in the political domain and all other aspects of social life. However, the primary, axiomatic ideological delineator cannot be exploited to "derive" all secondary elements of human activity.

On the contrary, classical Marxism hard-wires economic relations with political, moral, cultural, and all other aspects of life. In such a fossilized structure, there is no place for the concept of "freedom." In Marxism (and Leftism in general), the wealth distribution inside the society (excluding government) acts as a Grand Modulator of Everything. From such a viewpoint, morals and culture are more or less direct derivatives of intra-society economic relations. Conversely, the individual-state paradigm recognizes all these aspects of human life—religion, nationalism, culture, government, and morale—as semi-independent incarnations of social self-organization. If the individual-state paradigm acts as a Grand Modulator, it directly applies to only one category—freedom.

As conservatism maintains, man's wealth is paramount over government wealth in terms of absolute value, relative value, and control. It is the proper demarcation line, capable of enduring the test of time. Per Roger Scruton, "In

---

20. Note that none of Umberto Eco's 14 points describing Fascism deals with the primary question, the question of wealth allocation between the government and the governed. Meanwhile, all of Eco's 14 points are valid, but they represent the universe of secondary delineators.

the modern world, the State's role is inevitably extensive, but Conservatives believe its reach should always be subject to challenge. It is, therefore, time to reaffirm the fundamental axiom of conservatism, which is that the State is not an end but a mean" (Scruton 2014).

Conservatives' ideological and philosophical adversaries promote the primacy of government wealth over individuals's wealth. For clarification, conservatism favors a minimum ratio of government wealth to the total wealth of citizens. When there is no tangible mechanism for citizens to control their government, the phrase "consent of the governed" loses meaning and is frequently ignored by the government. That is the primary distinction between conservatism and those who hide behind an array of labels: Leftists, Collectivists, Progressives, Marxists, post-Marxists, Fascists, Maoists, Stalinists, Statists, and numerous others—the list is lengthy. We will interchange the terms Leftists and Collectivists while referring to other sister ideologies by their historical names. Hence, from the viewpoint of the individual-state paradigm, Conservatives are not distinguished from the axiomatic Right. Thus, Liberals, Libertarians, and Constitutionalists are virtually unrecognizable from Conservatives.

Conservatives' ideological adversaries promote the primacy of government wealth over individual's wealth.

In the definitions above, "government wealth" is not to be limited to material wealth alone. "Government wealth" here refers, in general terms, to both material wealth and all other forms of authoritative control, influence, and possessions that do not yet have precise monetary equivalents. For example, the Federal Government in the United States owns over a quarter of the country's landmass—approximately 630 million acres. Comparatively, John Malone, the largest private landowner, owns approximately three hundred times less land than the Federal government. Furthermore, the government owns over half of the state's land in five states. Government-owned land is practically impossible to estimate regarding monetary value; likewise, it is impossible to assess its political value.

Moral tenets—from the individual-state paradigm—are outside the domain of the primary question. Instead, moral norms belong to the pool of vast non-written laws and, in the long run, only those uncodified laws that have survived society's evolution. Morality is a set of uncodified rules outside the government-to-governed setting. It is not a superstructure that hangs over people (or is imposed by religion); on the contrary, it is a set of unwritten rules that have passed the evolutionary beating and have a proven record of positive cash value. Along with religion, nationalism, culture, and government, morale is the visible result of society's self-organization. However, this book primarily dwells upon only one of them—the government; morality and others (and interactions between them) are well beyond its scope.

Decadent art was spotted long before the term "decadent" was invented (as a matter of fact, decadent art was born at the same time as art itself). Likewise, unacceptable moral behavior was detected long before the term "moral" was invented. Each generation notes the regrettable "fall of morals," "decay of culture," and widespread counterculture or anti-culture. Yet, the invisible hand of social evolution selects the winners and preserves them for future generations. From the political philosophy standpoint, all these secondary attributes of society are relevant only if the government penetrates those domains. As long as culture, religion, art, business, sport, and many other activities are not the subject of government regulation, they play a secondary ideological role. If the government has nothing else to do but micromanage all these aspects of society, they become tools in the power struggle. Consider, for example, government intervention against something that it considers "decadent," "hate speech," or "wrongthink."

"Income inequality" (a "wealth gap" between the rich and poor), cherished by Leftists, does not play an overriding role in society's dynamics. If it did, why are people escaping societies with a low degree of "income inequality" to societies with a high degree of "income inequality" *en masse*? Hence, "income inequality" is often an attractor more than a repellent. In order for people to desert countries without regard to "income inequality," there must be some other attraction. The individual-state paradigm provides the apparent candidate—people are drawn to societies with a low ratio of government-to-citizens wealth and ignore intrapopulation wealth distribution no matter how high the rich-poor disparity is.

Consequently, the "wealth gap" is still relevant, but only in the context of the gap between government wealth and the wealth of citizens. Therefore, socialist equality is phantom equality; the same can be said for socialist equity. Intra-society inequality is natural, and uniformity and equivalence are artificial. Moreover, every time it was tried, implementing intra-society equality required violent homogenization.

Relationships between the government and the governed must not be confused with relationships among citizens. In any attempt to entangle these relationships, we are negotiating the beginning of tyranny since it implies a) the use of government political power to settle private, non-political matters, b) the expansion of government intrusion into pure political matters, and c) the establishment of total government control over the governed. By the way, Abraham Lincoln knew that government-to-governed equality must be maintained despite the fact that humans often behave unjustly toward each other, in accordance with the idea stated above.

There is no truth to the notion that the French Revolution was a rebellion against inequality. The people revolted not against inequality per se but against a system that gave them no perspective and offered them no hope for upward meritocratic mobility. The crucial factor is not the degree of intra-society inequality, but rather the impossibility of modifying the existing wealth distribution in a non-criminal manner. Wealth relations in France did not present a problem at a static level but at a dynamic level, as there was no possible legal pathway from one wealth cohort to another. According to this view, the rich have the right to go broke and become poor, whereas the poor have the right and legal mechanisms to become rich.

It also entails that, regardless of whether there are artificial or natural distinctions between groups, the government is responsible for treating them equally. That adequately embodies the idea that "all men are created equal." However, it does not imply that any such group is obligated to treat other groups equally; mutual respect is outside the single-axiom political philosophy. Yes, it means the equal rights of homosexual and heterosexual families— but only for engaging in government business. In other words, it does not mean heterosexuals must respect homosexuals outside the sphere of government business or vice versa. Essentially, society should ensure equal treatment of homosexuals by the government, but society's opinion about homosexuals could differ dramatically. It means society must enforce equal treatment of transexuals by the state, but transexuals must cast away any idea of sex rearrangement surgery on the taxpayers' dime. It means that black police officers must provide security for KKK torch marches, and Jewish police officers must provide security for neo-Nazi demonstrations—but the policemen in question have no further obligations. Outside government business, they may have opinions and reservations about the people they must protect—and vote accordingly. It means that a Jewish neurosurgeon fights for the life of an unfortunate Muslim teenager, and a Muslim FBI agent infiltrates a terrorist cell that plans to bomb a synagogue—while holding certain prejudices against each other's faith. Despite equal treatment from the government towards women and men, they continue to be treated unequally by society. Men will persist in classifying women into "Wifey material" and "Non-Wifey material." Women will carry on cataloging all men into two categories—"I am willing to take this guy's last name" and "I am not."

In every society, each person experiences a degree of freedom and a degree of non-freedom. The terms sound complementary, but they are not. Again, the word "freedom" is reserved exclusively for government-to-governed businesses. The word "freedom" does not apply to society, a domain of people-to-people interactions. In such a domain, only the term "non-freedom" applies. In a government that delivers a high degree of freedom, numerous attempts were made to alleviate some non-freedoms and taboos perpetually existing inside society by redirecting state power to intra-society issues. These attempts include the equalization of gays and the equalization of women. In both cases, we are not talking about political equalization, which exists by definition with a proper allocation of power between the government and the governed. Instead, we are talking about literal equalization inside the always intolerant and non-free intra-society business.

Suppose the political equivalency of men and women concerning their interactions with the government is a must. In that case, pushing artificial constructs like "menstruating men" and "penis-equipped women" will never become a norm. For example, the government must pledge political freedoms to women who consider themselves men. However, these individuals must understand that all bets are off in dealing not with the government but with other people. People may tolerate the political equality of LGBT folks regarding government affairs, but LGBT supremacism will never be accepted in society. The claimants of unenumerated constitutional rights, like "menstrual equity," will face an uphill battle.

If history teaches us anything, society will eventually reject such ideas due to their negative or close-to-zero cash value. Society is not as merciful as a government; ultimately, some ideas will be dumped into the status of fairies, goblins, and "knock on wood" cultural themes. Society is inherently inert, ponderous, and intolerant. This intolerance may be unrecognizable by the people living within it, but it is apparent upon reflection. Each member sees only the tip of the iceberg—the ruler, the government, the law, the celebrities—and ignores the vast governing negative freedom body under the surface that has an immense influence on his life.

As a result, conservatism carries anti-egalitarian and egalitarian vectors simultaneously—and this is not absurd. These terms are valid only in different domains: a solid egalitarian stance in the case of engagement with the government but commitment toward anti-egalitarian conditions in relationships between individuals. Thus, conservatism believes in the virtues of inequality and, at the same time, in the virtues of equality; being applied to separate domains eliminates all hints of cognitive dissonance. That is, in short, the perception of harmony amongst conservatives. The Declaration of Independence manifests this: "We hold these truths to be self-evident, that all men are created equal." The linguistic contortionism by left-wingers interprets the word "equal" here quite differently from the right-wingers. For Collectivists, "equal" means equality in everything, together with misery, while conservatives treat "equal" solely from a government-to-governed business mindset.

Leftists never worry about wealth disparities either. Instead, they weaponize the existing wealth disparity for a primitive power grab.

For conservatives, wealth disparities within society are never a source of concern. Instead, their primary concern is that those wealth disparities are contained within society and never, more than anything else, spill over into the government domain, where strict equality in government-to-governed engagements is a must. On the other hand, to be fair to Leftists, they never worry about wealth disparities either. Instead, they weaponize the existing wealth disparity for a primitive power grab.

In other words, the great watershed between right-wingers and left-wingers is the treatment of (unequal) wealth. The Right wants everybody to create new wealth. In contrast, the Left wants to redistribute existing wealth. (Basically, the assumption of "class" was introduced to facilitate the grand redistributive scheme). As such, the Left ideology leads to the politics of envy, revolutionary chaos, and subsequent misery.

EQUALITY AND INEQUALITY, IN WEALTH AND ELSEWHERE

Equality and inequality coexist because they are not opposites from the individual-state paradigm point of view: they are from different, incompatible, and incomparable domains. Like in quantum mechanics, these two states are in superposition. The trick is grasping that "equality" is the term concerning people-to-government business, while "inequality" refers to people-to-people business. Thus, each person is "equal" and "not equal" at the same time because "inequality" refers to wealth distribution between people; in contrast, "equality" refers to the equal political rights of all people in dealing with government.

In other words, conservatives can tolerate whatever measure of wealth inequality exists in society, even the existence of astronomically wealthy individuals—as long as their wealth does not penetrate government circles, or when it does, it is contained. When it does, however, it inevitably prompts social upheaval. Charles Hugh Smith named it "investing capital in the Capitol." One of the recent examples would be the participation of Internet-based social networks in purely government endeavors, like censorship and suppression of dissident thoughts based on demands of the surreptitious government-private ideological cartel.

Inequality in government-to-governed business is as perilous as equality in governed-to-governed business. Inequality in the former triggers social revolts, while enforcing equality in the latter eliminates all competition and removes all incentives for social and economic development. However, they are the two inseparable sides of the same coin: government business equality and intra-society inequality must coexist for the robust development of human civilization. Note that if equality's domain is the government-to-governed relationship, the modern Left's equity realm is intra-society relationships.

For American conservatives, the desirable law-making principle is: if it is in the Constitution, follow the letter of it; if it is not, follow the spirit of it, but all such laws must include a zero-sum game—if the government is allowed to do something, citizens must be given a properly working reciprocal mechanism. Otherwise, such a law shall be weeded out. For example, suppose the government administers a penalty for late or improper tax filing (quite a reasonable law, by the way). In that case, citizens must receive the same if their tax returns are not processed in a specified timeframe. Suppose the government places a person on the "no-fly list," "no-hire list," or any other "list of undesirable elements." In that case, citizens must be provided with a mechanism to review and challenge the decision. If the government wants to add some ingredients to commonly available gasoline—like ethanol—citizens must be provided with unrestricted access to ethanol-free gasoline.

Suppose the government wants to regulate the amount of water flushed in toilets. In that case, devising a rational reciprocal route is impossible, so such regulation must be eradicated. The alternative would be denying the power of law and affirming the law of power.

GOVERNMENT AS A REFERENCE FRAME

Each member of society signifies its frame of reference. All these frames are different; there are no two alike. Recall that one of the paper's results (Gindler 2020) is that people's knowledge and opinions diverge exponentially—similar to galaxies in the Universe. (An excellent demonstration would be a cake with raisins—when baked, all raisins are distanced from each other). That is why societies, in conformity with the individual-state paradigm, have realized a need for a single, universal, and absolute frame of reference against which everybody (well, almost everybody) has exact coordinates—the government. Any deviations from such design, however small, tend to compound over time and lead to a situation where "some animals are more equal than others."

From the physicist's point of view, a government is a stable reference frame against which (almost) all inherently and perpetually unequal individuals are regarded as equal. (Obviously, not all citizens fall into the "equal" category. There are exceptions: imprisoned criminals, slaves, and those explicitly denied equality, like serfs or medieval peasants.) Moreover, it is probably the only non-transcendental reference frame that provides such a feature, for any other reference frame carries a degree of inequality. The government appears to be a mechanism that maintains a stable cohabitation of unequal humans by providing a platform against which everybody is somehow equal. In any given process, the government acts as a giant political modulator: it decreases some people's power and influence while increasing others' power and influence, but only when it comes to government-to-governed affairs. That is, in theory. In reality, crooked political operators always try to distort that picture. Some of them, collectively known as Leftists, are trying to expand the "equality" maxim outside the government-to-governed domain.

Expanding the equality mantra into a wrong domain either produces an ungovernable public or exaggerates intra-society inequality. The common sentiment among Leftists is that they have identified a way out of this dilemma: forced intra-society equality, which, according to the permeating smell of naphthalene Marxism, makes any government no longer needed. Unfortunately, the reality is that such forced intra-society equality could be found only in concentration camps. That is right: Leftism claims to guide people out of Plato's cave but channels them into re-education barracks.

From the physicist's point of view, a government is a stable reference frame against which (almost) all inherently and perpetually unequal individuals are regarded as equal.

Thus, Leftism could be hypothesized as an ideological autoimmune disease. As a result, society turns on itself; as such, it clearly shows its evolutionary impasse. The Left symbolizes a philosophy of dissonance when stated objectives, operating methods, and end results conflict with one another. That dissonance is a fundamental feature, not a bug, of Leftism.

The apotheosis of freedom is not overindulgence. On the contrary, the apotheosis of freedom must be established as liberty in government-to-governed relations and, simultaneously, as unfreedom in governed-to-governed relations. In other words, the government must act as an absolute frame of reference against which everybody within heterogeneous populations with multi-dimensional inequality is treated equally.

The one side of the equality coin—equality in relation to government—is complemented by the other side of the same coin, namely, drastically unequal in all other imaginable respects of population. Therefore, any attempts to force inequality in regard to the government or force equality among the people with respect to one another are categorically opposed by the individual-state paradigm. If the former mindset is easily analogous with hyper-corrupt criminal territory ruled over by competing warlords, the latter is, without a doubt, the unreachable Collectivist Utopia.

Both outcomes were possible during the Revolutionary War by thirteen American colonies, albeit under different names. Both were unacceptable for the Founding Fathers, but that led to a seemingly impossible dilemma: to create a state that would be strong and weak simultaneously. The Founding Fathers decided to implement the crossover variant by implementing the idea of enumerated powers for the first time in history. The doctrine of enumerated powers was clearly stated by James Madison in 1788 (Federalist No. 45): "The powers delegated by the proposed Constitution to the Federal government, are few and defined. Those which are to remain in the State governments are numerous and indefinite." The "few and defined" powers had created a weak and, at the same time, strong Federal government. The "numerous and indefinite" powers had created strong and, at the same time, weak state governments. In other words, the young American Republic got a strong, hard shell and soft, delicate tissue.

There is no paradox in the shared sovereign scheme here, as the terms "weak" and "strong" must be applied to different domains. If the Federal government was tasked with mainly dealing in the international arena, the state governments were tasked with strictly domestic issues. In other words, the Founding Fathers assumed Federal and state powers were complementary and nonoverlapping, but that rosy theoretical scheme was easier said than done. The resulting tug-of-war between Federal and state governments extends to the present; the country is still too young to assign an accurate estimate to the cash value of varying balances of powers.

It makes applying the individual-state paradigm to the United States somewhat nuanced compared to all other countries. The United States is the only country in the world built "from the bottom up," while the rest of the world's nation-states were built "from the top down." The States created the United States Federal government from scratch, not vice versa. The Federal-State power balance strictly tackles the individual-state paradigm to State governments. As for the Federal government, it applies to federal powers only over specific enumerated domestic issues. The military, diplomatic, and political might of the United States Federal government in the international area is not directly limited by the individual-state paradigm. The individual-state paradigm affects the Federal government only tangentially.

The main danger arises when the mighty "hard shell" (the Federal government) spills over its unenumerated power (often erratically) into the "soft tissue"—the purview of State governments.

After that, the Civil War became a watershed event in the political history of the United States. Before the War, the Federal government was traditionally considered a mere servant to the individual States. However, the Civil War marked an unprecedented power grab by the Federal government at the expense of States' rights. Ask any Washington bureaucrat these days—nobody considers himself a "servant to the States" anymore. In the 21st century, such an idea would be laughed off by the unaccountable elites of the Washington Swamp.

The United States is the only country in the world built "from the bottom up," while the rest of the world's nation-states were built "from the top down."

In summary, the conservative view of the individual-state paradigm assumes equal treatment by the government of individuals who are unequal in all other respects. Essentially, conservatism views equality in dealing with the government—the "equal protection under the law"—as the only type of equality that a citizen may possibly experience throughout his or her lifetime. Equality between peers, on the one hand, and equality between peers and the government, on the other hand, are two distinct types of equality. They occupy unrelated domains and are destined to remain standing in their respective domains.

The breach of domain boundaries has numerous undesirable results. For example, consider a society where intra-society inequality extends into the government as a result of unequal treatment of citizens or where the government enforces equality across all aspects of the intra-society business. To conclude, the primary delineator is the determining factor that forces the government to respect the "consent of the governed."

In point of fact, it is not a paradox that countries dedicated to political equality were born with and maintain economic inequality. Besides, there is no contradiction because political equality (read: freedom) belongs to a category of man-to-state relations. In contrast, economic inequality belongs to a category of man-to-man relations. An idealized society has no overlap between these relationships. Realistically, they do overlap because certain people make their living from the government (public school teachers, military, etc.).

The absolute impossibility of legally changing property relations led to the emergence of numerous left-wing recipes, the meaning of which boils down to a simple "take away and redistribute."

However small, the government's economic power will always attract some people who try to resolve society's internal problems with the help of the government's might. Likewise, private wealth, however small, will always attract some people who will try to resolve the government's internal problems with the help of private capital. Right-wingers advocate disengaging the two economic spheres, while left-wingers always try to conflate the two, recruiting the government or private forces as political expediency dictates. From that view, political evolution may lead to two excesses: the hegemony of state power over society (Fascism and other forms of Socialism) or the political hegemony of selected private wealth. In both cases, people lose political and economic freedom, but we must distinguish between them because of their different roads to people's serfdom. The path of utilizing state power to settle intra-society scores has been tried many times in history and has consistently produced miserable results.

> **The absolute impossibility of legally changing property relations led to the emergence of numerous left-wing recipes, the meaning of which boils down to a simple "take away and redistribute."**

On the other hand, using selected private wealth to settle intra-government (read: political) scores has been known since the first pre-human tribes were formed and produced mixed results. The fundamental reason for these failures is cross-domain penetration due to a weakness in guardrails against excesses. For example, in the 21st century, we have witnessed numerous attempts to use the state's power to win culture war battles. The WEF (World Economic Forum) gives an obvious example of gravitating toward the Leftist Utopia by deploying private capital.

The individual-state paradigm sheds light on why many wealthy businessmen are on opposing sides of political barricades. There is a simple explanation for this. Businesses that serve millions of individuals usually lean to the Right, while those that deal primarily with the government often lean to the

Left. (As a side note, it clarifies why many wealthy Jews in the United States stay committed to the openly antisemitic Democrat Party and why Federal scientific grants over private funding play a critical role in shaping the American scientific community's political preferences.)

INDIVIDUALISM VS. COLLECTIVISM

A remarkable breakthrough was made by Copernicus in 16th-century astronomy when he shifted the fulcrum from the Earth to the Sun, making the movements of celestial bodies more simple, precise, and predictable. It is unfortunate that the simplicity and predictability sought by political philosophy are rarely present; we can only hope that the individual-state paradigm will fill the void. Per John Ray, "Leftism has the appeal of simplicity" (Ray 2004). The presented individual-state paradigm preserves that simplicity and adds much-needed simplicity to both opponents. In actuality, the elegance of the (generalized) one-dimensional ideological spectrum lies in its irreducible simplicity. The individual-state paradigm removes ambivalence and unnecessary complexity of ideological warfare. Similar to the success of Copernicus, who made a simple switch from one frame of reference to another, describing political philosophy from a different angle (read: frame of reference) should add much-needed clarity.

If the individual-state paradigm hypothesis is accepted, looking at what is happening in society from this angle will reveal rational meaning in many seemingly irrational events. Thus, meticulously framed as a dichotomy, the left-right issue eliminates all possible nuances that pundits, politicians, and pseudo-intellectuals love. However, real-world political forces rarely voluntarily adhere to such clean dichotomies as the individual-state paradigm.

Amidst the Left, it is generally believed that the Right places a high value on individualism. However, even if such an opinion has merit, it is not entirely correct. The Right operates under the premise of the primacy of individual wealth over government wealth. Individuals must possess more economic—and therefore political—power than the government to obtain this ratio of primacy. Individuals' economic dominance over the government results in individual liberty. In other words, individualism is not the cause; it is the effect of (relatively) small governments that cannot become tyrannous due to their (relative) economic fragility. Conservatives view efforts to circumscribe government as a cornerstone. Their ideological opponents work hard to constrain people, just like the previous 99 percent of Homo sapiens' existence, when government by coercion was ubiquitous.

Libertarians elevate personal freedom to the center of their ideology.[21] They understand personal freedom genuinely and unmistakably in terms of an individual-state relationship. However, they overlook that personal freedom is not an independent variable but a derivative of a more fundamental, material relationship between the government and the governed. As the government Leviathan grows, personal freedom becomes increasingly limited, not the other way around. Consolidation of government power can shape and ultimately override the wishes of the governed. Therefore, the fight for individual liberty per se, however noble, is misguided. This kind of effort is purely quixotic. Freedom is not a panacea since it deals with symptoms rather than root causes. The root cause is the material dominance of the government over the governed or vice versa, as expressed by the individual-state paradigm.

Individuals' economic dominance over the government results in individual liberty.

The perceived conflict between Individualism and Collectivism is non-existent; proper Collectivism's antagonist is Conservatism. Individualism is merely one of the features of Conservatism.

Libertarians assign the highest social value to individual freedom; as such, they use merely one of the primary problem's attributes, not the essence.[22] Conversely, conservatism maintains that personal wealth possesses the highest social value; individual liberty is a natural consequence of a fair distribution of wealth between the government and the governed. Note also that liberty and equality are not identical. Equality manifests itself during people's interactions with a government; on the contrary, liberty manifests itself through non-interaction with the government.

---

21. The paper "Introduction to Politiphysics" (Gindler 2019) provides a mathematical formalism for the individual-state paradigm and offers strict (in the mathematical sense) definitions of standard political science terms—freedom, revolution, etc. However, such a formalism is well beyond the scope of this book.

22. Adrian Vermeule wisely noted that "Liberty is a good servant but a bad master" (Vermeule 2021).

Since freedom of speech is a particular case of general political freedom, it must also be assessed from the same standpoint: it is a particular instance of the relationship between an individual and a government. It is not possible to have freedom without government; the right to free speech is rational only within this context. Any deviation from this framework may lead to silly paradoxes, such as issues arising from shouting "Fire!" in a crowded theater.

Without the government's presence in the equation, "freedom of speech" is meaningless.[23] That is not "protected speech" or one of the "commonsense restrictions." Such acts have nothing to do with freedom at all and with the absolutism of freedom of speech. There is complementary absolutism in addition to free speech—a complete lack of freedom for all intra-societal actions.

Therefore, there is freedom for vulgar, obscene, hateful, provocative, subversive, and blasphemous language, as any attempt to censor them would require a government-created definition of "undesirable speech" and, as a consequence, would provide intense pressure for regulating all aspects of speech. The idea is not to force rude language on people but to leave this aspect of human activity exclusively to the human mind. Thus, in most cases, society must manage expletives and harmful stereotypes, such as antisemitism. However, in cases that deal with property, it must be done through the court system.

> **Without the government's presence in the equation, "freedom of speech" is meaningless.**

The court system should be the only forum through which governments can participate in discussions concerning intra-society non-existent freedom of speech. Governments must enact and enforce laws that award compensation for tangible harm (not potential harm, feelings, discomfort, or what the government deems "disinformation") caused by one person to another.

Likewise, the First Amendment to the United States Constitution applies to people-to-government business only and does not apply to people-to-people interactions. If the freedom of speech exists unconditionally, in the absolute form, in the people-to-government domain, then speech (and manners) in

---

23. Recall a famous adage, common in totalitarian countries: "We do have freedom of speech. However, we do not have freedom after speech."

the society ex-government is under many written and unwritten rules, laws, taboos, superstitions, and cultural nuances.

The widespread misunderstanding of the applicability of the term "freedom" exclusively within the government-to-governed domain produces some strange and disconnected from the reality definitions of "freedom." One of the well-known (and incorrect) definitions is based on, first, negative conceptions, like "freedom is the absence of restraint." Second, it mixes up two distinct domains and applies that definition to the government-to-governed domain and the society itself. Personal freedom exists (or, better, freedom materializes) only during engagement with the government. When the engagement is over, liberty is over, too, for there is no such thing as "freedom" in engaging with other members of society. The presented location of freedom within the conceptual structure of conservatism is non-negotiable.

Like how temperature materializes only during interactions between a measured physical body and a thermometer, freedom materializes only during engagements with a government. Per Milton Friedman, "Government is necessary to preserve our freedom, it is an instrument through which we can exercise our freedom" (Friedman 1982, p. 2). In principle,

> **Personal freedom exists (or, better, freedom materializes) only during engagement with the government.**

there can be no freedom when there are no dealings with a government or even when there is no government at all. Thus, each person's existence is characterized by the superposition of two states: a certain degree of freedom traceable to a government and a certain degree of non-freedom caused by society.

In a speech before the Phoenix Chamber of Commerce in 1961, Ronald Reagan said, "Freedom is never more than one generation away from extinction. We did not pass it on to our children in the bloodstream. The only way they can inherit the freedom we have known is if we fight for it, protect it, defend it, and then hand it to them with the well-taught lessons of how they in their lifetime must do the same" (cited in Mann 2019, p. 119). What did the future president mean? He was undoubtedly referring to freedom in the context of government-to-governed interactions. He never meant the absolute unfreedom that dwells in intra-societal business. Freedom in government interactions is always accompanied by unfreedom within society. Intra-societal unfreedom is, in practice, passed to children in the bloodstream. The inherent danger is in mixing government-effectuated freedom and society-induced unfreedom.

In short, a person could be simultaneously free and unfree; his/her current state of liberty is a superposition of free and unfree components. There is no contradiction because the origins of these components are different. The "free" component comes from the relationship with the government, and the "unfree" component comes from society.

The relationship between these individual states of liberty is often inverse. For example, even in a country assessed as "free" (based on the government frame of reference, i.e., written law), an individual in society is surrounded by numerous unwritten laws, regulations, traditions, customs, and superstitions. An individual may have total freedom of expression, honored by the government. However, society may ignore government-related freedoms and impose strict, even draconian, written or oral speech restrictions. For example, a government may consider insulting or satirizing a politician acceptable. However, in some isolated cases, society may evaluate the situation from a distinct attitude—like an abhorrent attack on a parent of a disabled child—and reject it. Alternatively, a government may criminalize all attempts to ridicule a politician, while society would be OK with that. Obviously, mixing the term "free" emanating from different frames of reference is misleading and counterproductive.

Freedom in government interactions is always accompanied by unfreedom within society.

Racial antipathy is despicable, but government-enforced racial empathy is even more disgraceful. Whites must be able to sue for proven loss of wealth resulting from racism and prejudice, and blacks must be able to sue for proven loss of wealth resulting from racism and prejudice. A substantial monetary loss is a fairly good deterrent. Recall that the American Wild West was—despite ahistorical Hollywood movies—generally a polite and tolerant society, for all impudent fellows were bound to suffer a bullet between their eyes in due time.

Upon being loosed from the bottle, the genie of the primacy of the governed over the government can never return, as human history after the Magna Carta indicates.

English became the most popular language worldwide, even though many other languages represented great economic, financial, and scientific powers: French, German, and Spanish, to name a few. However, from one cardinal assessment, English is distinct from all other languages—since the Magna Carta, it has symbolized freedom.

Equality must be construed in the same circumstances as freedom—namely, within a relationship between the governed and the government. Outside that context, equality is grossly misconstrued. The danger is that dirty political operators could redefine the term's meaning as time passes. Historically, Collectivists have done precisely that. As a result of their misinterpretation, equality is no longer interpreted in terms of government-to-governed relations; rather, equality is understood in terms of governed-to-governed relations. The Leftists' meaning of the word allows them to play people, communities, and nations against one another while gradually, under the radar, increasing inequality in the traditional, government-to-governed sense. In the vast majority of cases, it breeds authoritarianism at the minimum and dictatorship at the maximum, all in the name of "equality."

In essence, the problem is that equality of political rights belongs to one category and equality of economic results to another. Equality of rights is in the government-to-governed domain, while equality of results is in the governed-to-governed domain. In other words, men and women who face the government are guaranteed equal rights. However, when they cooperate or interact with other individuals, "equality" has no meaning—just as "freedom" does not apply to interpersonal interactions. So, if the government is not part of the equation, then human rights do not exist.

It is pretty amusing that modern Leftists can redefine terms to mean their opposites. For example, previous generations of Leftists commonly accepted the term "equality" as a standard wealth redistribution scheme from the rich to the poor. The modern Leftist sister term "equity" means collecting and redistributing wealth from the poor to the pre-approved list of mega-wealthy politically correct and ideologically pure individuals—while the openly robbed population is somehow kept happy.

The endless debates about what is primary and secondary in a democracy, liberty or equality, are primarily misleading and widely incorrect. Also confusing are the notions that liberty and equality are somehow inversely related. The individual-state paradigm mandates that liberty cannot and never should be compared to equality unless a proper domain is explicitly specified. In the case of the people-to-government domain, liberty is simply a euphemism for equality. In contrast, in the people-to-people domain, equality is non-existent, and liberty is not applicable—both by definition.

To conclude, the distinction between the Right and the Left can be explained as follows: the Left aims to use equality of rights as a political weapon to achieve equality of economic results. This domain-swapping method is commonly called "bait and switch." On the contrary, the Right absolutizes the unrestricted power of the governed over the government and ignores inequality of economic results. Consequently, in order to accomplish its objectives, the Right must keep the material power of the government low relative to the governed. Likewise, the Left aims to increase the government's material power over the governed's objections.

The Left aims to use equality of rights as a political weapon to achieve equality of economic results.

Religion is understood as a relationship between a man and God. Freedom is understood as a relationship between a man and the government. Intellect is understood as a relationship between an individual man and the truth.

The trend has been unmistakable throughout the last five millennia: the ratio of government wealth to taxpayer wealth has steadily declined. Thus, the world generally moves toward greater freedom. However, the decline is far from uniform. Many countries are stubbornly absent from the process—the majority of them practice a form of organized religion (or an ideology elevated to the scale of religion) that is colossally difficult, maybe even impossible (by reason of the nature of religious foundations) to separate from a state. Often, organized religions became appendages to the ruling regime. Typical examples are countries that elevate a particular religion to the status of the state religion.

In other words, religion, as the relationship between a man and God, is confined to a private, individualistic sphere. There is no collective relationship between men and God unless a "religion" amalgamates with a government and becomes a servant of the state.

By defining religion as the relationship between a man and God(s), religion does not carry any ideological (read: left-wing or right-wing) payload.

In addition, it does not play a regressive or progressive role in society per se. However, what is currently known as "religion" has a scanty resemblance to the definitional relationship between a man and God(s). Modern religions survive evolutionary beatings. The most successful religions have joined forces with governments to, first, suppress competing religions and, second, make themselves indispensable for the state's existence.

Unmarried to the state religions may have their heyday occasionally. However, in general, they are in permanent decline. A typical example is the Deistic Cult of the Supreme Being during the French Revolution, which lasted just three months.

Deism does not accept the Holy Books of Christianity, Judaism, or Islam. They are considered insignificant "fairy tales" and unnecessary for the Deity's existence. It demonstrates that the religion stripped of its entertainment component cannot be widely accepted into society or government (in the United States, Deism followers constitute a fraction of one percent).

> **Religion is understood as a relationship between a man and God. Freedom is understood as a relationship between a man and the government. Intellect is understood as a relationship between an individual and the truth.**

CONSERVATISM'S BORDERS

In opposition to Libertarianism, National Conservatism places the nation's common good at the center of its ideology. As Libertarians lionize individual freedom, National Conservatives lionize the nation's welfare. In their view, economic relations are subordinate to the common good,[24] but by placing horses behind the carriage, they commit the same methodological error as Libertarians. It is not only possible for an overpowering government to redefine the common good; it will actually do so. While the common good certainly exists, all attempts to reach it are pointless because we learn about

---

24. The term "common good" is not even in the United States Constitution, which has the word "common" only in terms like "common defense" or "common law."

it only after the fact, *a posteriori*. *A priori* little is known about each of the so-called "common goods." Evolutionary competition among various "common goods" is as fierce as ideological and biological competition. To combat this, societies need some degree of freedom, which brings us back to a primary, pivotal issue: the balance of material power between the government and the governed.

Despite the shortcomings stemming from the individual-state paradigm, National Conservatism dispenses plenty of promising ideas on the culture war front from the secondary delineator's way of looking. Moreover, they appeal to younger generations, who overwhelmingly prefer reading books in electronic format and have no idea what a dust jacket is.

Collectivists have over-referenced the "common good" for two centuries, but it is one of the Left's misguided principles. The term itself assumes a certain primacy of the collective over an individual, which, as it is currently known, applies brakes to society's development. For example, a significant negative correlation exists between the government's size and economic growth (Bergh and Henrekson 2011). In terms of individual freedom, oppression by a government is indistinguishable from oppression by a collective mob. (Governments are well aware of this fact and have learned to exploit it. They emphasize that a government's action might theoretically be appealed, whereas a mob's judgment will always be final and unquestionable.)

It is not only possible for an overpowering government to redefine the common good; it will actually do so.

Conservatism, as defined via the individual-state paradigm, cannot be further radicalized, for it embodies the ultimate—single—cardinal axiom. Of course, there is wiggle room for the desired value of government wealth vs. the wealth of the governed ratio, but that is it.

Patrick Allitt emphasizes the first and foremost feature of all branches of Conservatism: strong anti-utopianism (Allitt 2009). Michel Gurfinkiel expressed this line of thought in terms of a tendency of conservatives "to think that communities and nations are best organized from the bottom-up—in a piecemeal, self-adjusting, idiosyncratic way—rather than from the top down through all-embracing rationalism imposed by means of social engineering"

(Gurfunkiel 2015). Overall, these cases support the view that anti-utopianism and the bottom-up approach are simple corollaries of the individual-state paradigm.

The recommended wealth allocation between the government and the governed must not be acclaimed as the grand elixir for all society's maladies. The hope of conservatism—an unsubstantial government under total control of the governed—stops at the border. In other words, the ideological jurisdiction of conservatism does not transcend the country's borders. Thus, what the individual-state paradigm does not explain—by definition—is foreign policy. The individual-state paradigm has nothing to do with international affairs, as it is axiomatically, purposefully, and narrowly focused on internal affairs as specified by just one fundamental principle. Even though there are numerous strains of Socialism, both National and International, there has never been and can never be an International Conservatism. Conservatism is axiomatically National—and, as such, is the archenemy of Globalism. There is no such thing as a "conservative foreign policy think tank" or "conservative foreign policy establishment." All such constructs are artificial, even if the dollar amounts they operate with are material. Friedrich Hayek emphasized this thesis by writing about the "close connection between conservatism and nationalism" (Hayek 1960). For the Leftists, the situation is the opposite; they treat foreign policy as domestic policy by other means.

What the individual-state paradigm does not explain—by definition—is foreign policy.

Naturally, the reality of life outside a country cannot be placed on the Procrustean bed of internal affairs. Any attempt to expand conservative principles beyond national boundaries would fail. Like any political philosophy, conservatism has its limits of applicability, either explicit or implicit. (By the way, refusing to define, hide, or ignore such limits is ideologically naïve and unproductive.) That is why, to the dismay of their diehard followers, some Republicans support Democratic presidents in their foreign endeavors and vice versa. That is why there are as many foreign policy "hawks" as "doves" within Republican and Democratic politicians: the primary delineator allows it because foreign policy portrays a secondary ideological attribute. There are as many interventionists and isolationists in the ruling and opposition parties as current political expediency dictates—and it is an acceptable political norm as it should be. As an aside, the export of right-wing ideologies should be encouraged since they accept the existence of below-par governments incapable of waging war or provoking conflict between neighbors. In other words, the export of conservative ideas instead of the export of democracy should be fostered in order to attain lasting peace.

At first glance, the situation appears contradictory; a meager government cannot protect national borders and acts as an invitation to foreign invaders. Thus, a government must be weak enough to secure freedom while simultaneously being strong enough to ensure unbreachable borders.

The United States Founding Fathers knew about this contradiction. The way they discovered a solution was genius: they decided to create a country where the government was weak and strong simultaneously—by breaking up government powers. The Founding Fathers gave practically unlimited powers (what came to be known as enumerated powers) to some avenues and forced the government to be inherently weak in other areas. They intentionally strengthened the security-related powers of the Federal government and purposely weakened the powers of government in freedom-related areas. Thus, the Federal government became a two-faced Janus: the first side, the tough one, was facing outward, and the second, the soft one, was facing inward. The conveyed scheme would work as long as those two faces did not penetrate each other's domains. Sadly, every reader is familiar with examples of such interpenetration, such as bombing feudal tribes in a faraway land into democracy or treating all white American males as "extremists."

Under Liberalism, there was not only a separation between church and state but also a separation of the economy and the state. Economic and political spheres should be kept far apart, but it is easier to say than to do. If in the 20th century, the penetration of the economy into politics was dominating, in the 21st century, the opposite winds are blowing. Currently, politics penetrates all categories of workers and management. Corporations are being segregated based on political preferences, especially the upper echelons of executives. The political stance of the corporate board routinely leaks out, sometimes deliberately—and it costs these corporations a lot of money. "Go Woke, go broke," says a famous Internet maxim. Note the apparent asymmetry in the process: if the politicization of capital—which leads to economic partisanship—mostly has negative consequences for businesses, the capitalization of politics mostly has positive consequences for politicians.[25] The total dominance of government in politics, economics, and culture transforms society into a *de facto* colony of the state.

Another limitation of the individual-state paradigm is that it provides necessary but insufficient conditions for a just society. Thus, the individual-state paradigm does not possess the only known mechanism for building a full-flavored and stable society—the separation of powers and enumerated powers. Only the separation of powers concept and the theory of enumerated powers lead to the creation of a government that is both sufficiently strong and necessarily weak. Characterized by a single axiom, Conservatism equals Liberalism, but that fact does not automatically lead society toward prosperity, dignity, respect for the law, and individual rights. It maintains that purely theoretically. Alternative ideologies could deliver the niceties mentioned above, but we should be pretty skeptical that other ideologies have not been tried and have survived the unmerciful social evolutionary selection.

Another limitation of the individual-state paradigm is that it provides necessary but insufficient conditions for a just society.

For instance, a society that does not protect breastfeeding mothers will vanish in just a few generations. It must be said that all such communities have disappeared without a trace. Like Ancient Sparta, a society that focuses on specific (military) physical abilities and ignores practically everything else is destined to fail. Likewise, a society that blurs the lines between men and women has no bright future.

Note that we are talking about society here, not the government. The point is that society, not the government, must care for young mothers, encourage competition among men, and separate competition among women. Inserting women into men's evolutionary competition, men into women's evolutionary rivalry, or inserting the government into such an evolutionary endeavor marks the beginning of the end of society.

---

25. Senator Ted Cruz offers terrific "behind the scenes" exposure about how the Cultural War is happening in Washington, DC (Cruz 2023).

COMMON ANCESTOR

Humans and apes share a common ancestor, and all branches of Leftism, including Communism, Socialism, Fascism, Statism, Marxism, Trotskyism, Maoism, and National Socialism, do as well. Moreover, that common ancestor is opposite to the Right—from the individual-state paradigm frame of reference—and the nuances between Leftist ideologies are simply the offered measure of the abolition of private property and the degree of the asserted control of the rest. Across the spectrum, there is a great deal of variation, ranging from the complete abolishment of private property under Communism to the limited possibility of private ownership by certain not-so-radical Leftists. Globalism may be the one exception. Even though the specifics remain unclear, it appears that private property is permitted under Globalism, albeit in limited circumstances. Only members of the supranational ruling demigods will be permitted to own property, rendering all others "quasi-slaves." "Slave" is an old-fashioned word; the proper term in Newspeak/Wokespeak has yet to be determined, but it is likely to be reminiscent of "free citizens."

There has always been a sense of uncertainty associated with Left-Right dualism. Two centuries ago, opposing political forces engaged in ideological wars that did not overlap, and this paradox persists today. The Right is primarily concerned with freedom in modern times, whereas the Left is concerned with equity. Occasionally, it is stated as follows: the Right prefers equality at the beginning, and the Left prefers equality at the end. However, it is inaccurate, given that they fall under distinct categories. In spite of this, there is some overlap in these ideological wars, provided that the individual-state paradigm is accepted. That is because freedom and equity are derivatives of the state-man paradigm. Therefore, they cannot be treated as independent variables in the political equation. Instead, they are direct effects of the distribution of wealth between the governed and the government.

An individual-state paradigm applies to all human societies, realized or unrealized, from cavemen to feudal systems to Utopias. In contrast, primitive class warfare is carried out exclusively in societies where a class is both relevant and well-defined. Consequently, there were no oppressed classes in the Soviet Union, but the government and the governed existed. Similarly, there are no "classes" in anarchist theory, but the non-existing governing body remains in charge, and the governed are still subject to it. Therefore, the inferred paradigm is applicable to even the most Utopian societies, such as Communism (which officially declares the dissolution of government but still maintains an all-encompassing government).

No matter the circumstances, the government and the governed will always exist, regardless of society's size, customs, or historical period. The individual-state paradigm generalizes and extends the Right-Left distinction outside the traditional domain of democratic countries and can now be applied to authoritarian and totalitarian regimes.

> **An individual-state paradigm applies to all human societies, realized or unrealized, from cavemen to feudal systems to Utopias.**

Of course, ideological competition in any country is characterized by more than one dimension, but a one-dimensional mode bears something much needed: absolute resistance to misinterpretation. For example, it eliminates the possibility of holding Right and Left views simultaneously (known as "ideological asymmetry" by those who do not like the term "cognitive dissonance.") It makes it impossible to be economically left-wing and culturally right-wing or vice versa. If one accepts axiomatic conservatism, it prevents terms like "conservative socialism," "Tory Socialism," "right-wing socialism," "green conservatism," "middle-way conservatism," "dialectical conservatism," and other similar oxymorons.

Finally, it offers a solid definition of ideological "center" as an ideology that aims to keep the government's economic and control power close to aggregate society's economic and control power. (It also brings forward the inherent political and economic instability of the "centrist" policy.) In other words, a single-axiom political philosophy *a priori* is just another model of society with some attractive characteristics worth studying.

DENIAL OF REALITY AND PASSIONATE BELIEF IN POSTMODERNIST UNREALITY

Richard Rorty's political stance is unambiguous: he was a committed socialist (he counted himself a "social democrat," though he eventually dropped that term in favor of "liberal.") Nevertheless, he was one of the first on the Left to recognize the dangers of Soviet Imperialism (Rorty 1987). He wanted to fight the ayatollahs in Iran and "nomenklatura in Moscow" simultaneously, calling them "gangs of thugs" (with a reservation that "much of what each gang says about its rivals is all too true.") Rorty was brave enough to declare that the left-wing critique of "bourgeois ideology" of "late capitalism" has "turned into self-parody." His view of Marxism "as an amiable, but fruitless, exercise in nostalgia" was seen as heresy on the Left.

Rorty harnessed a historically inaccurate but linguistically elegant trick. Like all Leftists, he revealed the grand theft idea of establishing a "social democratic utopia—a future to the human race in which Enlightenment liberalism is carried through to its limit." Namely, Rorty tried to constitute proof of a (non-existent) line of ideological inheritance between Enlightenment liberalism and Leftism (Marxian or non-Marxian). Furthermore, it seems that the real, behind-the-scenes reason for which the tenured Left presumed Rorty "controversial" was a mere slip of the tongue, almost in Freudian fashion.

The Left made a concerted effort during the post-World War II era to establish a lineage to the original classical liberalism of the 18th century. Nevertheless, the existence of two distinct strains of socialism, the International strain (in the Soviet Union) and the National strain (in Mussolini's Italy and the Third Reich, albeit only by name), taints the legacy of that lineage.

Like all other Leftists, Rorty re-labels (perfectly in accordance with canon) National Socialism as "right-wing" and places Reaganism, for instance, in the same category as Nazism. Yet his intellectual honesty prevented him from waving that "right-wing" flag perpetually. Instead, Rorty put together a decidedly telling reservation, saying, "...we should not try too hard to label philosophical views by 'rightist' or 'leftist,' nor waste too much time asking what 'ideology' they represent" (Rorty 1987, p. 574). Indeed, in-depth analysis of such questions is near the taboo tier for all in the Leftist commentariat—and the main reason for drafting this book. Considering the individual-state paradigm, the Left could not forge anything more conceptually impressive than vulgar Marxism. As a result, the modern Left is burdened by decades of ideological baggage and its ensuing derangements.

Rorty managed to ask a question dismaying for all Collectivists: "Why can we not yet point with pride to a non-capitalist democracy?" The answer is simple—there is no such thing as "non-free capitalism." Likewise, there is no such thing as "non-free democracy." Why? Since economic freedom and political freedom are two sides of the same coin. Human history has not shown an example of an economically free but politically repressive society or an economically prohibitive but politically open society. There are only isolated examples in literature in the form of various Utopian stories.

Collectivists are known for fanatical denial of reality and passionate belief in postmodernist Unreality. In Unreality, everything is a "social construct." Everything is subjective and ephemeral and stems from uncontrolled, unconscious thinking. Leftist dogmas, however, are off-limits. Essentially, the Left Cerberus guards the credos and prevents anyone from even considering "race is a social construct" or "equity is a social construct."

A positive outcome of unprecedented political polarization in the 21st century is the widespread recognition that authentic Leftist and Rightist ideologies are mutually exclusive. The political and economic primacy of the individual over the government, promoted by the Right, cannot be reconciled with the government's primacy over the individual, promoted by the Left. The irreconcilable, uncompromising disagreement manifests itself in every political issue, sometimes explicitly, sometimes implicitly. It is important to stress that the monumentally

Collectivists are known for fanatical denial of reality and passionate belief in postmodernist Unreality.

incompatible nature of the conflict should not serve as a deterrent, since such controversy has been a part of human civilization from the very beginning. The first step in resolving this primary conflict is to accept that the opposing side is not necessarily evil but simply wrong.

To illustrate, Leftism is not inherently evil. Its adherents need to learn how to identify solutions instead of just identifying problems. Collectivists are largely meticulous in identifying ills in society, but they quickly turn around and utilize the perceived victims of these problems as political cannon fodder.

ANCIENT AND MODERN CONSERVATISM

While "conservatism" is less than two centuries old, systematic conservative ideas go back to Medieval Britain and never deviate from the simple foundational principle: the primacy of men over concentrated government power.

Were the Whigs conservative? As specified by the individual-state paradigm, they were conservative long before the term was widely accepted.

However, all such bold statements must be complemented with a disclaimer stating that Whigs could be reduced to a single axiom. The reality is that the Whigs held not one but a bouquet of views, and they are inseparable from these views. Of course, it applies to both British and American Whigs.

The Liberal origins of Conservatism are well-known. The seminal 1958 book of Harry Jaffa, "Crisis of the House Divided: An Interpretation of the Issues in the Lincoln-Douglas Debates," offers a clear line of ideological inheritance between the Founding Fathers and the writings of Locke.

A novel strain of Leftism emerged around the turn of the 20th century, the Progressive Left. They proclaimed a new way to solve problems accompanying "wild capitalism," namely elevating a powerful central government to the center of the political universe. The progressive Left began with progressive taxes; however, they needed to take additional, unusual steps as part of their strategy. After stealing its identity from liberals, who dominated the 19th century, the Left initially reincarnated itself under the "reform liberals" name. Then they declared any opposition to Collectivist ideas as "conservative"—under the premise that the opposition resists revolutionary change. That word game proved successful because the Left-redefined terms "liberal" and "conservative" had entered the public conscience.

How come environmental sustainability, a pure conservative agenda at its core, suddenly became a battle cry for the Left?

One of the undisputed achievements of the Left is stealing not just identities but ideas. So how come environmental sustainability, a pure conservative agenda at its core, suddenly became a battle cry for the Left?

The drama's final act was the concept that "everything is a social construct." Under this concept, "liberal" and "conservative" terms are not what they are but what the government propaganda machine says they are. Truth be told, the Left here is, to some extent, correct—conservatism, undeniably, is a matter of resisting left-wing social experiments and revolutions. Nevertheless, such resistance is focused only on Left ideology (as one of the many zero cash value ideologies) and is never meant to be against the progress of society overall. Those who state conservatism represents "resistance to progress" and is a retrograde and reactionary ideology demonstrate their full acceptance of left-wing terminology. Thus, since the dawn of the 20th century, we have lived under two versions of liberalism: classical liberalism, or conservatism, and reform liberalism, or simply Leftism/Collectivism.

Here is another example of a recent case of "borrowing" and "switching" standard terminology. In the early 21st century, Leftists managed to reassign the color red to Republicans (partially right-wingers) and blue to Democrats (mostly Leftists). Though the color red has represented left-wing parties throughout the history of humanity (recall the flags of the Third Reich and the Soviet Union), this system was sharply reversed over the last several decades. The Left is delighted that the clueless right-wingers have accepted the change; they have even begun to vocalize slogans like "The Red Wave" foolishly. Thus, the modern Left has successfully disentangled itself from previous generations of the Left and their horrible deeds.

Classical liberalism and conservatism, stripped of myths and evolutionary misconceptions, are both remarkably similar and equivalent—thanks to a single axiom. There are, of course, nuanced differences, but these are exclusively associated with secondary attributes, which are subject to temporal changes. Both classical liberals and conservatives answer the question of who is to dominate whom in the same way: unquestionably, they affirm the absolute and undisputed supremacy of the governed over the government. Other human life and social organization elements have been purposefully relegated to the domain of secondary denominators: morality, religion, economy, political structure, culture, traditions, and all other aspects of human endeavor.

Another nuanced difference between Conservatism and Classical Liberalism was noted (correctly) by Yoram Hazony, "Enlightenment liberalism, as a political ideology, is bereft of any interest in conserving anything" (Hazony 2022, introduction).

Finally (and more precisely), Classical (Enlightenment) Liberalism embodies Conservatism's hard work, for it was the natural step in society's self-governing evolution. By maintaining a watchful eye (i.e., a negative feedback loop), Conservatism has always self-directed human society toward its own good.

Koselleck argued that "the dominant tendency of political theory since the Enlightenment has been to subsume the political under the moral" (O'Sullivan 2023). It is straightforward to see the fruitlessness of such subsuming from the conception of the individual-state paradigm: the political component is a material substance, whereas the moral component purports the transcendental aspect. Similar conclusions must be drawn for subsuming the political dimension under religious, nationalistic, or other non-material substances.

Another watershed between Conservatism and Collectivism is that the former wants to build an imperfect but decent world from inherently imperfect humans. At the same time, the latter aims to build a perfect Utopian world by reforging these incorrigible people into perfect human beings. All Leftist regimes were highly active in "bringing up new men" or "correcting human behavior" (and transferring those who resisted being reformed into "reeducation concentration camps.")

The individual-state paradigm elevates individual sovereignty above state sovereignty—just as the United States Constitution does. However, while reading the Declaration of Independence and the United States Constitution, some researchers experienced "confusion." For

The individual-state paradigm elevates individual sovereignty above state sovereignty— just as the United States Constitution does.

example, if the Declaration of Independence seems "liberal," the Constitution looks "conservative." It sounds pretty straightforward if one equips the terms "liberal" and "conservative" with hundreds of years of accumulated ideological baggage, predispositions, and openly stolen identities. If, however, a single-axiom procedure is applied, all of these misunderstandings are dispelled, leading to the conclusion that conservatism and liberalism are simply two different names for the same political philosophy.

What is the significance of two different terms utilized to describe the same concept? Well, this happens all the time in human history. For example, Bernard Shaw is credited with a clever, well-known epigram on a similar subject: "The British and Americans are two great peoples separated by a common language."

Strictly speaking, conservatism and classical liberalism are not identical; they are homologous, meaning they are descended from the same source. At the moment, that primary source does not have a single-word definition, but it might be referred to as the individual-state paradigm. The situation here is somewhat similar to that of electric and magnetic forces in physics.

Historically, they were thought of as separate forces of nature until James Maxwell proved in 1873 that they represent two manifestations of the same electromagnetic field.

It is essential to clarify the notion that Conservatism and Liberalism are not identical. Despite the fact that they are closely related, there are many areas—including often neglected but obvious timing issues—where these ideologies have acquired countless secondary characteristics over time. Long before "conservatism" and "liberalism" ultimately merged on the individual-state paradigm level, they diverged on a plethora of secondary delineators.

Adding the evolution of language and the corresponding evolution and beguiling redefinition of terms to this mix, we arrive at the repertoire of competing theories claiming to offer proof that Conservatism and Liberalism occupy either the opposite or the same side of the political barricades. Furthermore, ideological battles are often settled solely on the basis of secondary attributes, even though these attributes are not ideologies by themselves—such as authoritarianism or populism—but can be invoked widely by both the Right and the Left.

Monarchism can also be Left or Right. Monarchism in the form of absolutism clearly represents the Left. On the contrary, a parliamentary (constitutional) monarchy (like in Great Britain, for example) mostly belongs to the Right. As it is known, constitutional monarchies retain the sovereign's throne but deprive him/her of governorship. Similarly, the modern Left allows people to retain property ownership but denies property stewardship. It is owndom *de jure* and servitude *de facto*.

In its pure form, conservatism is liberalism as it was at its conception—the product of the Enlightenment era. In reality, such an immaculate Western liberal tradition has so little in common with modern liberalism that the narrative usually provokes an angry reaction from "modern liberals" and a muted response from modern conservatives. Rephrasing Margaret Thatcher, being a Classical Liberal is like being a lady; if you have to tell people you are, you are not. Moreover, Conservatism and Liberalism used to denote the same ideology in the past; they diverged but may converge in the future. Yet it is clear that the "modern liberals"—the Leftists—are the ones perpetrating ideological identity theft.

Noam Chomsky, a well-known and well-educated Leftist, gives another example of evolutionary political taxonomy. He states: "The terms of political discourse are not, at best, models of clarity. In fact, 'liberal' and 'conservative' are interesting in that they have just shifted around totally. What is now called 'conservative' in the dictionary sense was called 'liberal' in the late 19th century. There is a wholesome set of ideas called 'classical liberalism' represented by a lot of Enlightenment figures. Among the most important are [Wilhelm] von Humboldt, who inspired John Stuart Mill, and Mill himself, and it goes back to Locke and that tradition of classical liberalism. Nowadays, that is called conservatism. That is what should be called conservatism, when the term is used properly. It is opposition to state power. This is part of what the underlying conception of the United States government was before it became a state capitalist system in the 19th century" (Chomsky 1988, p. 655).

He continues: "The modern term 'liberalism,' however, means something soundly different. Certainly, since the 1930s, 'liberalism' has meant the commitment to the use of state power for welfare purposes, New Deal-type measures, etc. That is very different from classical liberalism" (Ibid., p. 656).

Is it possible to simplify the complex history of America's founding into a single philosophical narrative? The answer is probably no. Would it be possible to single out one, just one, philosophical idea that greatly influenced America's Founding Fathers? Was it the application of English common law? Was it the applicability of the political attributes of Ancient Rome? Or was it religious, moral, or economic considerations? Even though the Founding Fathers advocated political syncretism, their dominant theme was classical liberalism. However, the term "classical liberalism" did not yet exist during this period. Instead, the Founding Fathers discussed "Enlightenment liberalism" or "Lockean liberalism." It is well-known that Locke's political philosophy was the dominant mode of discussion among the Founding Fathers (Thompson 2019). However, eventually, they settled on the game plan of Scottish philosopher Francis Hutcheson (Curry 2023).

> **Freedom is the ultimate epiphenomenon of the individual-state paradigm.**

The American Founding Fathers viewed individual freedom as the cornerstone of the fledgling American state. Collectively, they acknowledged freedom within the relationship between a state and a man. Ultimately, this individual-state paradigm formed the basis of the new state (although the Founding Fathers never employed this term.)

Freedom is the ultimate epiphenomenon of the individual-state paradigm.

The Founding Fathers impeccably observed that the greater the state's involvement in a citizen's life, the less individual freedom one has, and vice versa: the smaller the state's role in a human's life, the greater individual freedom one has. Nevertheless, this postulate of classical liberalism of the 18th century came to be known as conservatism in the 21st century. Neo-Marxism has been misconstrued as Liberalism for an unimaginable reason, even though it has nothing to do with Liberalism.

Liberalism seems to glorify individual autonomy, but in reality, individual autonomy is the outcome of a more fundamental principle—the primacy of individuals' wealth over government wealth. As understood in terms of the individual-state paradigm, the primacy of individuals' wealth over government wealth has many consequences. The central principle of liberalism—individual autonomy—is just one of them. Further confusion stems from the fact that personages who call themselves liberals have, for all practical purposes, little or nothing to do with liberalism. Around the time of World War I, a hijacking of the term occurred, which passed almost unnoticed by the general public. There is nothing in common between Enlightenment Liberalism and modern, hijacked, big-government and welfare-state Liberalism. It explains a pseudo-paradox of our time: How did classical liberalism (read: "Right liberalism") morph into its opposite, progressive liberalism (read: "Left liberalism"), an ideology characterized by illiberalism, intolerance, and unfreedom? In contrast, modern conservatives have refused to relinquish the fundamental commitments of classical liberalism.

THE AMERICAN CIVIL WAR FROM THE INDIVIDUAL-STATE PARADIGM PERSPECTIVE

In applying the individual-state paradigm, certain historical events can be viewed from an unfamiliar perception. Consider, for example, slavery and the American Civil War (1861-1865). While the South believed in a small and limited Federal government, the North believed in a large and powerful one. For example, General Robert Lee, in a letter to Lord Acton in 1866,[26]

---

26. British politician Lord Acton authored the famous quote, "Power tends to corrupt, and absolute power corrupts absolutely. Great men are almost always bad men."

emphasized: "I can only say that while I have considered the preservation of the constitutional power of the General Government to be the foundation of our peace and safety at home and abroad, I yet believe that the maintenance of the rights and authority reserved to the states and to the people, not only essential to the adjustment and balance of the general system, but the safeguard to the continuance of a free government. I consider it as the chief source of stability to our political system, whereas the consolidation of the states into one vast republic, sure to be aggressive abroad and despotic at home, will be the certain precursor of that ruin which has overwhelmed all those that have preceded it."

Describing slavery as "unfreedom" is a misrepresentation. Of course, it is not technically false but absurdly reductionist. Freedom, palpable only within the government-to-governed relationship, does not apply to the institution of slavery. Slavery reduces a human being to the point of possession; slavery must be grasped only within a master-slave relationship. In such a relationship, a slave is bereft of freedom by denying the slave his human identity. The denial of freedom is the result, not the cause. The underlying cause is full ownership and complete control of a human being, labeled "slave" by the master. That ownership disengages slaves from government-to-governed business; slaves cannot be assigned "free" or "unfree" terms because they do not belong to the category of "the governed." Instead of being governed, slaves are owned by their masters; slaves are entirely shielded from the government by their masters. The government is not even permitted punishing slaves; slaves do not belong to government jurisdiction. Since Biblical times, only slave owners have administered punishment to their slaves. In the English-speaking world, it is known as the concept of "*respondeat superior*" (which means "let the master answer" in Latin).

The commonly misattributed cause of the Civil War, slavery, was not actually the cause. The despicable practice of slavery was used as a pretext, as a trigger, but everybody involved registered the primary issue at hand. Lincoln and the North were committed to preserving the Union at any cost,[27] and the North was willing to pay any price—especially if the payee was somebody else, namely the South. In a letter to Horace Greeley in 1862, Abraham Lincoln wrote: "My paramount object in this struggle is to save the Union, and is not either to save or destroy slavery. If I could save the Union without freeing any slave I would do it, and if I could save it by freeing all the slaves I would do it; and if I could save it by freeing some and leaving others alone I would also do that."

Writing about the Civil War in 1931, Robert Selph Henry stated, "One of the tragedies of the war between States while it lasted and for many years afterward, was that neither side could realize or appreciate for what the other side was fighting. To many of the North, the war of the South was a wicked and causeless rebellion undertaken to keep black men and women in slavery; to the like-minded in the South, the war of the North masking itself was a design of conquest and subjugation, hypocritically masking itself as a crusade for freedom" (Henry 1999, p. 13).

From the vantage point of the individual-state paradigm, the famous Lincoln-Douglas (Republican vs. Democrat) debates of 1858 were debates of two right-wingers. Per Jaffa, "As Lincoln held that no man was good enough to govern another without that other's consent, so Douglas held that no community of free men or group of such communities was good enough to dictate the domestic institutions of another community of free men" (Jaffa 2009, ch. 2). In other words, Douglas and Lincoln were fighting a non-overlapping political battle. While Douglas emphasized states' rights and self-governing as central issues and slavery as supplementary, Lincoln characterized Federal authority as the main issue and slavery as supplementary.

Both Douglas and Lincoln were leaning toward granting freedom to slaves. However, Douglas offered certain reservations: "...we ought to extend to the negro race, and to all other dependent races, all the rights, all the privileges, and all the immunities which they can exercise consistently with

---

27. Covering the Civil War for a Viennese newspaper *Die Presse*, Karl Marx on October 12, 1862, in an article titled "On Events in North America," praised Lincoln's ten-day-old Emancipation Proclamation specifically because it was "the most significant document in American history since the founding of the Union and one which tears up the old American Constitution" (Marx and Engels [1862] 1984, p. 249).

the safety of society. Humanity requires that we should give them all these privileges; Christianity commands that we should extend those privileges to them. The question then arises, What are those privileges, and what is the nature and extent of them? My answer is that that is a question which each State must answer for itself. We in Illinois have decided it for ourselves. We tried slavery, kept it up for twelve years, and finding it was not profitable, we abolished it for that reason, and became a Free State" (Jaffa 2009, ch. 2).

Neither Douglas nor Lincoln was a firm abolitionist or committed to pro-slavery. In 1858, both candidates for the Illinois Senate seat agreed upon the final destination but differed on the path. (What else should be expected from two right-wingers?)

At the end of the day, both must be designated wrong: Douglas was wrong for not supporting abolitionists unconditionally, and Lincoln was wrong for not supporting states' rights unconditionally. Note that both abolition and secession, per Jaffa, "were equally unconstitutional," and both "abolitionism and anti-abolitionism undermined respect for the law."

The United States Constitution provided a clear path to preserve slavery but not a clear path to abolishing it. In order to preserve the Constitution, Douglas pointed out a clever solution: expand United States territories to the West and create new states, all of which would be free states (no slavery allowed). According to Douglas, it might tilt the balance in Congress in favor of the free states. That could pave the way for ending slavery for good and, at the same time, protecting Constitutional norms. His motive was making the United States "an ocean-bound republic" and declaring "the area of liberty as broad as the continent." Jaffa openly credits Douglas with "the vision and determination that created the continental Union that Lincoln finally saved." He emphasized that "Douglas's proposal would have cut almost the whole Gordian knot of constitutional entanglements with the slavery questions."

At one point, Douglas warned his fellow Americans: "I am not pro-slavery. I think it is a curse beyond computation to both white and black. But we exist as a nation by virtue only of the Constitution, and under that, there is no way to abolish it. I believe that the only power that can destroy slavery is the sword, and if the sword is once drawn, no one can see the end" (Jaffa 2009, ch. 3).

Lincoln lost the Senate race that year to Douglas, but he won the Presidency of the United States two years later against Douglas (and two others). A political conflict eventually escalated from the state level to the national stage, where it became irreconcilable: the South subordinated the question of slavery to the Constitution, and the North subordinated the Constitution to the issue of slavery. We are all aware that the crisis was not resolved peacefully.

The noble objective of abolishing slavery was accompanied by the elimination of certain provisions of the Constitution. Jaffa offered the following brilliant passage describing the situation: "The crocodile tears that were shed for the Negro were only pretexts for destroying the constitutional equality of the states" (Jaffa 2009, ch. 4). In retrospect, that clash was inevitable for purely Constitutional reasons; it was repeated—for almost the same Constitutional motives—half a century later during the Prohibition fiasco.

The noble objective of abolishing slavery was accompanied by the elimination of certain provisions of the Constitution.

The relationship between the Democrat and Republican parties has improved slightly since the elections of 1860. Republican candidates are now permitted to appear on "Democratic States" ballots. It was not the case in 1860 when many Southern states forbade printing Lincoln's name on ballots. As a result, Lincoln won the Electoral College but received only 40% of the popular vote. In protest, eleven states attempted to withdraw from the Union.

The conflict's root cause was imperfections in the Founding Fathers' monumental work. "There was a question that had to be settled. It was a bedrock question, going to the very nature of the government...The fundamental question of the relation of the states to the government they had created" (Henry 1999, p. 13). From the point of view of Gödel's incompleteness theorem, the conflict preceding the Civil War could not be resolved through Constitutional means, even theoretically. A dispute such as this cannot be proven false or true in the framework of constitutional axioms enshrined in stone. The inclusion of constitutional amendments rectified some discrepancies in the Constitution,[28] but it is still far from perfect. As claimed by Gödel,

---

28. The Constitutional "three fifths of all other persons" (that meant black and white slaves) was a true political compromise—without that clause back in 1787, there would be no five fifths today.

this state of imperfection will be with us forever. Likewise, while following the letter of the law, the Dred Scott decision disregarded the spirit of the law and, for all practical purposes, nullified vital propositions of the Declaration of Independence, which back then, just like today, was not legally binding.

The Republican Party won the Civil War, but the Democrat Party returned the favor a century later—they employed a similar tactic of ignoring states' rights and imposing abortion issues (thoughtfully politicized by then) on all states. Later on, they imposed homosexual marriage on all states of the Union in the same manner. So, it is ironic that Republicans have been using the same arguments—tied to state sovereignty—to oppose "abortion rights" and "homosexual marriage" that Democrats deployed before the Civil War.

In retrospect, the ideal outcome of the slavery conflict would have been the South respecting the rights of blacks and the North respecting states' rights. The slavery issue, from the individual-state paradigm, was the *secondary* one because slaves had an infinitesimally negligible effect on the ratio of government-to-governed wealth. (Recall that slaves did not belong to the category of "governed," but to the category of "owned.") The Republicans won, leaving the country *de jure* without slaves but *de facto* without states' rights. A Democrat victory, on the other hand, would have left the country with slavery and states' rights. Both outcomes were unsatisfactory and remain so today, but both the winners and the losers in every war have a price to pay[29]. That is why the Civil War winners made the right decision and bluntly pardoned everybody who participated in the fighting.

Before the Civil War, the United States was a firmly right-wing country from the primary delineator standpoint. Despite the importance of this

---

29. The average price per slave in the years immediately preceding the Civil War was about $400-$500, or about $16,000-$20,000 in early 21st-century dollars—i.e., equivalent to a modest car. Back then, it was about five times the average annual per capita income in America. Using a car analogy, that ratio is still with us today—and it explains why so many Southern Democrats are still angry that Republicans cleared out their garages.

one primary issue, it was immersed into the atmosphere of many second-ary—but nevertheless screaming—issues, most of which were given their pre-fix "anti": anti-slavery, anti-black, anti-British, anti-Indian, and anti-Catholic. An immense amount of hatred was directed towards those despised parties, invoking an action of a mighty American hand. That hatred affected the North and South (except that anti-slavery sentiment appeared muted in the South). In the end, the "evolution of freedom," per Losev, has evaporated all these sentiments.

The American Civil War was not a result of moral, religious, territorial, or racial problems. Instead, it was a reaction to a more fundamental—*primary* in our approach—problem. The American dilemma is rooted in the practical implementation of the individual-state paradigm: the limits of government dominance over men and vice versa. Unfortunately, it is still widely misunder-stood, and the classical dictum "all men are created equal" has been misinter-preted. If "all men" is more or less appropriately understood, "created equal" is commonly misappropriated; it should be viewed exclusively in the context of government-to-governed relations, just as freedom is understood exclusively within that basis. In conclusion, "all men are created equal" makes sense only when the government is involved. The "created equal" argument loses validity if the government is out of the picture.

In other words, slavery was sacrificed in order to save the Union, but free-dom for slaves (which they deserved without question) was accompanied by the creation of the Federal Leviathan. The American Civil War—the bloodiest war the United States has ever experienced—illustrates the extreme brutality and uncompromising nature of wars waged by camps with the same primary delineator aimed at resolving the secondary issues.

Eighty years later, similar circumstances forced the Western elites to con-front Hitler—but, as Orwell suspected, "only at the price of accepting Stalin." World War II is an example of a bloody war based on the *primary* delinea-tor. The preceding World War I never touched the primary delineator, for a compilation of many secondary delineators caused it. Unfortunately, most of these secondary issues had not been resolved, leading partly to World War II. However, if the military history of World War II is well researched, the political history of World War II—at least from the individual-state paradigm point of view—is not written yet. Likewise, the political history of the Cold War is well known, while the military (and clandestine) history of the Cold War is not.

SPANISH CIVIL WAR

The formation of the Soviet Union triggered a huge "left wave" through European political institutions. In 1933, the National Socialists came to power in Germany by overpowering the previous—also Socialist—government of Germany, which was in charge for 14 years. In 1936, a conglomerate of radical left-wing ("Left" from both mainstream Marxism and the individual-state paradigm point of view) parties won the elections in Spain (which many believed rigged). It led to a bloody Spanish Civil War between revolutionary Leftists and various factions of Fascists under an umbrella named Falange, who established a National-Syndicalist economy along the lines of the original syndicalism.

However, "Ghosts of those propaganda battles of seventy years ago still haunt us. Yet the Spanish Civil War remains one of the few modern conflicts whose history had been written more effectively by the losers than by the winners" (Beevor 2006, p. xxvi). As it is known, the Falange was construed "right" by mainstream Marxism, but only in relative terms; from the individual-state paradigm, the Falangists were as "left" as they could be. (Recall the official name of Falange, *Falange Española Tradicionalista y de las Juntas de Ofensiva Nacional Sindicalista*).

"The Twenty-Six Point Program of the Falange" states, in Point 8, that "The National-Syndicalist State will permit all kinds of private initiative that are compatible with the collective interest, and it will also protect and encourage the profitable ones." Point 9 is the essence of the classical syndicalist idea: "Our conception of Spain in the economic realm is that of a gigantic syndicate of producers. We shall organize Spanish society comparatively through a system of vertical syndicates for the various fields of production, all working toward national economic unity." Point 10 explains a lot: "We repudiate the capitalistic system which shows no understanding of the needs of the people, dehumanizes private property, and causes workers to be lumped together in a shapeless, miserable mass of people filled with desperation. Our spiritual and national conception of life also repudiates Marxism." That single last sentence immediately positioned world Leftists against their heretical ideological comrades.

If Point 10 "repudiates Marxism," the next Point portrays classical Marxist exercise: "The National-Syndicalist State will not cruelly stand apart from man's economic struggles, nor watch impassively while the strongest class dominates the weakest. Our regime will eliminate the very roots of class struggle, because all who work together in production shall comprise one single organic entity."

There is no shortage of additional examples to support the view that the Falange promoted a set of classical Leftist ideas. They emphasized "redistributing arable land in such a way as to revive family farms and give energetic encouragement to the syndicalization of farm laborers." Their program called for "support the trend toward nationalization of banking services." The final Point 26 calls for "a revolution to implant this new order." These points confirm that Spanish Fascists, like their comrades, Italian and German Fascists, represented an austere aberration from mainstream Marxism-Leninism-Stalinism. The main deviation of Fascism from Marxism was the permission of private property, but under stringent government control, of course. Not only that, Spanish Fascism had openly stated something other Leftists euphemistically omitted: its imperialist ambitions (for example, Point 3 declares, "We have the determination to build an Empire.") Any attempt by any person to label the Falange and other Fascist parties as right-wing movements immediately indicates that such person is a committed mainstream Leftist, proficient in the standard Marxist-Leninist-Stalinist-Maoist lexicon.

In the same year, 1936, an alliance of left-wing parties won elections in France. These parties pursued a wide range of left-wing radicalism—from social democrats to communists. Under Prime Ministers Blum and Daladier, the left-wing coalition—The Popular Front—ran the French economy to the ground while declaring openly anti-fascist plans. This intra-Left struggle at the center of Europe ended with Germany's occupation of France in 1940. (To be fair to radical Socialist Daladier, he was one of the few who knew their ideological comrades in Germany all too well, so he accurately guessed that the National Socialists aimed toward "a domination of the Continent in comparison with which the ambitions of Napoleon were feeble").

The Russian Civil War of 1917-1922 is more complicated. On one side of the barricades were the Bolsheviks (later renamed Communists), the committed Leftists. However, their adversaries did not have any coherent political program at all. From the individual-state paradigm point of view, it was an amorphous conglomerate of participants of all ideological stripes, from the Left to the Right. Their flag was white, alluding to the restoration of the

Bourbon monarchy in France. Bolshevik propaganda painted them as monarchists—and some of them indeed were—but the so-called White Movement had only military targets: capture Moscow and restore the pre-Bolshevik coup democratic institutions of the interim government. Politically, the White Movement exercised a "non-predetermination" plan, assuming the deposition of Bolshevik usurpers would allow Russians to choose their own way with the help of democratic institutions.

So, in retrospect, the Russian Civil War was a war between the Bolshevik Left and the anti-Bolshevik Left, Right, and everything in between. That ideological unfoundedness led to the White Movement's defeat. That episode must serve as a dire warning for everybody involved in the struggle with the Leftists: military counterpunches are necessary but insufficient to defeat the Left. Ideological counterpunches are mandatory, but even if administered alone, they could lead to the Left's non-defeat.

The American Civil War was between two right-wing parties. The Spanish Civil War was between two left-wing parties.

To conclude, the American Civil War was a war between two right-wing parties. On the contrary, the Spanish Civil War was between two left-wing parties. Those two wars are textbook examples not contaminated by other secondary issues, like religion, race, or something else.

BIRTH OF REPUBLOCRATS

By the 20th century, the idea of the individual-state paradigm was formalized, and the tax burden was acknowledged as one of the tools for assessing the social system.[30] This (formal) scheme enables the comparison of state structures from different historical periods. Of course, we are discussing taxation here in its fullest sense, encompassing all forms—taxes, fines, administrative fees, "voluntary" contributions, confiscations, bribes, racketeering, etc. That is everything, one way or another, withdrawn from the governed by the government, regardless of its description.

---

30. The United States did not have an income tax until 1861. In 1872, the tax was abolished but re-established in 1913. Since the income tax was instituted, the government has grown exponentially—in absolute and relative terms.

Low-tax countries typically have a small government apparatus and, therefore, are characterized by great individual liberty. These are right-wing countries to which most developed capitalist countries belong at a certain stage of their development.

High taxes correlate with the low rank of individual freedom in left-wing countries. Furthermore, these countries possess a vast and omnipotent state apparatus, which tends to gravitate toward totalitarianism and tyranny, unlike right-wing countries. Thus, all countries that have chosen the Left (socialist) development path ultimately descend into some form of totalitarianism. Examples are the Third Reich and the Soviet Union.

The real, as opposed to the nominal, extent of taxation in the USSR may have been 90-95%. In the Soviet Union, only one-tenth of the budget was derived from citizens' income tax. The remainder of the budget consisted of corporate tax—extortionate amounts were taken from the profits of socialist enterprises. As a result of this decimation of profits, wages were also decimated. That is the reason Soviet citizens were so poor. It is known today as a pre-tax withdrawal of wages.

> **Extortionate amounts of corporate tax is the reason Soviet citizens were so poor. It is known today as a pre-tax withdrawal of wages.**

There are exceptions to every rule. Fascist Italy, for example, had relatively low taxes (for a society that identified itself as Leftist). However, Mussolini came across another equally powerful mechanism of total state control: syndicalism (equally delineated as Italian Corporatism.[31]) The owners of enterprises, workers, and trade unions in each industry were forced into syndicates, which formed the state's local administrative units. Mussolini's program found followers all over the world, not to mention the United States. The economic policy of Franklin Roosevelt (the National Recovery Administration was the American equivalent of Italian Corporatism) and Barack Obama's experiments with Leftist reforms

---

31. The idea of Corporatism was crystallized in the 19th century. It was formulated in more or less modern form by the German Jesuit theologian Heinrich Pesch and the French sociologist Émile Durkheim. The word "Corporatism" predates its ideological successor—Fascism, which is Corporatism to the extreme, the total unification of the state and business.

(reorganization of General Motors and the implementation of the Affordable Care Act) have flowed from syndicalism.

Taxation was not excessive in Nazi Germany either. The National Socialists, however, also ran across a novel way to assert control over the population through the government.

The idea that individual rights and freedoms are superior to the public (common) good is what led to the transformation of the backwater colonies of North America into the formidable United States of America. In the meantime, the dynamics of the development of political parties in the United States are far more complex. The one-dimensional scale of the individual-state paradigm does not always adequately reflect modern politics' multifaceted and convoluted reality. However, if we consider not only one but two variables—tax burden and the size of the Federal government—then a two-dimensional matrix of the political duopoly in Washington, DC, can be seen.[32] This matrix consists of four cells:

High Taxation Big Government (*Democrats*)	High Taxation Small Government (?)
Low Taxation Big Government (*Republicans*)	Low Taxation Small Government (*Conservatives*)

The Democrat Party of the USA is pictured in the upper left corner. This left-wing party advocates high taxes and massive government (i.e., a large Federal government budget relative to a country's economy). It is opposed (in the lower right corner) by Conservatives, whose position is predicated on low taxes and a small, limited government.

Only these two are internally consistent among the four ideologies presented in the matrix. More significantly, the inside logic of these ideologies

---

32. Of course, the size of a government directly correlates with the level of taxation. However, a political analysis must be based not only on official declarations but also on widespread cognitive and semantic dissonances between stated ideological positions and actual political stances. Such dissonances are all over the place, like in the case of Anarchism, for example.

is quite clear: a big government requires high taxes (Democrats), whereas a small government requires lower taxes (Conservatives). As is known, large governments are rarely the answer and consistently pose a problem for most societies. Leftists seek to govern without regard for legal or constitutional boundaries; therefore, the issue of big government is the foremost priority of the Leftists.

In contrast, the other two ideologies are characterized by internal contradictions that render these ideologies incapable of long-term survival. As far as history can show, one of these parties—the party of high taxes and small government—has never come to power in America, and it is unlikely that such a party has come to power anywhere in the world. High taxes and a small government cannot coexist. The party in question does not even have a name (indicated by a question mark in the matrix above). This party will be unable to avoid the temptation to move to the Left, to the place occupied by the Democrat Party.

The Republican Party also has a contradictory—indeed, senseless—ideology. A desire for low taxes is incompatible with a desire for big government. Large governments require massive amounts of money, so Republican ideology is mainly centered on borrowing money from future generations of Americans. In this regard, the Republican Party is in the same position as the Democrat Party. As a result, the United States' national debt increases by about one trillion dollars annually (slightly less than $2 million per minute). Such is the cost of supporting incoherent Republican ideology.

By the same token, the Democrat Party of the United States is a full-fledged accomplice of the Republican Party in withdrawing funds from the American people. Due to this, there are rumors that these two parties that alternately take power in America are factions of the same party, a Uniparty. Of course, that is not the case, but the above matrix illustrates the grounds upon which the rumors about a Uniparty are based.

Voters often criticize politicians for changing their stances on issues over time. These changes, however, generally relate to the *secondary* rather than the *primary* set of problems. In truth, each politician has pledged allegiance to one, and only one *primary* matter, and the opinions they express on *secondary* matters are all up for sale.[33]

---

33. Note that professional politicians never talk about the elephants in the room; they talk only about the issues they consider beneficial to their cause.

Unlike the Democrat Party, which is almost monolithic in its ideology (disagreements within the party can be attributed to different degrees of Leftism—from moderate to radical), the Republican Party comprises various factions. For example, a faction of conservative Republicans is referred to as the Freedom Caucus. There are also less formal factions, such as "moderate Republicans" and "Republicans In Name Only" (RINO). The RINO faction represents the party's left wing. It is a source of major internal contradictions since it is essentially identical to the Democrats when viewed through the matrix above.

Despite this, it has long been identified that Republican and Democrat political divisions are confined mainly to areas beyond the District of Columbia. In Washington, DC, the actual ruling party can be referred to as the Republocrats (Democrats and "big government" Republicans) or the Uniparty. However, the cynical description of political Washington as a fiefdom of the Uniparty is misleading since it emphasizes agreements between Republicans and Democrats only on peripheral issues. Contrary to this, the uncompromising tax war in Congress epitomizes a proxy political struggle over the primary issue, and it makes the primary issue as dirty as it can possibly be. Moreover, every "bipartisan tax compromise" in Congress ultimately results in an enormous tax burden and a redistribution of wealth from the governed to the government and its cronies. Nevertheless, it was precisely against the Republocrats that America voted in 2016. The American people voted against the party of professional bureaucrats, against the top experts in spreading American wealth around.

Republocrats prosper in Washington regardless of who won the last election. Republocrats have an impressive experience of survival in any election outcome, and this experience is customarily transmitted, for the most part, by inheritance. Donald Trump, from their point of view, was an outsider. He was not worthy of being in the White House because his roots are not hereditary Republocrat. Therefore, the only thing the collective Brutus set in motion in Washington during the Trump term was all-encompassing sabotage.

One of the branches of the Republocrats, better designated as the Democrat Party, has long forgotten its democratic, right-wing roots and has been taken over by supporters of the Left ideology. However, as we recall from Marxism, this socialist party selected only what was thought of as necessary. It rejected everything else as unnecessary (like the declaration of the inevitability of the proletarian revolution). This branch of the Republocrats is much more closely knit and almost always follows Lenin's norms of party life. (Note that modern American Leftists are not communists per se; they represent prevailing Leftist thought worldwide of being anti-anti-communists.) In contrast to the Democrat Party's founding principles of low taxes and a limited government, President Obama had completed the transformation of the Democrat Party into one that promotes high taxes and a big Federal government.

It is a much trickier situation for the Republican Party. The Republicans, like their Democratic counterparts in Washington, have been threatened with a takeover for many years. Several generations of conservatives attempted to reorient the Republican Party toward the Right ideology. However, the takeover by the conservatives was not crowned with success. Republicans are still loyal to their founder, Lincoln, and his views concerning a strong Federal government.

> **In contrast to the Democrat Party's founding principles of low taxes and a limited government, President Obama had completed the transformation of the Democrat Party into one that promotes high taxes and a big Federal government.**

That is the principal internal contradiction of the Republicans—the low-tax party is irreconcilable with the idea of a big Federal government.

Consequently, regarding a strong Federal government, the two branches of the Republocrats have come together and found common ground. Both Democrats and Republicans talk about Greater Washington, a strong centralized Federal government, but they are constantly fighting over the proportion of taxation.[34]

---

34. There are numerous calls to let go of the SETI (Search for Extraterrestrial Intelligence) program and begin searching for signs of intelligent life in Washington, DC.

For the sake of justice, it should be avouched that the position of the Democrats in this matter, although erroneous, is nevertheless not self-contradictory. However, Republicans' positions on the tax issue are astonishingly contradictory and inconsistent. A result of this internal contradiction within the Republican point of view is that Republicans often act simultaneously as classical Conservatives and as classical Republicans without even realizing that they are doing so. So, while Reagan-the-Conservative pursued a ruthless fight against communism, Reagan-the-Republican was responsible for the impressive expansion of the Federal government. On the one hand, classical Conservatives in Congress want to repeal Obamacare (because this law essentially raises taxes). On the other hand, the cancelation of Obamacare will reduce the Federal government's role, and classical Republicans cannot tolerate that.

The Trump administration was no exception.

Trump-the-Conservative reminded everyone of Reagan, Churchill, and Thatcher in his first genuinely ideological speech at the United Nations General Assembly in 2017. His words (written by Stephen Miller), "The problem in Venezuela is not that socialism has been poorly implemented but that socialism has been faithfully implemented," will enter the history textbooks. Just as Reagan's words entered the textbooks, "Socialism only works in two places: Heaven where they do not need it, and Hell where they already have it." Like Churchill's words entered the textbooks, "Socialism is a philosophy of failure, the creed of ignorance, and the gospel of envy; its inherent virtue is the equal sharing of misery."

Trump-the-Republican agreed with the leaders of the Republocrats about the increase in the United States' national debt.

On the other hand, Trump-the-Republican agreed with the leaders of the Republocrats about the increase in the United States' national debt. His Department of Justice confirmed the Obama administration's decision not to bring high-ranking officials of the Internal Revenue Service to justice for the financial wipeout of the pro-Conservative grassroots movement known as the Tea Party. Trump-the-Republican was so worried about the multibillion-dollar agreement for government contractors with Saudi Arabia that he decided to postpone the relocation of the United States embassy from Tel

Aviv to Jerusalem for a year. Trump-the-Republican conducted a thorough purge of the White House staff to the point that almost no conservatives are left. Nevertheless, simultaneously, Trump-the-Conservative filled vacancies of Federal judges with strictly conservative judges.

In the United States, "Federalists and Democratic-Republicans; Whigs and Democrats; Republicans and Democrats—all of them eschewed the 'conservative' designation, for more than one hundred and sixty years" (Lukacs 2005, p. 27). (Naturally, "one hundred and sixty years" is debatable). The Democrat Party took about two centuries to complete a 180-degree turn—from the right-wing party to the left-wing party—and the Marxists will never allow it to turn back (they are working hard to implement the Cloward-Piven strategy).[35] Democrats, like all Leftists worldwide, are waging a non-declared war on their constituencies. That is unconventional political warfare—they pretend to be on the side of the people while, behind people's backs, the Washington, DC swamp dwellers and their protégés in the states are working tirelessly to re-enslave the population. Likewise, the Republican Party remains a centrist and contradictory party, just like most political parties in the West, and its transition to the Right ideology is postponed indefinitely.

Interestingly, the major American political parties' shift from the Right to the Left began not with the Democrats, as many assumed, but with the Republicans. Following Lincoln's election in 1860, Republicans absorbed many old-fashioned Whigs and assimilated most Know-Nothings. This development gave birth to the two primary factions inside the modern Republican Party—conservative and left-wing (the Know-Nothings represented views that later on in the 19th century were labeled as "progressive"). Although the Republican migration toward the Left was slow and ended at the center of the political spectrum, Democrats' evolution began much later but moved much more quickly. They crossed the political center at the turn of the 20th century; by the 21st century, they became indistinguishable from other similar left-wing parties of the West (most of which are Socintern-affiliated). Currently, Leftists are the masters of the Democrat party, not its servants. In their separate, left-shifting ideological journeys, Republicans, for the most part, lost their spine, while Democrats lost their reason.

---

35. The strategy was proposed in 1966 by two radical socialists, Richard Andrew Cloward and his wife, Frances Fox Piven. The goal was to gain political advantage by exploiting manufactured crises.

The visible to the naked eye left-wing shift confirms that the Democrat and Republican parties represent anti-American and un-American parties, respectively. At the beginning of the 21st century, John Lukacs presented the known-to-everybody fact that "from a historical perspective, and using the proper terminology, we may say that generally speaking, in the United States the Republican Party has been more nationalistic than socialistic, while the Democrats have been more socialistic than nationalistic—the latter being perhaps the main cause of their relative decline during the last fifty years" (Lukacs 2005, pp. 41-42).

The "Sundance," anonymous author behind "The Last Refuge" blog, brilliantly described the situation: "The DNC is ideologically motivated. The RNC is financially motivated. The DNC uses money to get power, the RNC uses power to get money. The ideology of the DNC drives their donor activity, while the donor activity of the RNC drives their political ideology. This is the primary difference between the two corporations" (The Last Refuge, 2023).

Nature, as it is portrayed, does not abhor a vacuum. Furthermore, politics does not abhor a vacuum either. After all, there is one prominent ("Democrat") party in America and numerous small openly Leftist parties, but there is no major right-wing party, although there are many smaller ones. The ideological vacuum needs to be filled at one time or another. It is, therefore, essential to return to the constitutional foundations of our country. Hence, there is a necessity for a major right-wing party in America—a party of low taxes and correspondingly small and limited government. Who has enough political power to drain the swamp in Washington, DC?

BIRTH OF THE PROGRESSIVES

So, the Republican and Democrat parties were right-wing parties at a remarkably distant time. Nevertheless, both parties coexisted and fought for decades while firmly rooted in the same ideology. The irony here is that the left-right pair did not yet exist in the United States then. By the end of the 19th century, political currents split that right-wing unity, leading to the Progressive Era.

In America, the long-term tax legacy is as follows: the second and third items of Karl Marx's Communist Manifesto—the progressive tax and the inheritance tax—are fully and legally implemented. Few people think about why tax rates in America and elsewhere are progressive—the more money a person makes, the higher the tax rate he or she pays. The stance of progressive taxes has existed since ancient times, but only the Marxists turned them into a weapon of political struggle. Today, the phrases "progressive democrats" and "progressive humanity" are common. However, the term "progressive" originated from the idea of a progressive tax. It had nothing to do with technological or social progress but only with taxes.

The progressive tax system in the United States has progressed only in one direction: toward increasing societal polarization. Democratic tax reform resulted in the emergence of a negative tax rate, previously unheard of in human history. A progressive tax on the wealthy appears to be a simple wealth redistribution method. However, the progressive tax is a mechanism of deliberate corruption that forces the population to seek financial assistance from the state. Eventually, members of society become totally dependent on the government, both physically and spiritually.

Progressives believe they are making progress; however, nothing could be further from the truth. "Progress" in "progressive" societies was there, along with progressive tax—until it was not. That is, until society collapses. In all cases so far, cities, states, and countries run by "progressives" only get progressively worse.

What was the purpose of progressive taxation? *Divide et impera*—divide and conquer—a slogan that has been tested for centuries. Factually, the slogan originated with ancient Roman senators. Through this slogan, political operators are able to pit two factions of Americans against each other. Unfortunately, due to the extreme degree of progressive taxation in the United States, the nation is artificially divided into two groups: those who pay taxes and those who effectively do not. A substantial category of citizens makes their living by prostituting themselves to the government.

Two artificial factions of Americans—those who pay taxes and those who do not—are forcefully separated by a common Congress.

The "progressive" movement also borrowed the idea of an inheritance tax from ancient Rome. Emperor Augustus introduced it in order to pay pensions to his soldiers. Only the Emperor could have thought of such a thing—to declare the family property of a deceased Roman to be the state's property, with the proviso that the relatives of the deceased could obtain the property back by paying a new tax. Today, as in ancient Rome, this tax is viewed as nothing more than a state racket. As such, it should be no surprise that Marxists support this tax.

The imposition of high taxes is also a legalized political racket. All politicians prefer high tax rates to gradually hand over exceptions to the rules to lobbyists and create loopholes in tax legislation for individual companies or entire industries. Consequently, almost no company pays a high "nominal" tax on profits.

The United States has had a progressive income tax for over a century. Unfortunately, most people are unaware of what life was like in America before the income tax. Four or five generations of Americans have grown up in the conditions of progressive taxation, and they do not even realize that the tax burden can be different.

Four or five generations of Americans have grown up with progressive taxation, and they do not realize that the tax burden can be different.

This tax example is another illustration of the non-overlapping political battles in Washington, DC: the Left wishes to eliminate the rich, while the Right wishes to eliminate the poor.

Likewise, the "progressive" Left contributed to the politicization of science. For example, the evolutionary theory of Charles Darwin should remain what it is, the theory of species evolution within the framework of biology and nothing more. Darwin never intended his theory to be weaponized. Regardless, this theory was immensely popular with Leftists and has operated successfully as a weapon for over a century.

In many countries, including the United States, prisons are no longer titled "prisons," but "correction facilities." The prospect of "correcting" people by creating special conditions for them stems directly from Darwin's theory of evolution. Marxists borrowed precisely what they needed from Darwin's theory and dubbed it "Social Darwinism." Until today, one of the Leftist tenets is the unquestioned conviction that anyone given a chance will become precisely the person the surrounding environment demands. This approach is commonly known as Social Darwinism, but Darwin himself has nothing to do with that.

Until the end of the 19th century, the prison was a place of punishment and nothing more. Then, in the Progressive Era, Leftists began conducting mass experiments, using people as their unwitting subjects. A theory of "correction" of human nature states that placing a person in the appropriate prison conditions will "force" him to "evolve" in the direction of the government's ideals.

The idea of Social Darwinism has been put into service to "correct" all kinds of "enemies of the people" in countries where Leftists seized power. Thanks to the idea of Social Darwinism, the taking of power by the Leftists after a bit led to massive repression. As it is known, Darwin did not support the idea of Social Darwinism. (Despite the name, Herbert Spencer authored the theory. Not to mention, the cornerstone of Social Darwinism, eugenics, was put forward a year after Darwin's passing.)

Nevertheless, Karl Marx sent Darwin the second German edition of *Das Kapital I*, with the dedication "Mr. Charles Darwin / On the part of his sincere admirer / Karl Marx /London 16 June 1873," with Marx's handwriting on the title page.[36] In a letter to the German socialist Ferdinand Lassalle, Marx wrote: "Darwin's work is most important and suits my purpose in that it provides a basis in natural science for the historical class struggle. One does, of course, have to put up with the clumsy English style of argument" (Marx and Engels [1861] 1975).

(In a twist of fate, in 2020, the Natural History Museum's Charles Darwin collection in London was targeted by the Black Lives Matter mob and marked for "cancelation" because he had allegedly traveled to the Galapagos Islands on "colonialist scientific expeditions").

We all know how effective the "correction" is in these "correction facilities." Are the Leftists aware of this? Assuredly, they are aware. However, for some reason, they are attempting to hide the fact that the Soviet concentration camps under Comrade Trotsky (and later under Comrade Stalin) and the Nazi concentration camps under Hitler were initially conceived as institutions for "correcting" people. In the Third Reich, "correcting" was complemented by "creating an advanced human race." Nazis turned these camps into death camps later—when the number of Jews in the occupied territories

---

36. Darwin read no more than the first 105 pages of *Das Kapital*; the remainder of the book has uncut pages (i.e., unread). Darwin's copy is still in his library at Down House, Kent (Ball 1995).

of Europe became so substantial that Hitler was convinced of the possibility of a "final solution to the Jewish problem." Lastly, Trofim Lysenko attempted to "correct" the behavior of plants by placing them in proper "concentration camps" and forcing them to develop the desired attributes.

Other pseudo-scientific social experiments did not bypass the Leftists. At one time, Prohibition was the crown jewel of the Left's "Progressive Era" of profound scientific ignorance. It was repealed, but Daylight Savings Time, another legacy of the "progressive era," is still alive (though many countries and several states have given up on the silly notion of Daylight Savings Time). The alcohol prohibition was lifted promptly, but the ban on incandescent light bulbs stays in place. There have been many examples of using science as a political weapon: eugenics, the "natural global cooling" of the 1970s, and the "anthropogenic global warming" of the 1990s.

Another legacy of the Progressive Era is Labor Day, but—surprise—there is no Capital Day. However, any economist can confirm that labor and capital are inextricably linked. Labor Day celebrates socialist economics; why not have a Capital Day celebration of capitalist economics?

History and culture have long been the *idée fixe* for Leftists. The use of history as a political weapon often takes on an acute form with Leftists, who burn unwanted books and raze unwanted monuments. However, both books and monuments are here merely as tools, and the Leftist aim, following the principles of Social Darwinism, is to create such "external living conditions" as to have all political opponents shut up and "correct" their behavior.

Do Democrats and other Leftists consider themselves American patriots? By now, all readers should have answered this question spot on. The answer depends on the kind of America that we are discussing. Indeed, they are patriots of the United States, but their America differs from traditional America. As usual, the same word—America—carries different meanings for different groups.

THE LEFT, THE OTHER LEFT, AND FRANCE

What about the secondary, not the primary delineator? The conservative movement does not offer a dogmatic stance on secondary delineators. In contrast, conservatism allows a wide range of opinions on these vital but non-foundational issues.

No, conservatives do not share a uniform view on abortion—some conservatives support it, and some reject it. No, conservatives do not support a patriarchal lifestyle, but some like it. No, conservatives are not religious fanatics; some are militant atheists, and some are dedicated congregation members. No, conservatives are not racists. No, conservatives are not antisemitic, anti-Latino, anti-environment, or anti-whatever. No, conservatives do not have nostalgia for the monarchy (at least in America), but some conservatives thrive in constitutional monarchies (like Great Britain).

Conservatism has nothing to do with sexual orientation, immigration, water pollution, or the myriad of elements civilization worries about. What about chauvinism? What about nationalism? What about populism? They are non-foundational characteristics of both Left and Right ideologies and, therefore, cannot serve to differentiate them. Moreover, despite the much-needed clarification of various "isms," the primary delineator does not eliminate all questions. For example, some politicians studiously avoid associating themselves according to the primary delineator. Instead, they offer their constituencies a mosaic of various issues based exclusively on secondary delineators. They believe that they can hide behind these secondary issues forever.

A typical example is Marine Le Pen in France. Le Pen desires the working week to remain at 35 hours (the 40-hour working week has been forgotten in France for some time) and the retirement age to be lowered from 62 to 60. Plus, she supports taxing wealth (instead of income), raising import tariffs, and nationalizing entire industries. She seeks to increase social benefits (we know that payments go mainly to armies of loafers who have learned the art of "pity me"). Marine Le Pen definitely belongs to the Left wing of the political spectrum. The economic positions of Le Pen are far to the left of ordinary French socialists.

This is not surprising. Marine Le Pen's National Front is a socialist party with a nationalistic bent. Mass disinformation media call this party "extremely right," but where did you see the right-wing socialist parties? The French National Front is undoubtedly a Leftist party; its slogans are typically Leftist, while its economic and political policies are commonly Leftist. For example, the party is committed to nationalizing health care, education, and banks.

Le Pen wants all religious symbols—including Muslim scarves and the Jewish kippah—to be banned in public places. This war on windmills would have been ridiculed in pragmatic America long ago. Nevertheless, Le Pen does not stop at this—she plans to command France to be less hospitable to her non-French population by adding pork to the school lunch menu.

Unfortunately, elections are primarily around secondary delineators in post-World War II Europe. The primary watershed between two opposing political philosophies cannot materialize if all candidates profess the same— the Left—side. Under the helm of Le Pen—the Joan of Arc of the French Welfare state—France could face a dilemma: Global Socialism (Globalism) or National Socialism.

What past revolution do modern Leftists (read: American Democrats) trace their origin to? Do they trace it to the American Revolution or the French Revolution? Regardless of what definition of the Right or Left is used, it is evident that modern Leftists can be traced back to the French Revolution. It is widely known. Charles Krauthammer phrased it like this: "The line from Bastille to the GULAG is not straight, but the connection is unmistakable. Modern totalitarianism has its roots in 1789" (Krauthammer 2013, ch. 7). The connection between Liberalism and Leftism is also straightforward: Since the French Revolution, the Left has advocated for free, democratic elections of hangmen.

Amidst the critical differences between the Right and the Left is the static versus the dynamic property of intra-society wealth distribution. As believed by Leftists, it is nearly static, incapable of change without the participation of the "oppressed" classes in violent revolutions. Similarly, European conservatism tends to view the distribution of wealth as static. It can be argued that European conservatism, which incorporates issues of religion, tradition, authority, and freedom, has its roots in reaction to the French Revolution. In contrast, American conservatism has its roots in the American Revolution. The French Revolution happened at approximately the same time and for about the same reasons as the American Revolution. However, if France chose the Left development path, America chose the Right path. In the late 18th century, America chose liberty, and France chose equality. The results speak for themselves.

It seems the Left has singled out and decided to utterly obliterate France methodically—from the Revolution of 1789 to the Paris Commune in 1871 to the annihilation of De Gaulle's government during the ersatz revolution in the late 1960s. Since the French Revolution, Collectivism has piled on absurdity upon absurdity until it finally collapses under the weight of its own madness. Eventually, the French Leftists got rid of the King but installed the Emperor instead. Soviet Leftists got rid of religion but filled society with shamans of ideological religion instead. Chinese Leftists under Mao Zedong eliminated capitalism but later, under Deng Xiaoping, allowed capitalistic enterprises to flourish alongside the socialistic ones. Finally, German Leftists in the 1930s got rid of the nation's humiliation but, in the end, humiliated it even further.

Conversely, American—constitutional—conservatism views wealth distribution as dynamic. Accordingly, the static notion implies a static equilibrium of wealth relations. In contrast, the disinterested stand taken by conservatives on the intra-society wealth disparity must be interpreted in strictly dynamic terms. The picture of a society with static intra-society wealth inequality is ugly, for it means an absolute prohibition of the poor from becoming rich and a corresponding ban on the rich becoming poor.

Collectivism has piled on absurdity upon absurdity until it finally collapses under the weight of its own madness.

For conservatives, the intra-society wealth gap makes sense only in dynamic terms: people are free to move up and down the wealth ladder without any interference from the state.

Outside academic literature, there is no such substance as high or low inequality of incomes or an "international inequality standard." These "high" or "low" numbers of intra-society wealth disparity are essential only for those political operators who use them to divide and conquer. Low-income voters are naturally occurring political cannon fodder, and their ideological masters—the Left—intend to keep it that way.

All the mass delusions common to the Left are fanciful. However, none is more spectacularly irrational than the conviction that we can all become incredibly wealthy through the legal confiscation and redistribution of the wealth of others. The Nazi and Soviet economic triumphs, albeit temporary, never arrived in other socialistic countries, for they had not or could not run a massive property confiscation program. In just about all cases, after the initial spectacular phase of wealth redistribution, Socialism produces paralyzed, dysfunctional mafia-states or narco-states.

The Collectivists' economic illiteracy is breathtaking. Everywhere it was tried, Collectivism failed the test of endurance. In creating dystopias, Socialism has no competition.

The NFL: A Case Study in Socialism

It may appear as if it were magic, but financial independence and financial freedom translate into the freedom of conscience, free-thinking, and freedom from political oppression. On the contrary, financial dependence finishes in complacency, conformism, and varying forms of unfreedom. Both the Left and the Right have embraced such political banalities for centuries. However, as a rule, the Leftists managed to weaponize almost all secondary delineators in their quest for power.

In other words, the Leftists' quest to weaponize everything makes them pantophagous. They weaponize everything; nothing escapes their attention as potential political ammunition.[37] They weaponized poverty. They weaponized the movie industry. They weaponized gender. They weaponized race. They weaponized education. They weaponized religion. They masterfully weaponized courts by converting them into devices of mass financial ruin for defendants regardless of who wins the case. They weaponized many topics since Marx had weaponized classes. No wonder the Leftists weaponized language, too—by forcing pernicious reinterpretations of words—and the Internet. Leftists weaponized even such innocent and humanitarian initiatives as the food stamps program, morphing it into a pure population control mechanism.

Initially, sports became weaponized when the modern Olympic Games were established. During the 20th century, sporting events were weaponized for political purposes, reaching an apogee in National-Socialist Germany and the Soviet Union.

In the 21st century, China, along with the United States, holds the leading position in the politicization of sports. Recall the "kneeling NFL" saga—disastrous to football and its fans. It should not come as a surprise, since the National Football League, like many other sports leagues, is a socialist enterprise that parasitizes the capitalist economy. Moreover, most professional sports leagues in the United States are quasi-socialist enterprises within capitalist corporate America. Outwardly, the NFL looks like a successful corporation, but from within, this corporation has implemented principles of doing business that are alien to America.

---

37. Be careful with the constellation of Left-assigned neologisms, like neoconservatism, paleoconservatism, and Alt-Right. They have the same incoherent relation to conservatism as modern Antifa does to anti-Fascism or Black Liberation Theology has to Christian Theology.

In time to come, the conflict between the quasi-socialist paradise inside the NFL and its capitalist encirclement was bound to happen. Unfortunately, this smoldering conflict between serf gladiators and free citizens has been in the shadows for too long. Sports organizations have introduced as many socialist ideas into the sport as possible. Now, this genie is out of the bottle: since 2016, players have staged an anti-American *démarche*. They did not stand with their hands over their hearts for the National Anthem.

All NFL teams are formally independent and have their owners, as they should under capitalism. However, the profits of these supposedly independent organizations depend not so much on the quality of the game as on the collective agreement with advertisers. If there is a superstar on one of the teams who scores a lot, then all the teams become winners. The profit from advertising is distributed practically evenly between the teams, regardless of the game's quality and the championship place. The league champion earns only slightly more than the lowest-scoring team.

Forced leveling and coercive egalitarianism are practiced in most American professional sports leagues—that is, the worst team gets the best league players at the season's end via the draft. The worse the team plays, the better its composition becomes. That is the NFL's way of complying with Marxism's cornerstone: "From each according to his ability, to each according to his needs." Similarly, in the Soviet Union, only lagging collective plantations (collective farms) received state investments. As an argument, it was said that "weak farms should be helped." Thus, everything in the Soviet Union followed Churchill's words that socialism's "inherent virtue is the equal sharing of misery."

Another example of the socialist-leaning in the NFL is wage controls. The minimum salary for all gladiators is set in advance. If a player is drafted into the team, he automatically becomes a millionaire, regardless of the quality of the game. Doubtless, that is one of the critical features of the socialist economy. What is surprising is that not only the minimum but also the maximum salary in the NFL is also limited. How well a person plays and how many points he brings to his team do not matter. There is a salary ceiling that is impossible to jump over. Even in the Soviet Union, there was no such restriction; world-class athletes and show business stars' earnings were not subject to artificial restrictions. The quasi-socialism described here is one of the reasons American football has not spread to the entire planet, as soccer did, in which there are no elements of socialism.

Gladiators from the NFL made a strategic mistake and then foolishly proceeded to defend an indefensible position. In turn, American football fans reminded these quasi-socialist millionaires that the customer is always right under capitalism.

The weaponization of all aspects of human life could be observed in the multiple incarnations and extensions of the Left's central idea of government's primacy over individuals. Using this ground-laying idea, a significant quantity of left-wing movements materialized—from Socialism to Fascism to Communism. Moreover, springing from the single-issue foundational idea, the rich spectrum of the Left was equipped with a wide variety of multiple-secondary-issue movements. Equally important is that these manifold political movements, on the surface, have nothing to do with the government's primacy over men. Hence, nobody should be misled by the smokescreen of traditional Leftist governments' desire to micromanage all of their citizens' decisions.

The weaponization of all aspects of human life could be observed in the multiple incarnations and extensions of the Left's central idea of government's primacy over individuals.

The perpetual incompetence of socialist governments is not a bug but a feature of the underlying ideology. History has demonstrated that unsustainable socialist economies are always, without exception, short-lived artifacts. As soon as there are no more resources to confiscate, redistribute, or control, the initial boost phase, derived from massive redistribution or coercive control of wealth, ends. As a case in point, the Nazi's "economic miracle" was not a miracle at all, for it was based, at least partly, on the redistribution of confiscated Jewish properties.

To put it mildly, the situation of the Collectivists today is unenviable despite the never-ending flow of neologisms attempting to promote Marxism while publicly distancing themselves from it. In sports terms, Socialism is permanently down on the mat, looking up at the referee as he is about to deliver the count—but the referee either lost the ability to count or does not want to.

A FEW DAVIDS VS. AN ARMY OF GOLIATHS

As an example of an ultimate, single-axiom theory, the individual-state paradigm is a product of pure reason. Essentially, emotions are thrown into a jumble of secondary delineators, which may cause difficulties for some individuals, especially when they have an emotional connection to some secondary issues. As an example, it is practically impossible for a conservative to shake hands with an antisemite; similarly, some left-wingers find it impossible to befriend proponents of the Second Amendment.

Nevertheless, the political "big tent" exists in both camps. Both opposing ideologies have adherents, with many—sometimes contradictory—secondary delineators. There are plenty of right-wing antisemites and many left-wing supporters of the National Rifle Association—which is the reality we must deal with. The homoplasy between opposing ideological camps is notable. Both left-wingers and right-wingers have their share of interventionists, isolationists, fiscal conservatives, antisemites, and many others. While their core ideologies are irreconcilable, convergent ideological evolution has produced many striking similarities like this.

The Left has unity on the primary and the vast majority of secondary issues. On the contrary, the Right barely agrees on a single primary issue. That is because the Left operates on the principle of one idea-many people, while the Right assumes the many ideas-many people canon. Thus, the Leftist technique, the one-to-many relationship, is inherently more coherent—at least in general—while the disunity among right-wingers, the proponents of the many-to-many relationship, exists by definition.

> **The Left operates on the principle of one idea-many people, while the Right assumes the many ideas-many people canon.**

Collectivists are not isolated, disorganized individuals like conservatives, for whom individual freedom is almost a panacea. On the contrary, Collectivists look like well-organized colonies of adherents on an industrial scale. As a result, the political battles between the Right and the Left look like battles between a few Davids armed with Founding Fathers' quotes who do not talk to each other just because they were not properly introduced, and the monolith phalanx of numerous Goliaths, armed with a wall of spears. Conservatives are a band of individuals standing tall against the Collectivist storm.

As a rule, left-wingers are well-organized; they primarily focus on the Utopian goal, not the obstacles. Right-wingers, on the contrary, are primarily disjointed. For example, in the United States, there is no party whatsoever that wholly represents their interests. In the United Kingdom, such a party does exist, but, as the account of Winston Churchill—who meandered between parties—demonstrates, the Conservative and Unionist Party, also known colloquially as the Tories, counts as Conservatives only sporadically. Eventually, Winston Churchill became a towering conservative force for freedom who saved the free world from an ephemeral Collectivist idyll. It is a great mystery why society, in its natural development, had reached the state when the near monolith structure aimed toward the unreachable point, while the opposite, amorphous structure, had achieved an unprecedented quality of life.

It may be that now, in America, at least, Leftists are not as well-organized as they used to be. The current state of affairs for them from a nation-state point of view leaves much to be desired. After a century of picking off yet another "new revolutionary class," created the Left with too many competing and unnatural factions, and the overall structure is challenging to work with. Furthermore, if creating new revolutionary classes of "victims of capitalism" is a more or less agreeable point, the existence of the middle class is anathema for the Leftists. It is an existential threat for the Leftists because it disproves their written-in-stone pseudo-religious dogma.

"Is the middle class oppressive or oppressed?" For all Leftists, that is a great question. For non-Leftists, such a question has no meaning. Firstly, the simple rejection of the "class" (recall the fluid nature of the term) makes the question meaningless. Secondly, "oppressed" and "oppressive" in left-wing practice mean "socialist revolutionary" and "counter-revolutionary" correspondingly. However, a sizable number of men and women have no taste for characterizing their neighbors, relatives, or friends in such terms. As it usually happens, communist lingo has meaning only for its adherents.[38]

As it is known, Marx promoted a classless society. It has always been

---

38. Recall the old Soviet joke: "Under capitalism man exploits man; under socialism the reverse is true."

Marxists' stated objective. Well, they have come to the conclusion that they have waited too long and have rejected the notion that the political classes will eventually disappear on their own. Instead, they picked a target—the mega-inconvenient and disturbing middle class—and methodically tried to pillage it. They might succeed, but on their own terms, in a post-Marxian way, by simply altering the definition of "class." Carriers of Leftspeak are exceptionally skilled at such tricks. (While on the subject, the term "Leftspeak" first appeared in an article by Rorty in 1987, who claims Frederick Crows coined the term, but no citation could be found. Rorty knew well what he was talking about—he was raised in a family of committed Trotskyites and anti-Stalinists. Who authored the term "Wokespeak" is still unknown.)

Marxists argue that the entirety of social life is reducible to material reality—specifically, the disparity between the rich and the poor. Almost all collectivist states, such as the Soviet Union during its heyday, were driven by a paranoid obsession with reading everything that occurred on the planet through the lens of class struggle theory. Even though it is grounded in a material background, the individual-state paradigm does not maintain that social life can be reduced to a single principle. Instead, the emphasis is on the most critical material, highlighting the two opposing forces behind society's political development—the struggle between the government and the governed.

The emphasis of the individual-state paradigm is on the two opposing forces behind society's political development—the struggle between the government and the governed.

History suggests that such a struggle might coincide with the class struggle, as envisioned by Marx, but it would require, first, the existence of classes, and second, the classes themselves would need to be time-invariant. Moreover, to be universally useful, the definition of classes needs to be stable over many generations, which is impossible. The Leftists repeat their usual trick here: recalibrate the opposing classes' definitions at will to suit a particular political context. Whenever the situation changes, they change the participating classes as well. The individual-state paradigm does not follow that circular logic because human society always observes the existence of the government and the governed.

The other attractive feature of the individual-state paradigm is that it is resistant to negative attacks (telling people about conservatism and what it is not) and positive attacks (assigning conservatism to more than one foundational axiom). Finally, because the individual-state paradigm is one-dimensional, there is a simple method to determine if a specific "ism" is an ideology or a feature of an ideology. For example, if Right "ism" and Left "ism" exist, that "ism" is, most likely, just a feature of the underlying ideology and not an ideology by itself. So, populism or antisemitism could be left- or right-wing; thus, these "isms" are not ideologies.

WHO CONTROLS WHOM?

What is it that conservatives conserve? "It is a limp definition of conservatism to describe it as the desire to conserve" (Scruton 1984, p. 21). The common misconception is that conservatives maintain the *status quo*. The static viewpoint presented here is false since conservatives have never advocated freezing anything. Instead, conservatism should be viewed in dynamic terms. If conservatism preserves anything, it preserves society's undercurrents.

As an ardent follower of the European strain of conservatism, namely metaphysical conservatism, Russian philosopher Nickolas Berdyaev, at the beginning of the 20th century, manifested, "Conservatism supports the connection across time, does not permit of an ultimate breaking of this connection, it unites the future with the past" (Berdyaev [1923] 2015, p. 103). He adds that the conservative "principle holds in check the pressure of the chaotic darkness from below. And the meaning of conservatism, therefore, is not that it hinders movement forward and upwards, but rather in this, that it hinders movement backward and downwards, towards chaotic darkness" (Ibid., pp. 114-115). From Berdyaev's standpoint, conservatism prevents Western democracies from slipping into pre-Enlightenment obscurity. Finally, from Berdyaev's end of things, "The conservative principle itself per se is not opposed to development, it only demands that developmental growth be organic, that the future does not destroy the past, but rather should continue to develop it" (Ibid., p. 118).

Conservatism acts as a society's natural immune system that fights dangerous cashless ideologies.

Berdyaev presents a stark warning: "When conservatism is associated in the mind of the people with the hindering of development and hostility towards creativity, then in the land revolution awaits. Culpable in this become those conservative powers, which have permitted within them deadening and ossification in itself, and those revolutionary powers also, which rise up against the eternal principles, against non-transitory values and sanctities" (Ibid., p. 118).

Describing the current state of Liberalism in post-World War I Europe (by that time, Liberalism already had been hijacked by the Leftists and accepted the new title of Socialism), Berdyaev presented it in incredibly harsh words: "Liberalism has become so basically weather-bitten, has become so lacking in soul, that it is possible still to admit

Conservatism acts as a society's natural immune system that fights dangerous cashless ideologies.

some element of liberalism, but impossible already it is to be a liberal in faith, by one's ultimate worldview. Liberalism has ceased to be an autonomous principle, it has been rendered into something of a compromise, something of a semi-democratism or semi-conservatism" (Ibid., p. 144). In the opinion of Berdyaev, "It is impossible to ground liberalism on positivist a basis, possible only for it is a metaphysical basis" (Ibid., p. 142).

Nicolas Berdyaev postulated in 1923 in an essay, "Concerning Liberalism," what is presently acknowledged as Berdyaev's Theorem: "Freedom and equality are incommensurable" (Berdyaev [1923] 2015, p. 147). He continues, "Freedom is first of all the right to inequality. And equality is first of all an infringement upon freedom, limitation on freedom." Thus, the proper title of that philosophical essay should be "Manifesto of Right Liberalism" or, simply, in modern terms, "Manifesto of Conservatism," even though Berdyaev assigned a categorically different non-political meaning to "conservatism."

The proper interpretation of the incompatibility of freedom and equality is possible only by applying the individual-state paradigm. Therefore, although the described incompatibility is founded in different domains where the terms must be applied, freedom shall be understood exclusively in the government-to-governed fabric. At the same time, equality covers solely the intra-society business.

Berdyaev criticized the French Revolution because the "French Revolution completely confused equality with freedom." Between freedom and equality, "there exists not a harmony but rather an irreconcilable antagonism" (Ibid., p. 146).[39] Moreover, "The entire political and social history of the XIX century is the drama of this clash of freedom and equality. And the dreaminess about a harmonic combining of freedom and equality is merely an unrealizable rationalistic utopia. There never could be concord between the pretensions of the person and the pretensions of society, between the will for freedom and the will for equality" (Ibid., pp. 146-147). The beginning of the 21st-century events exhibits direct support for Berdyaev's warnings: "The thirst for equality always will be the greatest danger for human freedom," and "[t]he inner development of liberalism leads to democratic equality, which comes to be in an inevitable opposition to freedom" (Ibid., pp. 147-148).

The "border" between the government and the governed—deduced from a wealth allocation standpoint—is not sacrosanct. It is fluid. In a time of existential crisis (like a war, natural disaster, or other *force majeure* situations), the government's share of society's wealth goes up; when everything is back to normal, the government's share theoretically goes down. To be precise, the government's elevated share of wealth is *supposed* to go down after a disaster is mitigated, but, as history constitutes evidence, the government rarely does it voluntarily. The only time conservatives agree, albeit reluctantly, to increase the size of the government is during wartime. Alas, the Leftists got it, too. They know that each small war erodes capitalist society and contributes to the desired tyrannical outcome.

Leftists clearly learned a valuable lesson from this. They compared their desired state of affairs (total government dominance and control) with the natural proclivity of the government's allocation of wealth to increase in a crisis. It has been a long tradition for Leftists to thrive in a crisis. For example, the Great War (World War I) led to the Bolshevik coup in Russia and hyperinflation in the Weimar Republic, followed by the Great Depression. It boosted the chances of Adolf Hitler, just like the Great Financial Crisis catapulted Barack Obama into the White House. In general, dictators-in-waiting are activated *en masse* during crises and exploit them as gateways. Leftists have thus realized that the future Utopian society can be built without the help of

---

39. The central idea of Berdyaev's book, titled "The Philosophy of Inequality," is expressed by Berdyaev in very prophetic words: "*Freedom is first of all the right to inequality.*" Paper (Gindler 2019) offers a simple mathematical model that separates freedom and equality.

a single "Big Bang" event—socialist revolution—but rather through a series of endless crises. The following list contains recent (from the 2000s) crises (real and imagined) exploited by Leftists to cultivate fear and advance government control. Each item below was positioned and promoted as the end of civilization as we know it:

2000—Y2K computers scare
2001—Anthrax scare
2002—West Nile virus scare
2003—SARS scare
2005—Bird flu scare
2006—E. coli scare
2008—Financial collapse
2009—Swine flu scare
2012—The Mayan calendar predicts the world will end soon
2014—Ebola virus scare
2016—Zika virus scare
2020—Coronavirus scare
2021—Delta variant scare
2022—Omicron variant scare
2022—Monkeypox scare
2023—Disinformation scare

Of course, the ever-present climate scare over the last half-century must be included on the list. Note that the vast majority of these manufactured scares deal with microorganisms, invisible to the naked eye.[40] Each crisis, war, and new crime wave works for the Leftists. The Left is pleased when the population succumbs to an ideological, religious, bacterial, or virus epidemic. That is because, for them, it is irrelevant to which exact force citizens submit. As long as they submit, it is a step toward Collectiveville.

For Leftists, the answer to the question "Who controls whom?" is existential. The Right team mandates control over the government; the Left wants control over the governed. It is an understatement, for both opposing powers are totalitarian in nature: the Right wants total control over the government,

---

40. Many medical authorities worldwide—from World Health Organization to local health authorities—are still practicing medical Lysenkoism. In the United States, Dr. Fauci was one of them.

while the Left wants total control over the governed. As a result of that ideological totalitarianism, conservatism aims for the total truth—truth unobscured by the government in any way.

Both left-wingers and right-wingers feel the need to be free. However, if the Left wishes state power to be free from people's watchful eyes, the Right wishes people to be free from the state's watchful eye. For Leftists, collective (state) wealth matters more than the sum of individual wealth. For Conservatives, the rulers are answerable to their populations; for Collectivists, populations are answerable to their rulers. The Right insists that governments must be controlled; the Left dreams of the population to be controlled. The Left oversupplies mediocrity, while the Right oversupplies meritocracy. The Left parades fantasy, glamorized by selected elements of reality; the Right offers reality, sporadically sugared by imagination. While Conservatism has its roots in the Enlightenment, Leftism has its primordial principle in Enslavement.

The Left made a sizable contribution to dictatorship worldwide, delivering a great deal of agro-dictators, petro-dictators, narco-dictators, and communo-dictators. However, the Right can count only one person in the entire history of humankind—Augusto Pinochet.

Both Conservatism and Collectivism are forward-looking ideologies. Both change the present to achieve their vision of the future. However, in opposition to Collectivism, Conservatism inhibits altering the past and constrains society into focusing on changing only the future.

Leftists, therefore, are more belligerent than the Right. The left-wing elites want war; the right-wing elites want peace. Thus, while the Right prepares for war, the Left prepares the *GULAG* for the Right.

A good illustration can be found in the last World War. It was initiated by two socialist states with eerily similar chassis, the Third Reich (National Socialism) and the Soviet Union (International Socialism), against several capitalist countries. People forget that World War II was a multi-continent event where National Socialists and International Socialists tried to carry out a global assault against the capitalist West. They fought shoulder to shoulder for two years until one side decided there was no room for two on the Socialist Olympus.

WHAT DOES CONSERVATISM CONSERVE?

Both John Dewey and Richard Rorty analyzed the vital question of the relationship between an individual and society. They were trying to find a proper scale of the influence of society upon an individual. Dewey and Rorty consider the opposing imperatives of individual-societal as independent and given in search of a favorable dose of individualism in society. The situation here, however, bears some similarities to those mentioned above: electric and magnetic fields that cannot exist independently. The variations of an electric field produce a magnetic field, and vice versa, so their separation is artificial; it is just a result of the historical evolution of our analysis of these forces of nature. So likewise, a collection of humans creates society, which, in return, influences each member. The elusive dose of individualism both Dewey and Rorty were trying to find simply depends on the ratio of the sum of an individual's wealth to the sum of government (public) wealth. The higher the ratio (valued from 0 to 1), the higher the share of the individual. The closer the ratio is to 1—to the right of the scale—the more right-wing society is. If the ratio is close to zero—to the left of the scale—the more left-wing tendencies become evident.

> **Ibn Khaldun devised what later became known as the "Laffer Curve," which postulates the existence of the "optimal" taxation level.**

The surprising answer to Rorty's search for the proper demarcation line between an individual and society was provided six centuries before by Ibn Khaldun, a Tunisian philosopher who occupies (quite unfairly) obscure status. His seminal opus, "The Muqaddam," was dedicated to finding a way for just, fair, and sustainable taxation. Ibn Khaldun devised what later became known as the "Laffer Curve," which postulates the existence of the "optimal" taxation level. It is based on the discovery by Ibn Haldun that the overall level of tax revenue has two components: the arithmetical (linear) effect and the economic (non-linear) effect (Khaldun [1377] 2005). Furthermore, it was shown that high tax rates do not lead to high tax revenues because of a point of diminishing returns due to suppression of economic activity. However, the exact shape of the Laffer Curve is unknown; a paper by this author (Gindler 2019) offers the first analytical approximation.

Of course, conservatives do not consider government and government-enforced taxation an absolute evil construct or even a necessary gradation of evil. Per Berdyaev, "Vl. Solov'ev finely said, that the state exists, not in order to transform the earthly life into paradise, but in order to hinder it ultimately from being transformed into a hell" (Berdyaev [1923] 2015, p. 62).

From time immemorial, people realized they could not continue to be a mere collection of organisms at a certain point in society's development. People suddenly grasped that there was something—pretty elusive at first, but nevertheless reasonably achievable—beyond being a horde of mammals. This revolutionary "beyond an organism" idea gave birth to multiple self-organizational avenues: religion, art, culture, government, and science. They all had one common, uncodified, but easily understood pretension: to go beyond the individual organism's physical limitations. The government outlines a necessary level of structurization due to natural self-organization. The government structure, by design, carries less entropy (a lesser degree of chaos) than the individuals constituting a society. The Right perceives the shrinking low-entropy government as an inevitableness of individual freedom, while the Left considers the expanding low-entropy government a springboard to Utopia.

The government's entropy may exceed that of the governed society, which may lead to a revolution; such a government is deemed chaotic and dysfunctional and must be replaced. Such revolutions could be under the patronage of either the Right or the Left. Another reason for a revolution is when the government grows in size and becomes self-aware while its entropy is stable or drops down. Such a government unhesitatingly declares that the end justifies the means and begins uncontrolled growth until it consumes all aspects of human life. Such revolutions are exclusive to the Left.[41]

The popular myth (created by anti-conservatives) is that the conservative creed comprises aversion to change. This childish argument was concocted by self-anointed perverts who consider themselves the only drivers of social innovations. Conservatism offers protection from implementing ideas that do not have a positive cash value, but it does not prohibit the development of such ideas—as long as somebody is willing to pay for them. In other words, conservatism is not against innovations—simply because its ultimate role is to guide

---

41. To the horror of Leftists, the first true working-class revolution in the world was in Poland—and it was a revolution (spearheaded by trade union *Solidarność*) against Socialism and one-party dictatorship.

them. Since the Enlightenment, conservatism (known back then as liberalism and later as classical liberalism) has been guarding society against regressing to the pre-Enlightenment state. The proverbial "*status quo*" conservatives supposedly care for is commonly construed in a static sense. In reality, conservatism supports the dynamic *status quo*—the only static *status quo* it guards is society's vector of development.

Contrary to popular misconception, according to Berdyaev, conservatism does not prevent society from moving forward and upward; it prevents society from moving backward and downward. Conservatism is self-directing but not the driving mechanism of human society; it is a necessary but insufficient mechanism. The self-directing mechanism must complement a self-propelling mechanism of society that cannot be located within a single axiom. All necessary and sufficient systems of human progress are not exogenous to the individual-state paradigm. Using a car analogy, conservatism is not the engine but the steering wheel. To go on with the analogy, Fascism, Nazism, Leninism, Stalinism, and many other "isms" are all examples of Leftism driving over the speed limit.

Conservatism can be viewed as an ideological semiconducting diode that permits society to propagate only in one direction: forward and upward.

Reduced to its primary delineator form, conservatism can be viewed as an ideological semiconducting diode that permits society to propagate only in one direction: forward and upward.

Thus, conservatism establishes the asymmetrical evolution of human society. "Conservatives recognize that social order is hard to achieve and easy to destroy," affirmed Roger Scruton in the article "Totalitarian Sentimentality" (Scruton 2009). This evolutionary asymmetry requires a proper corrective mechanism, a compensatory feedback loop. Otherwise, society will ultimately proceed along the path of least resistance and reset back to a pre-civilized state. Conservatism is the epitome of a proper compensatory mechanism for society's evolution. In other words, one of the conservatives' mottoes could be "make the past predictable." Per Scruton, "Conservatives therefore maintain severe and—to many people—unattractive attitudes."

There is a straightforward analogy for conservatism in the world of classical mechanics. Consider the following mechanical problem: a large, heavy sphere is located at the tip of a needle. What is the direction of the sphere that is about to fall? Of course, the sphere's position in such an experiment is not predictable; it could fall in any direction. That is, it is not predictable, as stated. Consider adding one more condition to the problem: the sphere moves at a certain high speed in a particular direction. In this dynamic case, the existence of a needle becomes irrelevant. Even if the sphere is located on the tip of the needle at the beginning of the experiment, simple inertia will render the sphere's position at any time predictable. The static consideration above could be associated with the left-wing attitude, while the dynamic example could be bound with conservatism's role in social development.

In such terms, conservatism could be related to the inertial properties of a physical body. Yes, inertia resists changing the movement's direction, which is the essence of Leftists' opposition to conservatism. They constantly refer to conservatism as an ideology that "resists change" but never emphasize that it means "resist change from forward to backward." In reality, conservatism is change, but for the Leftists, it represents a change in the direction they do not like. Note that conservatism—made clear even by its spelling—seeks to conserve something. That "something" is the movement's direction. Of course, under the influence of the Leftist forces, society has been periodically led astray from its developmental path in its never-ending evolution of freedom. However, history shows that such fluctuations over the main trajectory are relatively short-lived everywhere they have been tried.

Conservatism is indeed in favor of the *status quo*, but that must be made out only in dynamic terms. The narrow, static *status quo* must be rejected because it has nothing to do with conservatism. Instead, conservatism favors society's development in the direction that maximizes its cash value. Conservatives consider that particular, dynamic meaning of the *status quo* fundamental and worth defending.

Assume that the entire society can be reduced to the scale of a single family. In that case, conservatism could be represented by a mother. She seeks a prudent path and directs the family ship through unstable currents. Mother offers care for her husband, kids, and the elderly. She maintains a certain degree of comfort and love onboard the ship. Note that some women do all this without paying much attention to the particulars of their husbands making money. The patriarch is the engine that propels the ship. The matriarch is the steering wheel at the helm. Family needs both, just as society does. Society needs a conservative, motherly hand to gently push the community toward prosperity and happiness. As a mother monitors her children's behavior, conservatism monitors the behavior of social ideas and rejects anything without a positive cash value. Just as a mother allows kids to play—but only on the condition of not rocking the family boat too much—conservatism prevents rocking society with dangerous ideas that could turn it over and lead to irreversible damage. In the same way that a child requires a father and mother, society requires a fatherland and motherland. To conclude, conservatism equates with the forces of Schumpeterian creative destruction; it must have accompanying forces of destructive creation to form a vibrant society.

By fostering a conception of only organic forms of change, conservatism acts as a ratchet that permits society's motion in only one direction. Conservatism is just another name assigned to society's self-correcting mechanisms. Moreover, Conservatism provides a medium for society's auto-correction. Society's regress is supported by adherents of illiberal and intolerant political operators associated with a Leftist ideological constellation. While the Leftists of the second half of the 19th century designated themselves "progressive," readers shall understand that the term was a gigantic pre-Freud Freudian slip, a clever word game based on the "progressive tax" scheme.

As one of the Founding Fathers, John Adams, wrote in a letter to his wife, Abigail Adams, on July 1, 1775, "Liberty once lost is lost forever." Conservatism is intended to prevent such losses. So, if one is still hard-pressed to clarify what exactly conservatism conserves, the veracious answer would be that conservatism watches over an orientation of social self-evolution. In particular, conservatives aim at thoroughly desacralizing the State, while the Leftists want to grant it sacrosanct status.

According to Michael Freeden and his morphological model, ideologies comprise core, adjacent, and peripheral concepts (Freeden, Stears, and Sargent, 2013). In these terms, the individual-state paradigm represents a single-core model; for the adjacent and peripheral items, we prefer to use the umbrella terms "secondary" or "derivative."

What are the differences between right-wingers and conservatives? The Right (like the Left) is a strict single-issue ideology formed on an economic foundation. In keeping with the True Right and the True Left, there is nothing beyond the individual-state paradigm. On the contrary, Conservatism is an umbrella term that routinely incorporates many *secondary* issues beyond the *primary* one.

The principal Right-Left watershed relates to the individual-state economic paradigm. Conservatism treats this distinction only as a primary delineator; many other secondary delineators exist. Conservatives rarely agree on secondary delineators. Specifically, conservatism, a right-wing ideology at its core, has a number of supplementary elements. Like the Leftists who were for free speech before they were against it, Conservatives unequivocally offer opposite opinions about secondary delineators at intervals.

From the individual-state paradigm point of view, Conservatism has many strains; this term encompasses multiple political movements under a single umbrella name. In contrast, there is a single Leftist ideology that is concealed behind various names. The same is true of the Left's institutions. For example, the notorious Soviet-Russian secret police, commonly known as the KGB, has many abbreviations: Cheka-VCheka-GPU-OGPU-NKVD-NKGB-MGB-KGB-AFB-MB-FSK-FSB.[42] Margaret Thatcher indisputably spotted the habit: "Socialists have always spent much of their time seeking new titles for their beliefs, because the old versions so quickly become outdated and discredited" (Thatcher 2002, p. 417).

Ancient Greeks had witnessed such a situation millennia before the term "Leftism" was born. Observing endless political fights, Greeks came up with the myth of the Hydra, an enemy that prefers to hide behind multiple heads (read: multiple ideological decoys.) Whenever one of the Hydra's heads is cut off, it instantly regenerates, creating another ideological smokescreen instead of the debunked one. In some versions of the myth, Hydra has one inseverable head, or two heads grow back to replace one lost. This emphasizes the hopelessness of some political fights, as Margaret Thatcher expressed: "Socialism is like one of those horrible viruses. You no sooner discover a remedy for one version, than it spontaneously evolves into another" (Thatcher 2003).

CAN THE INDIVIDUAL-STATE PARADIGM BE PROVED?

Is the individual-state paradigm the same dogma as Leftism? The answer is yes and no. The answer is "no" because, as noted previously, no set of axioms can prove themselves. The answer is "yes" because, by now, the two doctrines have run in parallel long enough to produce some incontrovertible results.

---

42. In Russian, these monikers are *ЧК-ВЧК-ГПУ-ОГПУ-НКВД-НКГБ-МГБ-КГБ-АФБ-МБ-ФСК-ФСБ.*

Where is the proof that the individual-state paradigm is true? Plainly, there is none since it is an axiom that does not need to be proven. Obviously, one cannot prove something based on the same thing (unless one is a Leftist who consistently uses circular logic). Thus, the validity of any axiom must be established by reference to external sources—namely, human history.

While an individual's political freedom is determined by the aggregate economic power of people vs. the government, the individual-state paradigm has no say about peoples' economic relations. Unfortunately, the term "freedom"—valid exclusively in the government-to-governed domain—often spills into the economic relations in society and produces such terms as "free-market capitalism." While it is inconceivable that a collective of free people would eventually evolve into some form of non-free-market economic relations, a single postulate does not warrant it.

A critical consequence of axiomatic conservatism is often overlooked: it makes no recommendations regarding the economic foundations of society. As a result, the individual-state paradigm is silent on whether the economy must be established on *laissez-faire* capitalism or something else.[43] It is not a bug but rather a feature of the advocated axiomatic system of thought. Per Gödel's theorem, within the confines of an axiomatic theory, it is possible to have accurate, factual statements that the paramount set of axioms cannot prove. In the same vein, the individual-state paradigm does not specify how society should be organized politically. For this reason, by the way, the word "democracy" does not appear in the United States Constitution.

Free-market capitalism happens to be the most compatible economic system with the individual-state paradigm. In other words, left to their own devices, free people (free in the template of the individual-state paradigm) naturally self-organize along certain economic principles. Capitalism was born around the same time as Liberalism and is one of the practical implementations of the idea of freedom. If left-wingers work on spreading the wealth around, the right-wingers work on distributing prosperity. Over the last several centuries, capitalism elevated so many people to an unparalleled amplitude of prosperity that no other economic system comes close. Capitalism is

---

43. Currently, it is customary to use the term *laissez-faire* alone. However, the proper usage is as a combination of *laissez-faire* and *laissez-aller*. For example, Karl Marx, himself an archenemy of both terms, is known to use them mostly in combination.

commonly analogous to pursuing profit, but that is just a part of the story. The whole story must include the freedom of using profit, for without freedom, profit could be taken away by the government. Therefore, as a derivative of liberty, profit must be viewed not as profit per se but within the blueprint of freedom to do with it, whatever one wishes. Unquestionably, capitalism has an organic connection to the individual-state paradigm.

What is more, the United States Constitution is practically mute in economic terms. In the economic arena, American citizens are granted property rights, and the Federal government is granted authority to mint coins, collect taxes, enforce contracts, and that is it. Undoubtedly, the Founding Fathers deliberately opened the newly created country to free economic experiments—in complete agreement with the Right side of the individual-state paradigm.[44]

According to widespread belief, the Right ideology effectuates capitalism, whereas the Left ideology catalyzes socialism. However, there is no direct relationship between the individual-state paradigm and capitalism—or socialism, for that matter. However, one crucial step between the individual-state paradigm and capitalism is meritocracy. The proper distribution of economic power between the government and the governed in favor of the governed and subsequent intra-society inequality leads to meritocracy; capitalism may follow later. For capitalism to emerge, meritocracy must join forces with money to create capital.

For capitalism to emerge, meritocracy must join forces with money to create capital.

Likewise, the individual-state paradigm does not mandate a particular form of political organization of society. Representative democracy, constitutional freedoms, and non-violent coexistence with political opposition are not directly linked to the primary delineator. Scruton emphasized that "we should not let our obsession with democracy blind us to its value" (Scruton 1984). Moreover, conservatism does not even mandate the creation and maintenance of any Conservative Party (it could be yet another excellent illustration of key distinctions between the Right and Left ideologies). This is due to

44. One of the icons of American progressives, Charles Beard, in 1913 offered the left-wing theory (now thoroughly discredited) that the actual purpose of the United States Constitution was wealth redistribution: from the poor class to the upper class, to which the Founding Fathers belonged.

the fact that conservatism views all these essential items as simply products of social self-organization through trial and error. Consequently, the government would do its best to stay out of the way of these natural phenomena.

Conservatism has proper answers to political, economic, and social questions, but these answers are drawn from sources outside the single axiom. To begin with, we should note that every time economic freedom was introduced to the community in human history, political freedom followed. Second, as the individual-state paradigm advocates, allocating government wealth as a small fraction of overall society wealth results in naturally developing capitalistic relationships since the government is not—even theoretically—able to "stand in the way." When a government's wealth is too small compared to society's wealth, it has insufficient muscle to mandate anything or only enough strength to enforce existing laws. In such a situation, as was argued by Margaret Thatcher in a speech on November 13, 1989, "When people are free to choose, they choose freedom."

Thatcher viewed herself as a student of Friedrich Hayek and Milton Friedman, Nobel Prize in Economics laureates of 1974 and 1976, respectively. In 1975, the daughter of a tobacco and grocery store owner from the provincial town of Grantham managed to describe the essence of the problem at hand in just two paragraphs. Comparing economic systems, she stated: "There are only two political philosophies, only two ways of governing a country. One is the Socialist-Marxist way in which what matters is not the community but the State. In which decisions affecting individuals' lives are taken from them, instead of being taken by them. In which property and savings are taken from the population instead of being more widely held among them. In which directives replace incentives. In which the State is the master of the individual, instead of the servant" (Thatcher 1975).

On the contrary, she continued, "A free economic system not only guarantees the freedom of each individual citizen, it is the surest way to increase the prosperity of the nation as a whole." Referring to the policies of British Conservatives, she pictured a free economic system, "[i]n which each individual is equally important but different in ability; equally entitled to rights, but equally free to rise to the heights of his talents. In which the family is the foundation of society and the desire of parents to give their children a better start in life is honoured as one of the most powerful influences for good. In which freedom to choose goods, services, education, and housing is steadily extended. In which savings and thrift are encouraged so that citizens become independent of the State rather than perpetually dependent on it. In which practical care and concern for others is not confined to demanding State benefits, but is a common purpose of daily life. In which the freedom of all is protected by a just and impartial rule of law" (Thatcher 1975).

In 1978, Margaret Thatcher offered another brilliant argument: "You can't make people good, kind, generous, thoughtful or dutiful by compulsion. True harmony comes from the willing cooperation of free men. It is not served by an over-regulated society. Socialists, on the other hand, believe in increasing the power of government, in reducing the choices left to the people, and hence in diminishing their liberties. Their methods are high taxation, regimentation, compulsion, closed shops and blacklists" (Thatcher 1978).

In fulfillment of the individual-state paradigm, an economically small government cannot possibly result in tyranny or compulsory economic relationships (e.g., socialism). However, despite the historical reliability of this thesis, it cannot be analytically "proven" from a single axiom. Truth be told, the individual-state axiom does not prescribe a particular method of conducting political affairs; it is just a means of creating an environment conducive to the free exercise of social self-organization. Thus, the individual-state paradigm does not directly lead to representative democracy (often referred to simply as democracy nowadays). However, as Winston Churchill contended, "Democracy is the worst form of government except for all the others that have been tried." (Note that the apparent cynicism of his speech in the House of Commons on November 11, 1947, could be explained by his crushing defeat in 1945 when he was ruthlessly thrown out of 10 Dawning Street despite winning the war against Germany just three months earlier).

The individual-state paradigm does not directly lead to representative democracy

Contrary to popular opinion, the keyword here is not the "worst." The key term is "have been tried." Tried, not imposed, and not dictated. The individual-state paradigm does not drive economic or political development—it establishes conditions for society's free, self-directed, self-organizing development with a particular pathway in mind. The individual-state paradigm highlights the most appropriate method of social progress—self-directed and self-organized evolution rather than revolution. As a fundamental principle of conservatism, it provides the most effective method for improving the lives of low-income individuals—by increasing their wealth in both absolute and relative terms. The population on the lower end of the income spectrum is encouraged but not forced to go up, and the well-to-do citizenry must not be obliged to go down. In other words, the Left's idea of intra-society equality inspires the poor to drag the rich toward the poor's financial level; the Right evangelizes to pull the poor up to the rich's financial level.

Conservatism is society's *modus operandi* to go forward, complemented by mechanisms preventing slipping backward. Collectivism is a scalar; conservatism is a vector. Conservatism is the only known human tool capable of orienting society's development axis precisely between the Scylla of chaos due to under-governance and the Charybdis of tyranny due to over-governance. The Right advertises the path but not the destination. The Left announces an unapproachable destination and follows an unintelligible path. Nevertheless, again, conservatism is not the engine—it is the rudder of society. Per Andrea Widburg, "Conservatives take facts and reach conclusions; Leftists have conclusions and sell them as facts."

The Left's idea of intra-society equality inspires the poor to drag the rich toward the poor's financial level; the Right evangelizes to pull the poor up to the rich's financial level.

One of the well-known secrets on the world stage is that the Right wants to improve people's lives. At the same time, the Left aims to sculpt life as miserable as possible for as many people as possible because that is the only path to eternal power the Left commissars feel compassionate towards. Of course, the Left's position is irrational, but who has ever met a rational commissar?

In the ideal conservative society, citizens are not concerned about how other citizens spend their money; sometimes, it is even considered bad manners to ask. Instead, everybody is concerned with how the government spends people's money. In the ideal collectivist society, it is quite the opposite: questioning government spending is either illegal or simply bad manners (depending on the strain of Leftism). So, instead, society focuses exclusively on discourse about other people's money.

LAISSEZ-FAIRE CAPITALISM AND LIBERTARIANISM

Ayn Rand's Objectivism is an interesting case from the standpoint of the individual-state paradigm. Per Rand, "In politics, Objectivism stands for *laissez-faire* capitalism, which means the separation of state and economics; as a corollary, we hold that men must deal with one another as traders, exchanging value for value, with no one being told that he must sacrifice for the sake of others or of the state" (Podritske and Schwartz 2009, p. 15). Objectivism's objections over conservatism look pretty straightforward: "'Conservative' is as loose a term today as 'liberal,' and most people who use it keep the meaning intentionally vague. There is no firm definition. Therefore, what I say does not necessarily apply to each individual who calls himself a conservative. I am speaking of the dominant trend and of the general impression people have of conservatism. By commonly accepted usage, a conservative is someone who opposes the welfare state and supports capitalism. In fact, however, most conservatives do not stand for free enterprise, but for various degrees of a mixed economy" (Ibid., p. 16).

In other words, Rand is concerned about one of the secondary delineators of the individual-state paradigm—namely, intra-society economic relations. Next, she emphasized in her opinion about conservatives that "many of them tie their political views to religion. They claim that mysticism—a belief in God—provides the justification for rights, freedom, and capitalism. Nothing could be more disastrous to the cause of capitalism—and nothing could be more opposed to Objectivism, which holds reason as the sole means of validating any idea or action" (Ibid., p. 16). In this instance, Rand is engaged in a quixotic struggle against secondary delineators, a collection of apparent features that are not the foundation of political philosophy. It is likely that Rand rejected any religious dictums due to the "negation of reason." She expressed a distaste for all religions at any given point (which might explain why her attractive philosophy never caught on—she alienated too many people unnecessarily.)

The Libertarian movement elevates personal freedom to the top of its movement, whereas the Objectivist movement uplifts *laissez-faire* capitalism. In contrast, as we have demonstrated, both personal freedom and (to a certain extent) *laissez-faire* capitalism are only naturally occurring corollaries of the more fundamental principle of the individual-state paradigm.

There is no ambiguity that Objectivists should accept the primary delineator as their foundational principle (Ayn Rand would undoubtedly accept it) since Objectivism, reduced to an individual-state paradigm, is not entirely different from the conservatism described in this book. One of Rand's most serious concerns with conservatism is solid: "Because conservatism is not sharply defined, it includes people of all shades of opinion. My main objection to any movement of that sort is that it is futile. It is disastrous to one's own cause to allow oneself to belong to an undefined group, or to collaborate with other groups, without any clear identification of basic principles or basic points of agreement" (Ibid., p. 17). These are wise and true words. Hopefully, this book will change some preconceptions and opinions about Objectivists and bring them back into the fold—after they finally comprehend that the free market is the means, not an end.

From the individual-state paradigm standing, Nicholas Berdyaev should be a household name for all modern conservatives; Ayn Rand should have joined him. Instead, these philosophers attain more or less "obscure" status for the same reason. That reason is religion. While Ayn Rand was a militant atheist who left Communist Russia in 1925, Nicolas Berdyaev was a devoted religious scholar who looked at political philosophy strictly through the prism of Christianity. If the divine world was the inspiration for Berdyaev, the material world was the inspiration for Rand. Both philosophers were (and still are) judged, perhaps undeservedly, too extreme for mainstream conservatism.

In 1922, Soviet communists initiated the expulsion of the non-conforming intelligentsia from Soviet Russia. Like hundreds of distinguished Russian intellectuals, the Bolsheviks arrested Berdyaev and expelled him from Russia onboard one of what turned out to be the infamous "philosophers' ships." All those world-renowned thinkers were counted as "elements ideologically alien to Soviet power." Another notable philosopher on the ship was Ivan Ilyin, the future founder of Russian Fascism. (The eviction policy of "non-desirable elements" never ceased until the end of the Soviet Union.) The forced exodus of the most famous Russian scientists was so successful that modern Leftists tried to emulate that success by deplatforming, cancelations, and superfluous ongoing technological methods of enforcing ideological conformity. So, it looks like culture, religion, family matters, education, and science are downstream of wealth alignment between the government and the governed, after all.

THE WAR WITH THE PAST

One of the most overlooked facts regarding pogroms in the 21st century in America is that Black Lives Matter and their sister gang Antifa pulled down many statues that have nothing to do with racial or Fascist themes. They are, however, symbols of a distant past. One of the rather unusual arguments predicting the inevitable failure of the current Leftist effort focuses on their poor choice of targets. In particular, they misunderstood and mischaracterized conservatism; in their warped view, conservatism is associated with everything that is old, outdated, or otherwise not "cool."

Unfortunately, the widespread (and wrong) perception that conservatism is somehow connected undividedly with the past has promoted these statues as symbols of conservatism. Leftists use their own antiquated but widespread definition of conservatism as the preservation of heritage. Thus, the drive to dismantle any heritage—statues, for example—because demolition is considered a part of the class struggle against "reactionary forces."

The war with the past in the West is not something new. Destroyed statues and burned buildings came from the distant past. As 19th-century historian Jakob Burckhardt stipulated, during the French Revolution, "men took upon themselves the right to indict the past as a whole" (Burckhardt 1943, p.43). It explains the absence of logic behind tearing down historical figures' statues to advocate equal treatment for blacks.

Moreover, it clearly exposes the "racial" smokescreen of these trans-Marxist perpetrators, who use racial and anti-fascist rhetoric to get more "useful idiots" on the streets. The Leftist crew cannot procure a prosperous future, so they must vandalize the bygone to ensure nobody remembers anything from the "reactionary" past. In waging war against the past, Leftists, as in discordant endeavors, pull off the same mistake: they concentrate on symbols of the past rather than the past itself.

The shocking toppling of American heroes' statues results from extreme political and ideological polarization. What is the root cause of this polarization in modern society? By now, the secondary delineators' conflicts had principally been fought for and practically exhausted. The world is moving toward an open, inevitable phase of the primary conflict—conflict regarding the primary delineator, the wealth allocation between the government and the governed. This primary conflict was never dormant (recall *Ecclesiastes*

1:6, "round and round it goes, ever returning on its course"). However, it was masked by a multitude of ferocious secondary conflicts (racism, religious intolerance, border disputes, human rights, etc.). There is a significant loss of intellectual power in the public sphere due to battles on the secondary delineators. Intellectual arguments about the ins and outs of economic policy, which can be regarded as a suitable proxy for the primary delineator, are fast disappearing.

Conservatism is characterized by its susceptibility to renaissances since freedom, like Mother Nature, always finds a way, together with the features of conservatism, to prevent dangerous regressive trends in society. The susceptibility to renaissances is a peculiar characteristic of left-wing movements, too, since the hatred of one cohort of humans by another can be relatively easily orchestrated and exploited by competent Kapellmeisters. That is why the recidivism rate of Left ideologies is high. Leftists' ideas rarely die; rather, they usually hibernate.

It leads to yet another paradox—the paradox of Marxism's prodigious vitality. As long as capitalism exists, the theory that promotes its inevitable demise will have its share of followers. It is well-established that the rise of Marxism's adherent base (and Leftism's, for that matter) occurs in antiphase to economic ascendancy and prosperity. However, regardless of the perturbations and never-ending crises of capitalism, all branches of Collectivism are unlikely to be able to go beyond the limits indicated by the original dogmatic theory. Collectivism is unworkable beyond a few generations, but their authoritarian ability to concentrate resources in one particular area (at the expense of others) produced some spectacular achievements, like Soviet space endeavors and almost total literacy of the Soviet Union population.

The late Soviet mathematician Igor Shafarevich was probably the first author to identify socialism as a recurrent social construct that can be traced back to ancient Egypt and Mesopotamia rather than a specific phenomenon of the last several centuries. In his view, "socialist ideology, while claiming to construct a distant future, in fact represents a regressive attempt to restore the primitive communality of the past" (Epstein 2021, p. 33). Unfortunately, Shafarevich walked away from that point of view in favor of a completely different, antisemitic mentality toward social systems.

One glance at world history shows that Leftism is not the only marginal theory with a substantial following. One possible escape hatch for Marxism would be lessening its political pretensions and strengthening its academic ones, but its inveterate adherents will probably never commit political *hara-kiri*.

With predictable periodicity, the Left does not allow the cruelties of the Leftist regimes of the past to fade from memory, along with its favorite tools—guillotine, gas chambers, GULAG, genocide, and ethnocide. By the 21st century, the recurrent ideological doom loop for Collectivists has begun. However, the coming reckoning will not be apocalyptic, for it will not be the first or the last. The seemingly endless cycle will keep going until the Collectivist ideology morphs into nontoxic superstition. Wokeness is the terminal stage of the current Leftist cycle.[45] The near-completed takeover of the education system manifests not Leftism's victory but the last breath before the inexorable crush of Leftism.

The reality is that there is no STOP button for the Leftists—only the PAUSE one. It is impossible to eradicate all strains of Collectivism completely. Every time it was tried, Leftists managed to press the REWIND (Revolution) button. Their behavior is always unnatural and revolutionary; on the other hand, conservatism operates on a naturally occurring evolutionary path.

According to Marx, "Communism is the riddle of history solved and it knows itself to be this solution" (Marx [1844] 1988, p. 103). However, only Marxists were obsessed with the "riddle of history." For everyone else, there is no riddle, for the dominant purpose of history is the evolution of freedom. All world events can be viewed as deviations from history's path. Periodic ugly setbacks and regressive periods are well known, as well as breakthroughs. Leftists are the ones who offer sporadic obstructions and put a spike on evolution's wheel. However, they cannot stop the overriding trajectory of human social development: from a low to a higher level of freedom.

---

45. As it is known, what is called "pizza" outside Italy is simply an Americanized version of pizza; likewise, Wokeness is an Americanized version of Mao's Cultural Revolution.

Chapter 3

Globalism as the Highest Stage of Left Imperialism

By the beginning of the 20th century, theoretical Marxism had become a spent force. Marxism was in crisis because, contrary to orthodox Marxism, the proletariat—the primary "victim of capitalism"—did not develop into the driving force of the communist revolution. With the rise in culture and quality of life, the proletariat emerged without the main characteristics of a victimized class. Specifically, the proletariat has lost its appeal to Marxism as the primary representative of the "oppressed class."

Recent evidence suggests that by 1917, the reputation of Marx and Engels was in shambles; they were mostly unknown outside the academic and labor insiders. In part, that resulted from the fact that "Marx was mostly unoriginal when he was right and original when he was wrong" (Watson 2010, p. 24-25). In a Foreword to Isaiah Berlin's classical book "Karl Marx: His Life and Environment," Alan Ryan wrote: "Marx's economics were not taken seriously other than on the Marxist left." Based on the number of citations in books, magazines, and newspapers, they were also peripheral figures in public and academic circles (Magness and Makovi, 2022). Marxism founders' reputation (and citation index) was elevated only after the communist coup in Russia in 1917.

Describing Karl Marx's academic achievements, Thomas Sowell emphasized that "Marx's legendary fame today makes it difficult to realize that he was an obscure figure with no substantial following in the early 1860s, that his writings were largely ignored, and that even a man as knowledgeable as

John Stuart Mill could live for twenty years in the same city, writing on the same topics, in utter ignorance that someone named Karl Marx even existed" (Sowell 1985, p. 176). Marx was either ignored or assumed to be a laughing-stock in 19th-century academic circles. He, along with Engels, was retroactively idolized by Russian communists.

In a letter written in 1852, Marx confessed, "I do not claim to have discovered either the existence of classes in modern society or the struggle between them. Long before me, bourgeois historians had described the historical development of this struggle between the classes, as had bourgeois economists their economic anatomy. My own contribution was 1. to show that the existence of classes is merely bound up with certain historical phases in the development of production; 2. that the class struggle necessarily leads to the dictatorship of the proletariat; 3. that this dictatorship itself constitutes no more than a transition to the abolition of all classes and to a classless society" (Karl Marx [1852] 2010).

Von Mises noticed that nobody—pre-Marx, Marx himself, or post-Marx—ever provided the scientifically acceptable definition of "class." (It is commonly noted that Marxism's vague vocabulary is one of its strong political features). Marxist thought always revolved around the existence of special groups of people called "classes," naively assuming their presence everywhere and anytime. One of Mises' clever challenges was the question to Marxists of how a particular "class," as an eternal being, is formed in the first place. "One first had to explain the formation of groups before one could explain the struggle between them. But all struggle theorists, Marx included, failed on this front" (Hülsmann 2007, p. 535).

In a sense, Marxism is a heretical form of Leftism because it singles out just one revolutionary class—the stalwart proletariat. As a result of Marxism's crisis, it underwent a stage of revisionism and alterations contingent upon the search for suitable revolutionary classes. Unfortunately, Marxism had no coherent answers back then, and the modern Pleiad of Leftists still does not have them.

Some Collectivists have offered radical deviations from mainstream Leftist thought to resolve the dilemmas posed by the Marxian concept of class. (In a process, all other heretical branches of Leftism were customarily labeled as "thought crimes.") Marxism developed into numerous branches; they differed primarily in the class of victims it selected. Meanwhile, all strands of Leftism worship the state. In this respect, all subsidiaries of Marxism, neo-Marxism, and post-Marxism are united, without exception. It is the primary impetus of Communism to create an egalitarian society, a principle inherent in the definition of the word "communism." There are even contradictions within the party, formed by factions of Leftists united in choosing a specific class of victims but unsure how to use them as an instrument for political power.

Under classic Marxist thought, the primary victim of capitalism (i.e., the primary source of the revolution's momentum) is the "oppressed proletariat." On the contrary, Russian Marxist revolutionary Vladimir Lenin chose colonies as such victims, "oppressed" by the metropolitan, imperialistic states. For example, even though Russia was formally an Empire at the beginning of the 20th century, it was economically and financially peripheral. The country's status was that of raw material and agricultural subsidiaries to European metropolitan power countries. It was a classic Lenin example of the proverbial "bait-and-switch": he unmistakably described the Russian Empire as a "prison of nations," like any other Metropole. However, Lenin had to use pretzel logic to bend Marxism to the desired outcome. He asserted that other, more powerful empires oppressed the Russian Empire, thus elevating the country to the desired "victim status," a colony, an "agricultural appendix" of European powers. Unquestionably, it was Lenin who perpetuated the notion of the dual self-perception status of Russia—as a victim of imperialism and, at the same time, an Empire itself.

> **In classic Marxist thought, the proletariat was the primary victim of capitalism. Vladimir Lenin chose colonies as victims "oppressed" by imperialistic states. Mao Zedong chose the peasantry as the victim.**

As is widely known, it was Chinese Communist Party Chairman Mao Zedong who chose the peasantry as the victim. He complemented it with the proviso that the proletariat (a virtually absent group in China at the time) would remain in control over the peasantry. In contrast to European or American socialists, Mao Zedong understood socialism sincerely. According to his thesis, it was a stage in the transition to communism, characterized by the simultaneous existence of capitalist and communist economies (as we are currently seeing in modern China).

Notably, the Italian Fascists chose a nation-state as their victim (Italy was considered "oppressed" by Europe's more powerful industrial countries). Fascists in Germany chose their victim to be a race that did not exist, the Aryans ("oppressed" by the winning coalition after World War I). Apparently, Adolf Hitler effectively enhanced Marxism by switching focus from "class" to "race."

In 1934, Frederick Schuman pointed out the significant difference between the Italian and German flavors of Fascism: "German Fascism, unlike its Italian counterpart, developed and perfected its doctrine through fourteen years of struggle before it came to power, instead of fabricating a doctrine after seizing control of the machinery of the state" (Schuman 1934, p. 211).

In the case of Aryans, "the race myth plays the same role in the Nazi cult of racial nationalism as the class myth in the Marxian world outlook" (Schuman 1934, p. 218). Schuman, being a communist himself, knew the subject.

Thus, Hitler "borrowed" the term "National Socialism" ("Nazism") during the 1920s from Mussolini's Fascists, who, as it happens, were the pioneers of National Socialism in Italy. If we were to use the language of the Left, it would be Racial Socialism (more precisely, Aryan Socialism) synthesized in the Third Reich. Hitler "borrowed" from Mussolini not just the "National Socialism" term, but also the Roman salute and legion standards (Schuman 1934, pp. 210-232). Fascism's origins are not in the esoteric depths of the German soul. The German national character simply made Fascism more acceptable to the citizens of the left-wing Weimar Republic. As a result, Germany's Fascism reached its logical conclusion faster than in other countries, producing almost a pure form of Leftism.[46]

It is important to recall that Marxism was only a theory before 1917. No one, not even Marx himself, was aware of how to transition from capitalism to communism. They have been in a ruthless battle over the best way to accomplish this for decades. Prior to the 1917 communist revolution in Russia, two main camps developed. First, the Mensheviks ("members of the minority") supported the evolutionary transition. Second, the Bolsheviks ("members of

---

46. Monographs by Jonah Goldberg (2008) and Dinesh D'Souza (2017) offer mesmerizing details about Fascism's origins.

the majority") supported the revolutionary transition.

The Mensheviks (the irony here is that "the minority" was, in fact, the majority) were clustered around the theories of the Fabian Society. In their view, the transition should be conducted smoothly and gradually, with the assistance of democratic institutions and via incremental legislative codifications. Otherwise, they argued, the revolutionary confiscation and property redistribution would become a bloody feud.

After the coup of 1917 and the horrific civil war in Russia, Leftists faced a new challenge—maintaining power in a socialist country surrounded by capitalist countries. The left-wing intellectuals across Europe agonized over the future of the newly minted socialist civilization. In a process, the Mensheviks and the Bolsheviks split again. Therefore, the main Leftist ideologies have changed to four. We will designate them honoring terms that are currently established and do not necessarily correspond to the historical categorization of these ideologies:

- Leninists-Stalinists ("Bolsheviks") argued that terror could hold socialist power for a sufficient period to establish communism in a single country. History confirmed the fallacy of this venture.

- The Trotskyists ("Bolsheviks") argued that no terror would retain power in one socialist country in a capitalist encirclement; it would be necessary to engage in socialist revolutions/coups in all countries without exception. History has confirmed Trotsky's assertion that terror cannot hold power exclusively.

- Fascists ("Mensheviks") argued that the bloody redistribution of wealth would discourage the population from embracing socialist views. Instead of confiscating it forcibly, the proposal would engineer totalitarian state control over private property. However, history has demonstrated that this method does not work either.

- Globalists ("Mensheviks") believed that socialism could succeed by implementing it simultaneously in all countries in a peaceful, democratic way. Therefore, they chose the method favored by the Italian Communist Antonio Gramsci as a primary means of socialist transformation—"Cultural Marxism." The process of socialist transformation was to begin with the transformation of education, culture, literature, journalism, cinema, etc.

As Claude-Frédéric Bastiat observed in 1850, "Socialism, like the ancient ideas from which it springs, confuses the distinction between government and society" (Bastiat [1850] 1998, p. 29). Gramsci corrected that; he was probably the first to split the human collective into a state and society. While imprisoned by fellow socialist Mussolini,[47] Gramsci introduced a deviation—even a heresy—from classical Marxism. His ideas of proletarian revolution differ from Marx's, who emphasized a direct attack on a state (as the main oppressor). Instead, Gramsci uncovered the non-linear feedback loop between a state and society and offered the idea of "Cultural Marxism," which captivated and agitated most left-wingers. Moreover, Gramsci changed their priorities—instead of directly attacking a state, he suggested gradually altering the society itself, its culture, its traditions, and its institutions. Over time, the feedback mechanism will do its thing, which would greatly simplify the attack on the "oppressive" state (or whatever would be left of it).

Thus, Gramsci redefined Marxism; in track and field terms, the reoriented Marxism switched from sprinter to stayer. Instead of aiming for a swift socialist revolution at the start, the new mission is a long march of mass indoctrination with the revolution at the end.[48]

Gramsci's idea of sabotaging existing cultural and societal institutions proved very popular with Leftists. One of "Cultural Marxism" ambitions is to establish a critical mass of voters who will support Leftism unconditionally, like religious zealots, without regard for the awful living conditions the Left delivers. The ability of the Left to convince these low-information citizens of the benefits of self-mutilation is endless.

GLOBALIZATION: THE BEGINNING

Globalization was primarily an economic phenomenon in its infancy. As a result, all Western industrial heavyweights experienced de-industrialization as manufacturing was transferred to countries collectively referred to as the "third world" at that time.

Observing the massive de-industrialization of the West, Leftists concluded

---

47. Gramsci disagreed with Mussolini's efforts to strengthen the state to achieve Socialist goals.

48. "The Long March through the Institutions" phrase that brilliantly describes Gramsci's approach was coined by German radical Leftist Rudi Dutschke.

that it would serve a dual purpose. First, it would provide a conducive environment for the rising class consciousness of the proletariat in third-world states. Second, it—by means of "spreading the wealth around"—would impoverish "oppressed" workers in the West while increasing the profits of the "oppressors," thus accentuating tensions in society.

It is likely that globalization (with the small "g") of the world economy will continue to improve the lives of millions of families and reduce poverty even further if it is able to maintain its current pace. Yet, in spite of this, one particular group of humans—politicians—decided to reap the benefits of the rational, natural, and desirable process of economic globalization.

While this is still an open question, it appears that political globalization may have preceded economic globalization. Consider Wilsonian small-g globalism, for example. In compliance with the previous chapters, the Left and Right designations are strictly related to domestic affairs, and therefore, there is no such thing as left-wing or right-wing Wilsonian globalism. The only thing that could be said conclusively about Wilsonian globalism is that American Leftists practiced the purest form of it. In any case, globalism vs. nationalism is not a fight between the Left and the Right.

> **It is likely that globalization (with the small "g") of the world economy will continue to improve the lives of millions of families. Capital-g Globalism is a parasite on the body of small-g globalism, just as most Leftist movements are.**

This brings us to Globalism, a political movement with a capital "G," created by the international Left to achieve economic and political objectives. After successfully hijacking ideologies and identities in the past, the Left saw hijacking world commerce as a valuable tool to achieve their ultimate objective. It should be noted that capital-g Globalism is a parasite on the body of small-g globalism, just as most Leftist movements are. It feeds on the construct of economic globalization; as a consequence, modern Collectivism is literally consuming itself and devouring the infected societies in the process. To a degree, Leftism is inherently cannibalistic.

As an economic phenomenon formerly known as "Americanization," globalization is approaching its end. Americanization has greatly contributed to the availability of first-world luxuries to virtually every citizen of the world. Having assumed control over the economic processes of globalization, the Left has moved into ideological and political domains. Therefore, it would be naïve to assume that economic globalization will carry out in its previous "Americanization" form. Capital-g Globalization is a purely ideological project that has a very attainable intermediate outcome: communism for the rich in the name of communism for the poor.

Contrary to trendy belief, we do not carry on living in the world envisioned by the Frankfurt School of Socialism. It cannot be denied that the modern, imperialistic Left is far more sophisticated and equipped than its predecessors. The world they have created is categorically more ideologically Left than the Frankfurt School could have imagined in their wildest dreams. The late Marcuse, along with Lenin, Stalin, and Mao, would be incredibly proud.

From several strains of National Socialism and a multitude of strands of International Socialism, Leftists have jumped onto the Supranational Socialism bandwagon.

The natural and inevitable process of merging and interconnecting national economies—globalization—was weaponized for political purposes.

The natural and inevitable process of merging and interconnecting national economies—globalization—was weaponized for political purposes. To further confuse the situation, the Left has adopted the same term to describe its latest trek to reaching a Socialist Utopia—globalization. Economic globalization, which refers to the unrestricted movement of goods, people, and capital across borders, is a naturally occurring and inevitable phenomenon. Political globalization, on the other hand, is a fictitious construct that hides behind the same word but uses it to enact ideological aspirations. The focus of the Globalists is to establish post-national states. There will be no place for the immortal component of social life known as nationalism in these countries.

In terms of timeframes, it is straightforward to identify when the Collectivists successfully hijacked Globalization. It occurred just before the media stopped referring to it as Americanization, as it was initially termed. Since then, Globalization has no longer been about the economic expansion of American multinational corporations.

The ideological foundation of Globalism could be summed up like this: "The principle of a sovereign nation-state is outdated. Thus, the existing states desperately need a supranational governing body with such enormous economic and control power that the nation-states must play a purely ceremonial role if they wish to continue." The Third Reich's slogan *"Ein Volk, Ein Reich, Ein Führer"* is replaced by "One Ideology, One Empire, One Sovereign." Globalism is a trans-Marxist Trojan Horse for the project of global Collectivism. The Left Imperialism is a tool to implant a one-world collectivist government.

From the outset, the Globalists encouraged and facilitated the well-observed power shift from governments to joint government-corporate syndicates. That blurring of the distinction between government and corporations offered the Globalists new effective methods of population and mind control. Furthermore, this two-faced Leviathan provided participants with an attractive option: the government could hide behind corporations and blame them for all society's troubles. Conversely, corporations can hide behind government policies and blame them for their workers' low wages.

Revolutionaries fall into two categories: those who seek to undergo a sea change of government-to-governed relations while disregarding much of the intra-social business and those who wish to remodel intra-social affairs while keeping the majority of the ruling elite intact. However, it is pertinent to note that these are extremes; real revolutions are always a combination of these approaches. Both revolutionaries faced a difficult, uphill battle. However, the common view is that a *coup d'état* against the ruling class generally has a higher probability of success. Therefore, flipping rulers is much more common; it is worth mentioning the last two (failed) attempts to change society after coups: the Soviet Union and the Third Reich. Globalist revolutionaries are of the same type. Thus, *Homo sapiens* have taken side trips to *Homo sovieticus* and *Homo fascisticus* on their way to Davos-promoted *Homo servus*.[49]

The concept of Fascism does not imply tyranny, dictatorship, or concentration camps—at least not in theory and propaganda. (It must be said that the majority of Leftist ideologies may look pretty good on paper, while right-wing ideologies are, on the whole, inarticulate). However, being a strain of Leftism,

---

49. The term *Homo sovieticus*—a clear dog Latin phrase—was coined by Soviet propagandists. In 1974, they proudly informed the creation of the highest type of *Homo sapiens*, a new biological specimen—*Homo sovieticus*. Alexander Zinoviev, an exiled Russian philosopher, popularized the term in the eponymous book.

Fascism followed the predetermined path toward the innate trait of the Leftist genus—totalitarianism. In terms of the biological evolutionary tree, *Homo erectus* is a common ancestor of *Homo neanderthalensis*, *Homo bodoensis*, *Denisova hominins*, and our species, *Homo sapiens*. All of these *Homos* are different, yet they all belong to the same evolutionary branch and share many characteristics. In the same way, Marxism, Fascism, Maoism, Stalinism, Leninism, and many others fall under the same category of ideological evolution. Even though they have many differences, they belong to the same Leftist family or genus.

Homo neanderthalensis is not directly related to modern humans, although they have a common ancestor and represent a failed evolutionary branch of humans. The bifurcation between *Homo neanderthalensis* and *Homo sapiens* happened around a half-million years ago, and the extinction process terminated approximately fifty thousand years ago. Likewise, *Homo fascisticus* are not directly related to modern *Homo collectivismus*, although they have a common ancestor and represent the failed evolutionary branch of Leftist ideology. In this example, we know the exact year of the split, 1921, and the precise year of *Homo fascisticus* extinction—1945.

Globalism differs from all other Leftist movements in that it is politically omnivorous; it accepts all types of "victims" into its ranks.

By the 21st century, three of the four Leftist branches mentioned above have virtually disappeared (apart from Venezuela, Cuba, and North Korea). If they exist, the Leninists, Stalinists, Trotskyists, and Fascists are almost always marginal groups that rarely remember (or do not wish to remember) their past. For example, many modern National Socialists have entirely forgotten their Socialist and Fascist roots and are concentrating primarily on one point (out of 25) of the official Nazi party program—racism.

The fourth branch of neo-Marxism—Globalism—goes on to spread. Globalism differs from all other Leftist movements in that it is politically omnivorous; it accepts all types of "victims" into its ranks. Unknown to the "victims," they are destined to perish in the hecatomb arranged by their ideological overlords.

Conservatives have engaged in numerous ideological battles throughout the years, sometimes among themselves but mostly with various well-defined factions of the Left. Traditionally, the Left hid behind a constellation of names. However, in the 21st century, conservatives face an entirely new foe: an enemy without a specific self-assigned name. Before, Leftists proudly wore self-assigned and sometimes stolen identifiers, such as Progressive or Liberal. As yet, they have refused to openly associate themselves with the term "Globalists" openly.

It is easy to understand why Antonio Gramsci, so revered by Globalists, wrote about the 1917 communist coup in Russia, that it was "a revolution against Marxism" and why "the Bolsheviks rejected Karl Marx." The reason is that Globalism is not only the most cynical but also the highest phase of Marxist revisionism.

Marxism "dissolves" in other collectivist theories and makes itself almost invisible, but even in small concentrations, it smells of war, hate, misery, and suffering—the themes Marxism is presumably against. Moreover, the genetic drift of Marxism toward all aspects of society is a matter of fact; recall the "achievements" of the Frankfurt School.

Globalists frequently claim that "true socialism" has not been attempted. Yet, even though socialism has resulted in the collapse of society in all countries where it has been practiced, the Globalists are, to some extent, right here. Obviously, we are referring to those terrible socialist regimes that ruled many bygone countries. Globalists' ultimate objective, however, is an immaterialized version of the global Leftist dictatorship on which they have been working tirelessly for nearly a century. As a result of the revised strategy, the bottom-up approach cherished during the 20th century will be reversed. A radically unique way of doing things is based on supranational forces. There remains a role for gangs of thugs on the streets, but they are no longer harnessed as revolutionary cannon fodder. Instead, they are employed to bring chaos and widespread crime to shift social consciousness in a new direction. The proponents of the new direction would demand a strong government and gradual—not revolutionary—decay of political freedoms.

BRINGING MARXISM BACK FROM THE DEAD

For political power, control is paramount. The Marxist dogmas of abolishing private ownership and the inevitable establishment of collective ownership did not age well beyond the 19th century. The original idea was realized in the Soviet Union and its satellites only by using unheard-of-before terror. Many

Western Marxists and Leftists rightly argued that forced wealth redistribution would lead to bloody civil war, citing the Soviet Union's experiment as an obvious example.

That left Leftists in search of some novel ideas to revitalize Marxism. They did so by (temporarily) dropping the involuntary wealth redistribution requirement. Instead, while possessing the same strategic intent as classical Marxists, they decided to introduce quite different tactics designed to smooth society's transition to the Utopian worker's paradise.

At the beginning of the 20th century, the Leftists' thought process looked like this: business owners control all their businesses' aspects. Why? Because they own it, fair and square, *de jure* and *de facto*, as a matter of law and as a matter of fact.

Essentially, classical Marxism aims to dump *de jure* and *de facto* ownership, eliminating the legality and tangible ownership components. However, what would happen if only one of the two components was dropped (albeit temporarily and reluctantly)? What if the *de facto* ownership requirement is eliminated, but the *de jure* requirement stays? As a result, the non-Marxist Leftist ideology came to be known as Fascism. In comparison to Communism, Fascism was designed to be much less bloodthirsty. (Consider also the contrary situation, where the *de jure* requirement is dropped, but the *de facto* ownership stays. The resulting non-Marxist, Leftist society would resemble a mafia enterprise on a state level, also known as a plutocracy.)

There were many ways in which the Fascist idea was implemented in practice. First, it was implemented in Italy by a group of prominent Socialists, with Mussolini, an orthodox Marxist, at the helm. Mussolini's credo, expressed in a speech on May 26, 1927, was "Our formula is this: everything in the state, nothing outside the state, nothing against the state." Then, in the 1930s, he managed to get all Italian industries and finances under state control while keeping private ownership primarily intact. He described this state-run capitalism as "true socialism." The second, predetermined step—the national government taking over all private ownership—was announced in due time but did not materialize thanks to the Allies' invasion in 1943.

Another obvious example is the National Socialism of the Third Reich. However, from a purist's rendition, real National Socialism was established in Italy, not Germany. Mussolini, who was already a well-known statesman when Hitler was just a nameless community organizer, was furious when he learned that Hitler had "borrowed" (read "embezzled") the term. "National Socialism" redefined "Fascism" by incorporating antisemitism and racism into it; the Third Reich's actual ideology shall be described as Aryan Socialism.

Reforms in fulfillment of eliminating *de facto* ownership while keeping *de jure* ownership sprang up in many counties on both sides of the Atlantic. The simplest version of the idea assumes near-total control of an enterprise by the government, while legal ownership still lies with the rightful owners and their heirs.

Did owners revolt? Did they protest? Anywhere? Anyone? Nope. Stripping owners of any control of their enterprises was mainly met with jubilation. Hitler never hid the eventual aspiration when he confronted German industry tycoons with the ultimatum on February 20, 1933: "Private enterprise cannot be maintained in the age of democracy; it is conceivable only if the people have a sound idea of authority and personality" (The Farben Case 1949, p. 558). The Third Reich never ran a nationalization program, with just a few notable exceptions (like the expropriation of Junkers airplane factory with more or less fair compensation to the owners).

German business leaders poured millions of dollars into Nazi party coffers. Because the transfer of control to the government removes owners' perpetual worries about competition, the environment, labor laws, strikes, and profits.

For their part, German business leaders poured millions of dollars into Nazi party coffers. Why is this so? Because the transfer of control to the government removes owners' perpetual headaches. Owners no longer need to worry about competition, management, the environment, labor law, strikes, profits, unions, taxes, and myriad other burdens. Everything has been taken care of—go to Davos, Miami Beach, or Courchevel and enjoy the life of nobility while the government, through its ideologically purified agents, does the heavy lifting.

In the closing arguments for the conviction of Nazi war criminals, the chief United States prosecutor at Nuremberg, Robert Jackson, describing the February 20, 1933, meeting, stated, "Hitler and Goering explained their program to the industrialists, who became so enthusiastic that they set about to raise three million Reichsmarks to strengthen and confirm the Nazi Party in power." For example, Gustav Krupp pledged one million Reichsmarks on the spot. As a result, Hitler appointed him a toothless but ultra-prestigious title, "*Führer* of German Industry," on May 4, 1933. Two days after that meeting, Krupp issued a memorandum that "expressed to Reich Chancellor Hitler the gratitude of approximately 25 industrialists present for having given us such a clear picture of the conception of his ideas" (The Farben Case 1949, p. 562). Krupp also emphasized that the industrialists, like Hitler, "consider that the object of every regulation is to benefit the interest of the German people as a whole, not that of individual professions or classes" (Ibid.) If the term "stakeholder capitalism" had been widespread back in 1933, Krupp would have made use of it without hesitation, along with Nazi bosses. Instead, he used the "interest of the German people as a whole."

Why did such an idea become so popular? The reason was uncovered by Adolf Berle and Gardiner Means in 1932. In their book *The Modern Corporation and Private Property*, the authors pointed out the overlooked consequence of corporate growth. Namely, the growth of the number of owners (shareholders) translates into the separation of ownership and control. In particular, the "separation of ownership and control has taken place through the multiplication of owners" (Berle and Means [1932] 1999, p. 5). As a result, control over the enterprise is consolidated in the hands of upper management (in Thorstein Veblen's terms, "engineers"), which does not necessarily represent shareholders. Thus, it was just a matter of time before politicians would weaponize and exploit the separation of ownership and control. In the political sphere, it became known as Fascism—the quintessence of usurping control without actual ownership, expanded to all spheres of life.

Berle and Means were trying to assert that "the corporate profit stream in reality no longer is private property" (Berle and Means [1932] 1999, p. 219). As such, "giant corporations are no longer private property and do not deserve to be treated or protected as private property by the government" (Hessen 1979, p. xii). In addition, Berle and Means deduced that corporations lack legitimacy because they are not private property, and that immediately propelled the authors to the top of the Leftist must-read list. Consider, for example, the following eloquent passage: "It is an odd paradox that a corporate board of directors and a communist committee of commissars should so nearly meet in a common contention. The communist thinks of the community in terms of a state; the corporation director thinks of it in terms of an enterprise; and though this difference between the two may well lead to a radical divergence in results, it still remains true that the corporation director who would subordinate the interests of the individual stockholder to those of the group more nearly resembles the communist in mode of thought than he does the protagonist of private property" (Berle and Means [1932] 1999, p. 245).

That attempt to "institutionalize the alliance between big business and National Socialism" (Manchester 2017, ch.15) is still in the Leftists' playbook. Collectively, the Left Imperialists reject the "clear warning about the risks inherent in any close relationship between business and state and what can go wrong when political objectives and the pursuit of profit become dangerously entwined" (Jeffreys 2008, prologue). Thus, before the Germans lost their democratic freedoms, German industrialists lost control over their capital, factories, and workers. Before many Germans found themselves in concentration camps, German businessmen found themselves in financial concentration camps. Then, in 1934, after the "Night of Long Knives," National Socialists utterly eliminated the influence of big business on politics.

China's current state of affairs scrupulously follows the Fascist template. The Chinese do it under a different name, of course (Fascism—surprise!—got a bad reputation). Thus, their followers in the United States and other Western countries are trying to foist their aims under separate banners, too (and for the same reason).

> **China's current state of affairs scrupulously follows the Fascist template. The Chinese do it under a different name, of course.**

The dirty little secret amongst the post-Marxists is that they temporarily, at least during this transitional phase from capitalism to a leftist Utopia, ignore economic components entirely and care only about unrestricted political power and total societal control. Until the workers' revolution is successful on a global scale, and worldwide wealth redistribution is a done deal, comprehensive control—the *de facto* part of ownership—is all that drives the would-be-revolutionaries.

In the United States, we have not reached a total control phase. However, today, we see suspensions, demonetizations, terminations, and other cancellation methods and digital executions practiced by para-government agents commonly known as "social networks." For the time being, these agents still own all these famous Internet tech giants *de jure*. However, *de facto*, they carry a baton from 20th-century book burners into the 21st, enthusiastically enforcing the nomenklatura demands of the post-Marxists.

The United States, we has not reached a total control phase. However, we see suspensions, demonetizations, terminations, and other cancellation methods and digital executions by para-government agents— "social networks."

The Federal government institutionalized censorship by simple outsourcing. None of the FBI/CIA/DOJ plants at Twitter/X headquarters received the second salary from their previous positions in the Federal government. Formally, they are not Federal employees anymore, so the First Amendment no longer applies—or so they thought. In reality, the First Amendment does not look into the payroll stream; on the contrary, it, in essence, prohibits censorship on the government's behalf, period.

Despite all controversies, social networks that have operated until now have been neutral platforms, but not neutral concerning free speech. Initially, these platforms were developed as neutral data and intelligence collection platforms. Then, during phase two of their development, they were transformed into propaganda outlets and censorship nomenklatura. Finally, the third phase—the primary one—is creating a culture of self-censorship, which is the main ingredient in population control.

OWNERSHIP AND CONTROL

The difference between ownership and control is perfectly illustrated by recent United States election fiascoes, where the logistical fight for ballot harvesting and middle-of-the-night ballot dumps has replaced the political struggle for votes. The modern Left has done better than the previous generations in all election endeavors. As a result, it eventually surpassed Stalin's motto, recorded by Bazhanov: "I believe that who and how people in the Party vote is unimportant. What is extremely important is who counts the votes and how they are recorded" (Bazhanov [1930] 1990).[50] Stalin said it in the context of internal Bolshevik Party elections. It took the battle-hardened international Left a half-century to re-interpret, weaponize, and expand it to all elections. It has become a preferred and meticulously polished left-wing practice world-wide to emphasize counting ballots instead of getting votes.

Consequently, convincing the electorate has been transformed into a Machiavellian game of gerrymandering, distributing, collecting, and counting ballots. The election process has been transformed into a ballot collection contest. During this process, the term "ballot harvesting" was coined; the Left traditionally renamed it "ballot submission assistance" when electoral tactics were exposed. The previously crucial details of campaigns, such as candidate quality, messaging, and endorsements, no longer matter; the mechanics of handling ballots are the focus.

By doing so, the Left has achieved the unthinkable: it has disconnected elections from reality. According to the new "ballot collecting" paradigm, economic issues do not influence election results. Candidates' qualities are no longer able to influence their electability. Traditionally, the Left out-games its competition in the realm of voting mechanics. In this mindset, debates and political rallies are viewed as unnecessary and outdated by those who understand perfectly well that the appropriate ballots have been preprinted, distributed, and, in many cases, collected well before the election. There is a tendency among Democrats in the United States to turn Election Day into Election Week (or weeks). In many competitive races, Republicans receive more votes, but Democrats collect more ballots.

Ballot harvesting brings up ballots from utterly apolitical people. Every society has such individuals: they may not vote but play a vital role in the political process. Many of them are "independent" because they do not engage in politics due to pressure from anybody. Whatever the source of political pressure, they shut it down. Their part in social evolution is to be deliberately uninformed; they ignore political battles because they have other important things to do. They are generally good people. Think of them as incarnations

---

50. Boris Bazhanov was Stalin's assistant and secretary to the Soviet Politburo. He escaped the USSR via Persia and then India (both illegally) in 1928 while Stalin's assassins chased him; thus, he became the first high-ranking Soviet defector. In the West, Bazhanov became anti-communist and escaped several more assassination attempts.

of Rick Blaine, owner of *Café Americana* in the 1942 movie *Casablanca*, before he dropped the mask of a cynic and turned into a fighter.

Additionally, ballot harvesting may be regarded as coercion when people are forced into decisions based on the ignorance they possess. In most situations, such decisions are stupid, and if recent elections in the United States resemble fools who elect other fools, it has merits. Trying to force these leave-me-alone people to vote is comparable to forcing them to compute pi's 15th digit; most will randomly pick any number from 0 to 9, and the same is true when collecting ballots. Due to these factors, many 21st-century elections are not a left-wing or right-wing wave but rather a tsunami of gray, nescient biomass.

It should be remarked, however, that the invention of ballot harvesting is merely a symptom and not the cause. It is a sign that the Left has run out of suitable categories of victims. Hence, they decided to stop the search and extract ballots from the unsuspecting, inexperienced, never-before-voted, low-information citizens.

FRANCE BIRTHS A MONSTER

The political adage "if you cannot beat them, join them" has been well-known for centuries. So, the Left made one extra step and arrived at the "if you cannot beat them, lead them." The Left has been trying (unsuccessfully) various methods to eliminate capitalists and private property. Eventually, Leftists learned their lesson and decided to preside over private property instead of confiscating and spreading it around. Lenin used it (the so-called "New Economic Policy" in the Soviet Union 1921-1928), Mussolini used it, Hitler used it, and Mao Zedong used it (his campaign is still alive and well in China). It is a blatant violation of a well-demarcated borderline between the government and the governed, but by now, it is the cornerstone of Globalism.

However, the systematic and deliberate infiltration of the state into private economic affairs did not begin with Mussolini. In 17th-century France, for example, Chief Minister Cardinal Richelieu established state-sponsored and state-directed cartels. That resulted in public-private entities that were granted monopoly status in their respective fields. The official policy of the Chief Minister was the subordination of all cohorts of French society to the will of the state (read: the will of the monarch). Richelieu's aim was not to build a proto-fascist state per se; his cravings were more down-to-Earth: France had a war to win. Nevertheless, he deployed state power to consolidate state power even more. His offer to the French merchants was one they could not refuse: guaranteed profits under the protection of the state or guaranteed imprisonment at the Bastille. The resultant economic landscape in France in the middle of the 17th century comprised numerous, stable, privately owned cartels controlled directly or indirectly by the government. Nevertheless, it did strengthen and consolidate French economic power, especially concerning rivals—the Habsburgs and England. However, the other side of the same coin was unavoidable—the government-chartered monopolies, insulated by the state from external competition, pressed the brakes on innovations. In the end, Cardinal Richelieu led the Habsburgs to bankruptcy and France to the dominant power on the European continent.

In 17th-century France, Chief Minister Cardinal Richelieu established state-sponsored and state-directed cartels. That resulted in public-private entities that were granted monopoly status in their respective fields.

England and her colonies were provided more economic freedom during the same period. That sealed the fate of two revolutions at the end of the 18th century. The French had no choice but to continue their Left turn. On the other hand, the thirteen overseas British colonies turned Right (note that Americans were the wealthiest British subjects by the time of the American Revolution).

The story of the proto-fascist policies of Richelieu demonstrates the theme observable in all future left-wing economies: a short-term boost in economic activity due to crushing, inescapable state intervention, and then, in the long run, unavoidable decline and stagnation. As it is known, the Soviet Union, Nazi Germany, Cuba, Venezuela, and the entire Soviet bloc post-World War II followed this course. The demise of Communist China is inevitable for the same reason. A similar fate is awaiting the Davos Oracles of "stakeholder capitalism." From that outlook, all four of Dumas's three musketeers and the rest of the French nobility and peasantry were the first proto-anti-fascists.

Richelieu learned most of his ideas from the book *Traicté de l'oeconomie politique,* published in 1615 by French economist Antoine de Montchrétien, where he advocated for a paternalistic form of government. That paternalism manifested itself in the creation of new, government-chartered business enterprises. In 1600, the English government chartered the East India Company, the first business with government-like duties on the chartered territory.[51] Between 1594 and 1602, multiple companies from the Netherlands were active in Asia; the competition was fierce and unmerciful. Finally, the Dutch government forced all these small companies to merge in 1602 into the Dutch East India Company. The merger thus achieved two goals. First, kill competition. Second, granting exclusive quasi-government duties and monopolist status to a private company gave proto-fascists (and later the French and Italian Fascists) the idea of achieving absolute state control over commerce.

Also, "Cardinal, as soon as he came into office, turned his attention toward colonization" (Palm 1920, p. 26). In other words, a government that subdues business to its liking—even without owning it—immediately develops imperialistic plans. The French colonies in the Caribbean still exist, but the African possessions gained independence in the 20th century. All of them were chartered using "patents," issued by the French government to grant a monopoly for a particular territory for a specific time—just like France's English and Dutch predecessors. However, the French quasi-government enterprises were less successful than the English and Dutch ones. One of the reasons theorized by researchers was too much centralization, protection, and patronization offered by the state.

However, Richelieu never saw the government as merely in control of commerce. On the contrary, the Cardinal's openly stated push was to constitute the government (read: the King) not just a holding and management company, but a key business owner. That was the standard rendering of the term "absolutism." Furthermore, the message to the public was that "when he attacked any class or sect of individuals, such as the Huguenots, he did so for the public good, that is, the benefit of all" (Palm 1920, p. 32).

---

51. The Reedy Creek Improvement District of Florida, also known as Disney World, is a quasi-government private entity that has existed since 1967. Far from having the power of the East India Company, Disney World still enjoys the self-governing and monopolistic powers on the chartered territory, including a power of eminent domain even outside the district. It can build anything it wants without following the state of Florida's construction codes or zoning board approvals.

The "public good," similar to the traditional Leftists' motto, was also apparent in Richelieu's treatment of the French noblemen. Due to his reforms, the nobility "were no longer independent of the central government socially, politically, or economically. They were subject to the will of the state" (Palm 1920, p. 33). There were no hard feelings. After they were deprived of political power, the nobles were offered an attractive escape route: to serve the state in a political, military, or commercial capacity. As it is well-known, that conduct had been greatly expanded by 20th-century proponents of Fascism/Corporatism by making everyone—not just noblemen— wholly dependent on the state, the ultimate employer and handout distributor, explicitly or implicitly.

> **The "public good," similar to the traditional Leftists' motto, was also apparent in Richelieu's treatment of the French noblemen and clergy.**

The Chief Minister wanted clergy to serve the state, too. His central-ized-state-building efforts even assumed that "the king has the right to do anything, even though it is against religion, to save his state" (Palm 1920, p. 30). While conducting a program to separate church and state, Richelieu treated that separation very specifically. He taxed churches; the church was expelled from politics, and, as he wrote, "the King must be obeyed, by great and small, and he must fill the bishoprics with wisely chosen and capable men" (Palm 1920, p. 37).

The Richelieu strategy has been reviewed, analyzed, copied, and refined over centuries. Unsurprisingly, the Left proudly considers him its mentor. As stated by Palm, who authored the book about Richelieu long before Mussolini published his famous "nothing outside the state," "the Cardinal built up everything for the interest of the state. That was the central part of his political and economic philosophy" (Palm 1920, p. 38). Despite the pop-ularity of Dumas's claims, Cardinal Richelieu dealt with no-nonsense issues concerning the foundation of a proto-fascist state. Queen Anne d'Autriche's pendants were not a concern to him.

While working on modernizing France's finances, Cardinal Richelieu, independently from Ibn Khaldun, rediscovered the non-linear feature of taxa-tion, currently known as the Laffer Curve. Progressive taxation was one of the pillars of his economic reform. He stated, "Sovereigns must, if possible, make use of the abundance of the rich before they bleed the poor" (Palm 1920, p. 43). Palm commented: "This remark has a socialistic tinge which is rather out of place in the seventeenth century" (Ibid.)

Along with traditional methods of promoting state capitalism, Richelieu exploited non-traditional techniques. For instance, he encouraged wealthy individuals to finance desperately needed government projects with the promises (which were fulfilled) of ennobling them, as with the Braire Canal. In spite of the fact that it was not a novel concept and was not unique to post-feudal France, only Richelieu made it an official tool in the toolbox of a state supremacy regime. Another example was the postal system, chartered by the government but operated by private carriers, entirely dependent on the state. Carriers participating in the program were granted monopoly rights over the roads on which they traveled. Moreover, the first periodical in France, the *Mercure François*, was privately owned but downright controlled by the Richelieu government.

Cardinal Richelieu established a form of stakeholder capitalism in France, where the government served as the only principal stakeholder.

The tradition of entanglement between industry leaders and the state spilled into the 21st century, although the forms have changed. For example, while nobility is no longer widely regarded as a worthy prize, aspiring entrepreneurs are highly motivated by ambassadorships, civil decorations, and invitations to White House dinners. Using these, governments can achieve their intentions without spending money on them. For example, the United States Federal budget allocates no funds for censorship or propaganda. However, being outsourced to private Internet social network companies, censorship and propaganda are rampant.

Another recent example is Obamacare, a state-superintended health insurance program operated by numerous private insurers. Under Obamacare, private insurers depend entirely on the state, but that is the price to be paid for ensuring profits.

To use 21st-century terminology, Cardinal Richelieu established a form of stakeholder capitalism in France, where the government served as the only principal stakeholder. Upon the predictable failure of the Left Ideological

Caliphate, all junior stakeholders will find themselves in the position of the proverbial bag holders.

State-managed "stakeholder capitalism" was known in the 1600s as mercantilism. The mid-17th century was the height of the mercantilist doctrine, "which centered everything economic and political in the hands of the state" (Palm 1920, p. 18). Adam Smith's lengthy critique of mercantilism is classic in modern economic thought. "Part of [Adam] Smith's critique of eighteenth-century mercantilism was that it exacerbated the potential for international conflict. Thanks to its beggar-thy-neighbor conception of wealth, mercantilism encouraged governments to think that national prosperity could only come at others' expense. This mindset stimulated national rivalries, whether it concerned territory in Europe or colonies and trading rights in the Americas, Africa, and Asia" (Gregg 2022, ch.7).

Corcoran, describing Klaus Schwab, founder of the World Economic Forum, stated that "Schwab's real trick is to attach the word 'capitalism' to stakeholder, and claim to have created a new model called stakeholder capitalism. But it is not capitalism" (Corcoran 2021). Klaus Schwab is not the originator of the term "shareholder" (he claims that the idea was born with the establishment of the World Economic Forum in 1973). However, the idea was introduced only in 1984 by R. Edward Freeman, a professor at the University of Virginia. Per Freeman, "a stakeholder is any group or individual who can affect, or is affected by, the achievement of a corporation's purpose. Stakeholders include employees, customers, suppliers, stockholders, banks, environmentalists, government and other groups who can help or hurt the corporation" (Freeman 1984, p. vi).

A list of entities that could potentially help or harm the corporation does not pose any problems per se. However, the problem arises when the wrong priorities are assigned. In a classical corporation, shareholders are the sole and exclusive responsible parties, while other parties may play a role in determining the success or failure of the corporation. Shareholders have an ultimate say in all corporate affairs because they own the corporation. In Freeman's view, legal owners should be regarded as just a small part of the corporate iceberg, as one of many significant stakeholders. When other groups attempt to gain control of the corporation (without being significant shareholders themselves), the rightful owners—shareholders—are left behind. When a particular entity—the government—uses hostile takeover tactics, the situation becomes even more interesting. A merger of corporate power and political power often results in the creation of monopolistic entities under the protection and patronage of the state. History is replete with examples of such entities.

Those who are not shareholders (thus, do not have any stake in the company) appear as loosely defined "stakeholders" with the self-assigned status of overseeing all corporate affairs. From the outside, it appears a corporation semi-voluntarily cedes control over the business to government-appointed commissars; in human history, this event has been well documented.

When other groups attempt to gain control of the corporation (without being significant shareholders themselves), the rightful owners—shareholders—are left behind.

Per Klaus Schwab, the World Economic Forum advocates a "stakeholder-centered approach" (Schwab 2021). Unfortunately for the Globalists, the "shareholder-centric paradigm prevailed, particularly in the United States" (Ibid.) Nobody better describes the essence of shareholder "capitalism" than Schwab himself: "The world currently knows two prevailing and competing economic systems: shareholder capitalism, which is dominant in the United States and in many other countries in the West, and state capitalism, which is championed by China and is gaining popularity in many other emerging markets. Both have led to tremendous economic progress over the past few decades. They left us with a world that is more prosperous than ever before. But each has equally brought about major social, economic, and environmental downsides. They led to rising inequalities of income, wealth, and opportunity; increased tensions between the haves and the have-nots; and above all, a mass degradation of the environment. Given the shortcomings of both of these systems, we believe we need a new, better global system: stakeholder capitalism."

Describing the 20th-century economy, the Davos Maestro lists typical Leftists' grievances about classical shareholder capitalism: "The power of unions evaporated, and the ability of national governments to act as an arbiter declined" (Ibid.) While praising China's "state capitalism," Schwab writes, "[the] state is considered the most important stakeholder and retains power over individual shareholders. The government achieves its dominant role in at least three ways. First, it keeps a strong hand in the distribution of both resources and opportunities. Second, it can intervene in virtually any industry. And third, it can direct the economy by means of large-scale infrastructure, research and development, and education, health care, or housing projects" (Ibid.) However, "state capitalism too has its fundamental flaws. Most importantly, given the hegemony of the state, corruption is a constant threat" (Ibid.) Schwab concludes, "In both shareholder and state capitalism, the dominance of one stakeholder over the others is the system's greatest flaw. In shareholder capitalism, shareholders' aims are often the singular focus; in state capitalism, the government wields too much power" (Ibid.)

Schwab publicizes "the third way," "stakeholder capitalism," as the ultimate solution. His "capitalism" must be quoted because it corresponds to free-market capitalism in only the remotest sense. Note that National Socialists of the Third Reich also run under the banner (or, rather, the smoke-screen) of "the third way." Schwab is painfully aware that "the stakeholder concept competed head-on with Friedman's notion that 'the business of business is business'— and it ultimately lost out" (Ibid.) There are no surprises here; based on the individual-state paradigm, Schwab's "stakeholder capitalism" is just a reformulated branch of Leftism, rebranded for the 21st century, commonly known as Fascism. Of course, it is not a replica of 20th-century Fascism; it has been updated and modified to incorporate "climate change," digital technologies, and the pandemic and has expanded global outreach. "Planet's health" becomes the central stakeholder in the global economic system.

> **Schwab publicizes "the third way," "stakeholder capitalism," as the ultimate solution. Note that National Socialists of the Third Reich also run under the banner of "the third way."**

To illustrate the difference between control and ownership—in other words, the difference between stakeholders and shareholders—consider promiscuity. Like infidelity, promiscuity is problematic for society because it negates the pride of ownership by the legitimate partner. Every spouse who cheats hands away control over his or her body to somebody who is not a legitimate owner. In light of this, the annual pilgrimage to Davos is a process of cheating on all of us.

WHERE THE NAZIS COME IN

The German corporation law of January 30, 1937, was a milestone in "share-holder capitalism," as it codified the idea of a hostile government takeover of private businesses without acquiring ownership of those businesses.

Contemporary observers in many countries praised the German corporation law of 1937. For example, in 1938, William Kessler published a not-negative review of the law in the United States. In his remarks, he highlighted the Nazi law's core appeal: the extensive powers the government was given to interfere in the business affairs of corporations. Moreover, a foundational principle of leftism was meticulously codified in the Nazi law of 1937: "*Gemeinnutz geht vor Eigennutz*" ("common good before individual good").[52] That was the 24th point (out of 25) of the official German Workers Party (DAP) program in 1920. Later that year, the party adopted the familiar name of the National Socialist German Workers Party (NSDAP).

Kessler underlines that "the state was to be granted more power over the corporation. It could approve the selection of the Board of Directors by the stockholders and reserve veto power over any actions of it, the Board of Managers, and the stockholders in order to protect the public interest" (Kessler 1938, p. 654). Kessler described the law further: "The Nazi rule that 'Politics leads economics and not vice versa' has been followed" (Ibid., p. 660). Finally, "The result is that the state can exert the power of life and death over a corporation both before and after its charter has been granted" (Ibid.)

The tectonic legislative shift was written in paragraph 70 of the law. There, it stated that the "board of managers must direct the company for the good of the employees and for the welfare of the people and the Reich" (Ibid.) Moreover, the law made corporate management "no longer responsible specifically for shareholder interests but for all groups having a stake—figuratively—in the company, including the Reich" (Fohlin 2007, p. 265). Kessler concludes that "law thus places considerable power in the hands of the state, a state which, it must now generally be realized, is not at all friendly disposed toward capitalism and liberalism" (Kessler 1938, p. 661). Even if many parts of the 1937 law were articulated under the left-wing Weimar Republic, the Nazis made the step still cherished by Leftists: they forced corporations to serve the state, not the shareholders.

---

52. Third Reich silver coins had the same slogan as the edge inscription "*Gemeinnutz geht vor Eigennutz.*"

In his description of the 1937 Nazi law, Thilo Kuntz emphasized that "the new law allowed dissolving a corporation against the shareholders' will if the corporation endangered the 'common good' (Gemeinwohl)" (Kuntz 2018, p. 219). The "common good of *Volk und Reich*" and not shareholders' profits became the official purpose of a corporation, and "all the corporation's matters are subordinate to those of *Volk und Reich*" (Ibid.)

However, the most relevant today is that "the main pillars of modern German corporate law remain firmly grounded in the 1937 reform" (Ibid.) Other researchers confirm that "as with many rules, regulations, and laws enacted during the Nazi period, the 1937 German Stock Corporation Act continued to operate largely intact for a substantial period after the end of World War II" (Chambers et al., 2016, p. 33). Caroline Fohlin concluded that the law of 1937 "was not seen as a major problem by many politicians in Germany after World War II" (Fohlin 2007, p. 266). For example, the *Führerprinzip* was abolished only in 1965 (Ibid.)

Wirtschaftswunder, or the economic miracle, as it was known in post-war Germany, was the result of breaking apart the fascistic, corporatist organization of the economy and reassembling it, according to the Marshall Plan,[53] in the image of a free-market economy. However, the Marshall Plan did not utterly break down the "shareholder capitalism" of Germany and Italy. Indeed, it appears that the Marshall Plan contributed to the success of Nazi corporate reform in Germany and Italy. Schwab witnessed this structure in the 1960s and 1970s and did not hesitate to enhance it by leveraging Freeman's intellectual foundation. In essence, the modern Left confessed that the Marxist war on private property was over. Long live private property—but under government control.

As is known, the United States government did not have the money to rebuild Europe after World War II. It was American taxpayers who funded the Marshall Plan: about eighty dollars per capita, or about 1/40 of the median annual income (over a thousand dollars in today's money). The primary objective of the Plan was political, not financial. After the liberation of occupied Europe, the uncompromising system of Nazi economic controls was still in operation, posing severe economic difficulties for the creators of

---

53. The United States Marshall Plan offered European countries massive financial support in the post-World War II years. It ran from 1948 to 1952 and aimed at economic recovery in war-torn countries.

the Plan. Unlike its effectiveness in Germany and Italy after World War II, the Plan was successful in previously occupied continental Europe because it dismantled the National Socialism-confirming economics and replaced them with more liberal and profit-driven practices. The Marshall Plan was a mechanism to transition from stakeholder capitalism back to shareholder capitalism.

The Marshall Plan was a mechanism to transition from stakeholder capitalism back to shareholder capitalism.

In a sense, the Marshall Plan could be re-evaluated as an example of Right Imperialism, an ideological attack against control-based economics. As the Soviet bloc countries were aware that the Marshall Plan was intended to obliterate socialist economics, they made a logical decision to reject it.

Supra-sovereign imperialists on the Left are plotting to grant themselves a charter similar to that granted to the four-century-old East India Company and Dutch East India Company, however, this time without any geographical or term constraints. (Deliberately sidestepping many essential details, the European Union was established, at least in part, around post-World War II Germany and its Nazi-influenced corporate policy). Political Globalism can be described as the reformatted colonialism of the digital age, the continuation of the *Volk und Reich* formula for the 21st century.

The old, unresetted capitalism stressed the importance of unity between capital and labor, since these two cannot carry on separately in any meaningful way. Globalism replaces the unity between capital and labor with the unity between capital and state. Accordingly, if old capitalism made it impossible to conduct business without labor, the modern Left Imperialists have made it impossible to conduct business without the government. As a result, the labor is pushed aside—all in the name of workers. Consequently, modern Leftist ideology is fundamentally elitist by nature.

WHAT IS GREAT RESET?

The Great Reset is not a plan of merely reconfiguring the world economy; it is a plan of global wealth redistribution and, as such, amounts to the biggest threat to human civilization the Left has ever concocted. The plot's astounding scope complements the planned changes' unprecedented arrogance.

Lenin observed three components of Marxism; Klaus Schwab just followed the tradition.[54] Per Schwab, "The Great Reset agenda would have three main components. The first would steer the market toward fairer outcomes" (Schwab 2020). Who will be in charge of that? The Davos Oracle insists that "governments should implement long-overdue reforms that promote more equitable outcomes" (Ibid.)

The promotion of "more equitable outcomes" follows with the second component, "equality and sustainability" (Ibid.) Finally, "the third and final priority of a Great Reset agenda is to harness the innovations of the Fourth Industrial Revolution to support the public good, especially by addressing health and social challenges" (Ibid.) The very first component of the Great Reset aims to eliminate intra-society inequality—known to be one of the engines of society development. It blatantly violates intra-society relationships by penetration (read: rape) of the boundary separating a government and society. Society, per Schwab, must be "steered" so that the boundary between government-to-governed and intra-society relationships would be erased.

> **The Great Reset is similar to Fascism without the contaminating effects of concentration camps, war crimes, or the Holocaust.**

Per Hanson, "talk of a distinct corporate world and government is anachronistic under the Great Reset, since the two would be fused into one entity" (Hanson 2022).

Obviously, history repeats here. Schwab makes the case that Mussolini would be proud of—soldering government, social, and business institutions into new, "reset" administrative units denominated "syndicates." That is somewhat "pure" but nevertheless reformulated Fascism. So, the Great Reset is similar to Fascism without the contaminating effects of concentration camps, war crimes, or the Holocaust. The reformulation part addresses the global scale on which Left Imperialists operate. Their analysis of previous attempts during the 1920s and 1930s shows that limiting themselves to state borders would be ineffective. That is because the "old," unreformed capitalist

---

54. Klaus Schwab keeps a bust of Lenin in his office.

countries could execute deals with competing versions of Leftism and crush the newly formed Fascist states.

Less than a year after being introduced, the Great Reset was channeled via traditional Left evolutionary treatment: rebranding. The reformulated Great Reset is now labeled "stakeholder capitalism" or a "private-public partnership." One of the latest modifications is "inclusive capitalism." All traditional Leftist normative components are still there; rebranding simply makes them less visible. Of course, all these monikers do not add clarity, which is by design. Rephrasing Lenin, "renaming, renaming, and renaming" is the motto of Leftists.[55]

According to Klaus Schwab, we must "bring our thinking and behavior once more into harmony with nature" (WEF 2020). So, how exactly should American billionaires voluntarily rearrange their financial deals to get "into harmony with nature"? As German industrialists did in the 1930s, modern billionaires are willing to exchange their freedom for the assurance of uninterrupted, worry-free, and sanctioned profits. The famous but apocryphal phrase commonly attributed by left-wingers to Lenin, Marx, or Stalin, observes that "the capitalists will sell us the rope with which to hang them." The "sell us the rope" metaphor illustrates the phenomenon of voluntarily placing corporations under government control without renouncing ownership during the 1920s and 1930s, reincarnated toward the end of the 20th century. Using the false banner of "decarbonization," the Great Reset implements the Great Control Reset program, accomplished by molesting and bringing on board economic titans.

It is imperative to note that Fascism facilitates a symbiotic power exchange between corporations and governments: governments gain economic power, and corporations gain political power. However, that exchange, while mutual, is not symmetrical: Corporations lose a bit of their economic power, while governments do not lose an iota of their political power. As a result of this asymmetry, a corporation is regarded as the junior partner of a state under a Fascist government. Further, it is not influenced by the ideological slogans or the specifics of the propaganda practiced by a particular fascist state. However, the mutual penetration of two distinct—political and economic—powers is so

---

55. Lenin's original phrase is from an 1899 article, in which he talked about those workers who "study, study, study, and turn themselves into conscious Social-Democrats—'the working-class intelligentsia'" (Lenin [1899] 1964).

widespread that it would be challenging to identify isolated instances in which such interpenetration does not occur.

As a result, one can apply a notion of not just a binary but also a continuum (theoretically, ranging from zero to 100 percent) of Fascism. Many proto-fascist public-private institutions remain in the United States, such as the Federal Reserve Bank (Central Bank of the United States)—a monopoly of twelve private banks operated under strict government supervision. Its Board of Governors is a Federal Agency directly accountable to the United States Congress. It is important to note that the United States Government does not own the money held in the Federal Reserve vaults but exercises absolute control over it. The Federal Reserve was a foretaste of government-public "shareholder capitalism."

Roger Shaw witnessed and vividly described the penetration of Fascist ideas on American soil in the 1930s. Shaw, a left-wing writer, stated in 1934, "New Dealers, strangely enough, have been employing Fascist means to gain liberal ends" (Shaw 1934, p. 559). By "liberal," he meant "socialistic," as it was customary to do in the 1930s. In addition, Shaw described Roosevelt's National Recovery Administration (NRA) as the institution "most of which was adapted from Fascist Italy" (Ibid.) The Fascist governments practiced widespread intervention in the economy, which coincided with the global trend of the 1930s. In the same article, Shaw openly listed those contemporaries he considered Fascists outside Roosevelt's administration: Mrs. Roosevelt, Mayor La Guardia, Mohandas Gandhi, Margaret Sanger, and many other celebrities. "The NRA, with its code system, its regulatory economic clauses and some of its features of social amelioration, was plainly an American adaptation of the Italian corporative state in its mechanics. It was recognized as such by Mussolini and Hitler" (Shaw 1934, p. 562). Describing the NRA, Ralph Nader wrote, "Franklin Roosevelt saw the NRA as a form of federalization of corporations" (Nader, Green, and Seligman 1976, p. 68).

Senator Joseph O'Mahoney, a Democrat, enthusiastically supported Roosevelt's New Deal. He promoted the idea and later served as chairman of the secretive Temporary National Economic Committee from 1938 until 1941. His attitude toward corporations was that "a corporation had no rights; it has only privileges" (Nader, Green, and Seligman 1976, p. 69). In his opinion, if a corporation does business across state lines, it must receive a charter from the United States Federal government. Ralph Nader cogently stated,

"As power begets power, large corporations are able to pursue their activities beyond the law, above the law, or against the law—a state of affairs clearly incompatible with democracy" (Ibid., p. 8). Nader also liked the centuries-old British, Dutch, and French ideas for issuing charters. His solution would grant the Federal government external control of internal corporate affairs. Nader insisted on a charter-based system to control all major American corporations "whereby a government gives the corporate entity existence and that entity, in return, agrees to serve the public interest" (Nader 1975, p. 1310).

As maintained by Wilhelm Röpke, "It has already been pointed out that the name of this system is, except for publicity purposes, absolutely irrelevant; the economic policy of the Third Reich amounts, for all practical purposes, to the same thing, and even the motley fabric of the New Deal shows a strong thread of this striking color" (Röpke 1935, p. 97).

Section One of the 1933 United States National Industrial Recovery Act openly voiced what was commonly recognized by contemporaries as Fascism/Corporatism.

Italy's Procurator General, Senator Silvio Longhi, "defined the essence of corporatism as being that 'the state recognizes and safeguards individual property rights so long as they are not being exercised in a way which contravenes the prevailing collective interest'" (Bosworth 2006, ch. 11).

Section One of the 1933 United States National Industrial Recovery Act openly voiced what was commonly recognized by contemporaries as Fascism/Corporatism: "to provide for the general welfare by promoting the organization of industry for the purpose of cooperative action among trade groups, to induce and maintain united action of labor and management under adequate governmental sanctions and supervision."

Currently, there are not many witnesses who can testify to the exact details of the establishment of the government-corporate bond in Italy and Germany during the 1920s and 1930s. There are, however, several events in the United States that follow the same pattern. One of the examples is Obamacare (the government graciously permits private medical insurance companies to exist, but their business is almost 100% directed and regulated by government bureaucrats). Another example is the establishment of draconian censorship in the United States. Although the government is prohibited from doing so, it outsourced the censorship business to friendly media magnates, especially modern social network companies.

Last but not least, the most desirable status for an American corporation is "too big to fail." No matter what the circumstances are, this status guarantees profits. All companies entitled to the status of "too big to fail" participate in the asymmetrical economic game choreographed by Leftists: they keep all profits while taxpayers absorb all losses. In the words of the Third Reich contemporary, "Fascism is steering between a competitive and a collectivist economy leads, in practice, to a heavily monopolistic-interventionist society adorned by terminological and phraseological ornaments, with extensive governmental control of prices and capital investments and large 'socialization of losses,' whereby the capitalistic institution of bankruptcy is, to some extent, replaced by concentration camps" (Röpke 1935). The Modern Left believes that Fascism was a disgusting, regrettable, but disappointing failure for the previous generation of revolutionary Leftist fighters; it must be tried again, but without concentration camps. The digital concentration camps remain legal.

> **Internet technology giants operating social networks have obtained unofficial charters from the Federal government to monopolize censorship and control public discourse.**

In essence, Internet technology giants operating social networks have obtained unofficial charters from the Federal government to monopolize censorship and control public discourse.[56] The loss of control of such a platform (as with Twitter/X) triggers a hysterical reaction from the Left because "the issue is never the issue; the issue is always the revolution."

A New(-ish) Socialist Worldview

In December 1620, the ship Mayflower anchored in Plymouth Bay in the New World. The daredevils landed on a deserted, cold coast, which is now in the state of Massachusetts. Plymouth Rock now symbolizes the approximate

---

56. Seamus Bruner devised a brilliant term for social network titans: Controligarchs (Bruner 2023).

landing site. The city of the same name still exists, as does the country founded by the Puritans: The United States of America.

One hundred and two people, contemporaries of Cardinal Richelieu, were set off by ship from Plymouth in the Old World, but on the way, one man died, and one boy was born. Unfortunately, one of the team members also died. Puritans, religious dissidents, adventurers, and merchants were among the travelers. All the passengers on the Mayflower were daring and brave people. They can be safely referred to as pioneers—but not only in the geographical sense.

They were the first to establish socialism in North America.

The word "socialism" had not yet been invented. However, we know all the details of the Puritans' socialist epic from the diaries of William Bradford, one of the Plymouth colony leaders for a third of a century. By the time the pilgrims landed, Thomas More's "Utopia" had already been through dozens of editions (the English translation of Utopia was published in 1551). Thus, the ersatz-socialist ideas were widespread in Europe. As it is known, Utopia's hypothetical state was based on the primitive idea of the monastic community. While still in exile in Holland before sailing to the New World, the Puritans had already begun introducing communal elements. They arrived in the New World with a clear plan for a collective community.

The Spaniards, who established colonies in the New World long before the British, also attempted to extend communal monastic rules to their territories in South and Central America. The Spaniards viewed the discovery of America as Divine Providence, and it was America that was to become the place for the creation of the ideal, Utopian-like state-community. All the communities they established have sunk into oblivion, but the idea persists. That may explain why South America still has a disproportionate number of Leftist regimes.

The Puritans had signed an agreement on what the community would be like before landing. The Plymouth colony's beginning was traditionally socialist—anyone who refused to sign the document was prohibited from landing. There is nothing extraordinary in this one-page document by modern standards, but it was the first document establishing democratic self-government in the New World. The Puritans agreed that power in the community should belong to the Law. However, the problem was that laws were adopted in this utterly democratic way.

Understanding why the colonists chose the socialist way of organizing the commune is pretty straightforward; it should be mentioned that after Thomas More, the ideas of the commune spread so widely in Europe that many of his followers and many other Utopian models were born. For example, in 1619, even before the Puritans' landing, Johann André's *Reipublicae Christianopolitanae* (known as "Protestant Utopia") was published, and in 1623–"The City of the Sun" by Tommaso Campanella.

These Utopias bore all the features that were fully manifested when the wave of socialist upheavals swept the planet in the 20th century. The highlights include total control, brutal social engineering, political power belonging to the elite, and forceful egalitarianism (which, of course, did not extend to the elite).

Like the Spaniards, the Puritans viewed America as the second Promised Land. From a religious point of view—from the Anglican and Catholic churches' purview—they were dissidents. Still, their initial beliefs about society's economic structure did not go beyond the commune with its primitive collectivism.

In the Plymouth colony, collective ownership of everything except women was established, and the recognition of private property did not exist at all.

In the Plymouth colony, collective ownership of everything except women was established, and the recognition of private property did not exist at all. The harvest and prey of the hunters were distributed equally among the colonists. Women were required to cook for all men and wash all their clothes, and men had to work to provide for other people's wives and children.

For the next two years, each colonist worked for everyone else and not for himself. As a result, labor productivity was disastrously low. The consequence was not long in coming—by the summer of 1621, about half of the colonists had died of hunger and disease.

It should be recognized that this experience is not unusual in human history; it has been endlessly and unsuccessfully repeated, and with the same devastating results—for example, collective farms in Russia and the first kibbutzim in Israel. The statistics here are unambiguous—all egalitarian communes collapse sooner or later. Nevertheless, the Plymouth collective farm differs from the others because the Puritans quickly realized and corrected their mistake in just a few years. Unfortunately, other similar social experiments lasted for decades.

In the spring of 1623, the colonists' wives rebelled after two and a half years of hunger, poverty, and despair. They did not want to prepare meals for other women's husbands anymore. They regarded the forced service of other men as *de facto* slavery. As a result, after a lengthy debate, the colonists made a decision that laid the foundation for modern American society—each family received its piece of land. Furthermore, only 70 years after these events, John Locke intellectually substantiated the right to private property.

As soon as the colonists forgo collectivism and allowed private property, prosperity came. The first harvest in 1623 was a celebration of abundance. The colony became so thriving that it even welcomed a new wave of immigrants. Contrary to myth, it was not the Indians who fed the colonists in 1623, but the colonists who saved the Indians from starvation. Thanksgiving, which America now celebrates every year, is, if truth be told, the 1623 harvest festival of the Plymouth colony based on private property.

As soon as the colonists forgo collectivism and allowed private property, prosperity came.

As a religious people, the Puritans believed that Divine Providence showed them the right way out of a demanding situation. Therefore, Thanksgiving Day is not as much gratitude for a bountiful harvest as gratitude for pointing out the suitable economic solution to the problem from Heaven.

If the Plymouth colony's rejection of socialism was almost instantaneous on a historical scale, then the reverse transformation—from capitalism to socialism—has been brewing in America for four centuries. In four centuries, America transitioned from Thanksgiving to Thankstaking to Thanksredistirubuting.

At the end of the 19th century, Edward Bellamy uttered probably the very first plan of transforming the United States into a socialist country. The plan assumed that the Federal government "would take over ownership of industry and operate it collectively for the public good" (Stabile 1987, p. 36). Thorstein Veblen further developed Bellamy's ideas. While "Veblen's earlier works emphasized workers as being agents for social change" (Ibid., p. 35), he eventually set aside the classical Marxist ideas. He developed his non-Marxian political philosophy of socialism. In his theory, the primary driving agents behind any social change would be not workers vs. bourgeoisie but bourgeoisie (he tagged them "leisure class" or "business class") vs. technocrats (commonly known at the beginning of the 20th century as "engineers" or simply "technicians").

In Veblen's view, there is an antagonistic relationship between the owners of an enterprise and the well-educated technical elite that operates it. According to Veblen, the distinction between them is not just occupational; it is fundamental: owners are in the business of making money, while technocrats are in the business of producing goods and services.

According to Veblen, the primary purpose of business is to gain a profit, which differs from the industry's primary objective, which is to produce goods and services. In this regard, Veblen looked at earning money to be a "predatory activity" in contrast to the productive work undertaken by engineers. Thus, he reformatted the classical Marxist antagonism between the haves and have-nots by substituting the proletariat with engineers inside the have-nots category. That way of thinking took deep roots and survived into the 21st century, but for Veblen personally, the price was high—his non-orthodox socialism is still not deemed "true" socialism by fellow socialists. In his opinion, a corporation's ownership should be restructured as a collective entity rather than an individual one.

According to Veblen, the primary purpose of business is to gain a profit, which differs from the industry's primary objective, which is to produce goods and services. ...Currently, Veblen's ideas play the role of the second pillar of Left Imperialism.

Veblen's scheme is sometimes called "scientific collectivism," contrary to classical Marxism, which argues for "scientific socialism." (The Left loves the word "science." Note that Progressives appraised eugenics as a legitimate "scientific racism." The modern Lysenkoist Left wants to change the planet's climate by painting roofs white and eating bugs.) Currently, Veblen's ideas play the role of the second pillar of Left Imperialism. Note also that Klaus Schwab, the mechanical engineer himself, initially imagined his Davos thing as a club of the technocratic *patrizi*. Currently, it is an exclusive club for grandiose emirs of Leftist Nomenklatura. Finally, it is astonishing to note that the radical Nouveaux Left slowly but indeed evolved into the radical rich.

Veblen was always skeptical about the revolutionary potential of the technocrats. He stated that "the technicians can, in a few weeks, effectively incapacitate the country's production sufficiently for the purpose of overthrowing the business" (Veblen [1921] 2001, p. 103) but, in his opinion, "sabotage is not revolution" (Ibid., p. 57). Gradualism, the evolution toward socialism instead of a revolution, was the idea he supported, based on his deep belief in Social Darwinism. "Thorstein Veblen considered himself to be a follower of Darwin. His version of social Darwinism, however, unlike that of conservative defenders of business, was aimed at determining what features of the social structure presented the potential for evolution into a socialist system" (Stabile 1987, p. 36). Therefore, "Veblen can not be seen as promoting a *coup d'état* by an elite of engineers" (Ibid., p. 45). Nevertheless, per Don Stabile, some authors consider Veblen's book *Engineers and the Price System* as the "Communist Manifesto" for technocrats—and the Davos globalitarian technocrats as well.

Peter-like denials are not something unusual for the Left. Communist leaders do it all the time. For example, Gorbachev was forced to reject Stalinism to save Communism. In another example, after Italy invaded Ethiopia in 1935, the New Dealers in the United States abruptly stopped glorifying Mussolini; the "old" New Deal was promptly renamed "First New Deal." Next, the "Second New Deal" was put up that had nothing to do with Corporatism and shielded the Roosevelt administration from all criticism and accusations of flirting with Fascism (Whitman 1991). Whitman also emphasized that "the history of American interest in Italian 'corporativism,' an ill-defined industrial policy involving official state sponsorship of industry cartels and labor unions, remained something of a taboo topic. Indeed, the very word 'corporatism'—the commonly used shortened form of 'corporativism'—became a term of opprobrium, rarely used to describe any of the policies of the New Deal years" (Whitman 1991, p. 749). The so-called Green New Deal runs along the same Corporatism lines but is enhanced with environmental rhetoric.

Since the late 19th century, Japanese industrial monopolies, known as *zaibatsu* ("financial clique" or "wealth clique"), have enjoyed benefits from a significant degree of state patronage. One of the ways Japanese governments controlled enterprises was through taxes (including excessive tax rates for those who dared to demonstrate disobedience). The government also determined the corporate dividends and income of the owners. Some well-known *zaibatsu* conglomerates from the end of the 19th and the beginning of the 20th centuries still exist, like Mitsubishi or Nissan.

Like in the West, government-chartered corporations in Japan and their private owners were isolated from financial losses. Likewise, "[t]he banking system was protected by the government but also enclosed and cut off from real decision-making; the government could simply remove and replace any of the handful of people who controlled the banking system if they so desired" (Addicott 2017, p. 9).

Numerous lucrative contracts between the government and *zaibatsu* fueled the Japanese Empire's military adventurism. Eventually, paired with the military taking control over many *zaibatsus*, civil government was pushed aside, creating a *de facto* military dictatorship in the 1930s Japan. By 1940, Japan made one last (and predictable) move: they switched toward a planned economy, where the government mandated production quotes (and prices) for corporations. The end of the Japanese occupation of Korea in 1945 gave birth to the *chaebols*, the Korean version of the *zaibatsu*. Some large *chaebols*, like Samsung and Hyundai, are well-known outside South Korea.

In 1976, Ralph Nader penned the book *Taming the Giant Corporation*, which is dedicated to the reincarnation of issuing charters to corporations. In the book, Nader admirably illustrated the shortcomings of capitalism (all Leftists are proficient in that area). As believed by Nader, "It must be realized that private property is not a gift of the gods but a bundle of rights created by our Government; it hardly seems valid to condemn the Government for legally rearranging this bundle of rights when it created them in the first place" (Nader 1975, p. 1313). Moreover, long before Schwab, Nader compiled a list of the pre-ESG corporate disclosures,[57] like "what is the racial composition of employees and new staff" (Nader 1975, p. 1315). What Nader missed, however, is that, per Hessen, corporations are the result of "voluntary associations created by contract to conduct business" (Hessen 1979, p. 40).

---

57. ESG (Environment, Social, and Governance) is the Social Credit Score System for businesses, analyzed in detail later in this Chapter.

"Much like marriages, corporations are recognized, but not created by the state" (Greene 2022). The government is a mere registrar who has "the role of *protector*, not creator" (Hessen 1979, p. 33).

Nader's socialistic crusade against corporations—which he calls private aggregation of power—was a pure left-wing ploy. To fight the perceived "private aggregation of power," he uses the old Leftist tactics of bringing the government—public aggregation of power—into the fight. Instead of keeping corporations as far from political power as possible, Nader wants political power to take over private power and, in effect, merge the two. Nader proposed a new United States agency, the Federal Corporations Agency, to place American businesses under government control.

From the WEF's glance, Nader's "national stakeholderism" was just child's play. They wish to establish such an agency—international stakeholderism—throughout the planet.

Like everything the Left proposes, Nader's solution is "state-oriented." The term "state-oriented" was introduced in 1994 for "people or organizations bidding for collective benefits through changes in state policies" (Amenta, Dunleavy, and Bernstein 1994, p. 679). Similar to Huey Long's "Share Our Wealth" radical socialist political platform, Nader's inclination "benefited some groups and punished others" (Ibid., p. 680). Pressure from Long and other left-wing organizations paved the way for the Second New Deal, including the "soak the rich" tax bill and other wealth redistributing measures. From the WEF's glance, Nader's "national stakeholderism" (the term coined by Terence Corcoran) was just child's play. They wish to establish such an agency—international stakeholderism—throughout the planet. Thus, Klaus Schwab's entourage should be considered Ralph Nader on steroids.

THE GLOBALIST PHOENIX FROM THE SOVIET ASHES

Well-educated progressives know that an economy based on socialist ideas is not sustainable. Therefore, they are obsessed with "sustainability," another Freudian slip masked by rhetoric about decarbonization.

The dissolution of the Soviet Union in 1991 provided conclusive evidence of the unsustainable character of the socialist economy. With its fall, progressive intellectuals were forced to find a new source of inspiration and income, with the latter being their primary concern. Therefore, the myths conceived by the previous generation of Leftists had to be revised so that "global cooling" quickly turned into "global warming." As for the new source of income, the international Left panicked for many years until it realized that its quintessential enemy—capitalism—could be exerted to combat capitalism.

From that account, the WEF's ascendance as the international Left's *de facto* leader directly resulted from the Soviet Union's crash of 1991. The WEF was founded in 1971 under the name of the European Management Forum, when cracks in the Soviet Union became an open secret. Shortly after, a campaign began to rehabilitate Corporatism (Whitman 1991, p. 750). By the time of renaming the European Management Forum into the World Economic Forum in 1987, the term "neo-Corporatism" had sufficiently emasculated from any links to old Corporatism/Fascism. Despite this, the organization went unnoticed for over two decades, remaining in the shadow of more powerful socialist organizations. The tool the WEF used to win the international socialist race was not its invention: they just modernized the old 1930s Leftist "guaranteed profits" thesis of getting political power from the semi-educated by utilizing control mechanisms instead of ownership redistribution. Thus, the evolution of the WEF runs in parallel with the revival of Corporatism.

By the time of renaming the European Management Forum into the World Economic Forum in 1987, the term "neo-Corporatism" had sufficiently emasculated from any links to old Corporatism/Fascism.

The bloody socialist experiment in the Soviet Union came to an end in 1991. Before sinking into oblivion, however, it passed the ideological baton to those whom Soviet communists had carefully groomed for many decades, starting in the 1930s, collectively known as "useful idiots." Talented "useful idiots," of course—otherwise, they would not be able to prove the Left's imperishability.

There is an element of excitement involved in the immense task that the Great Resetters have set for themselves, but it can also be very discouraging.

To date, the Globalists have not even implemented a uniform metric system in the United States. As brought forward by Napoleon in 1799, the metric system has been legal in the United States since the 19th century, but on a voluntary rather than a mandatory basis. The push for the metric system enforcement was restarted shortly after establishing the WEF's predecessor, the European Management Forum. Immediately after assuming the brand-new name in 1987, the Globalists forced the metric system, but only onto the United States Federal Government. Despite this, the rest of the country upholds the imperial (British) system.

The push for the metric system looks strange because, according to postmodernism, any measurement system is a "social construct," but there is no such thing as a better or worse social construct. As postmodernists maintain, all "social constructs" are equal, but this does not explain the irrational preference for one measurement system over another.

The imperial system continues to be practiced in all fifty states. This arrogant display of measurement sovereignty is a significant irritant to the modern Left, who still cherish the achievements of the French revolutionary Leftists. As a result, the radical Left would like to punish non-conforming and non-recalibrating countries and expunge all references to sovereignty from all languages.

The New Left became known in the 1960s; the "New" in the title meant that they were—contrary to the "Old Left"—independent from Soviet ideological orbit.[58] After gaining their independence, "Fidel Castro, Ho Chi Minh, Mao Zedong, and Che Guevara replaced Lenin and Stalin as revolutionary icons" for the New Left (Gonzales and Gorka 2022). In 1989, "American Marxism was being liberated from Moscow's shackles" (Ibid.) By the second Obama presidential term, the WEF had decisively won the evolutionary struggle with fellow left-wing peers. Davos became the ecumenical council of the New Left Caliphate, and the race for Assets Under Management was catapulted to the top Leftist strategies. Davos is where the blossoming romance between the rich and the left-wing *beau monde* happens.

Everything suggests that, in the Leftists' mindset, the value of control over private property has displaced the value of private property ownership.

---

58. Comparing the "New Left" and the "New Right," the latter is an oxymoron because there is no such thing as an "International Right" to get independence from. Right-wingers are, by definition, limited to country borders and are independent by definition.

So, Assets Under Management is the new game in town—and on planet Earth, for that matter. In the economic game, the overall net worth is the score. In the political game, commanding the net worth is the score.

After decades of preparatory work, the Left Imperialists eventually showed their rabid character by using the pandemic as a pretext. "The Covid-19 pandemic caused Davos Man to break out of his Alpine closet and reveal the secret but suspected plan: the whole world is to become a giant Davos—humorless, style-less, unspontaneous, unrelievedly materialistic, as long as the accumulation and application of capital is directed by the little Alpine gnomes of Davos and their underlings and disciples" (Black 2022).

> **Everything suggests that, in the Leftists' mindset, the value of control over private property has displaced the value of private property ownership. So, Assets Under Management is the new game in town.**

The Davos gatherings are a microcosm of what the Left has in mind for the rest of the world. Davosians cling to one of the strictest caste societies, indicated by the color of their badges. Meritocratic considerations do not solely determine the ranking of these individuals in the WEF hierarchy. The color ranking in Davos is loosely based on a person's position in the outer world. However, like all other left-wing movements, the actual hierarchy in the WEF strictly adheres to inner-Davos priorities—the distance from the party *Führer*. The Alpine resort town of Davos has emerged as a symbol of modern anti-capitalism, but that is only half true. Indisputably, Davos has been propelled to the top of Left Imperialism executives and become the *de facto* Olympus of left-wing half-men-half-gods. They genuinely believe they have found the cornucopia and met Goddess Abundantia, who has changed her name to State.

Davos attendees demonstrate progressive rhetoric of status-seeking ideological *nouveau riche* and status-confirming luminaries of ideological decadence. Confidently, Leftists are pathologically obsessed with conforming their adherence to official dogma; they are hyper-conformists. Like Jews who claimed they converted to Christianity in Torquemada's Spain, all converts into Leftism must carry unambivalent outward indications that they did—daily. Otherwise, they could be prosecuted by an ideological Inquisition. Unfortunately, the term "Inquisition" had been taken, so the Leftists had to settle for another one—"cancel culture."

Per Conrad Black, "Davos is for democracy, as long as everyone votes for increased public sector authority in pursuit of green egalitarianism and the homogenization of all peoples in a conformist world" (Black 2022). In other words, modern Leftists are trying to institutionalize the disconnect separating a person's decisions, actions, and consequences. Unfortunately, the ideas developed at Davos are not only Utopian, but also irredeemably flawed. Reformulated, partially castrated, and adapted to the digital era, Marxism has not moved toward asserting undisputed control upon any more or less significant country. (However, the ascension to the British throne of King Charles III offers Globalists some hope).

FASCISM IN NEW CLOTHES

Of course, one should not mix the modern treatment of a corporation with the Fascist understanding of it. In contrast to the conventional argumentation of corporations as having limited liability, the Fascists assign and enforce unlimited liability to all businesses—at least concerning government decrees. By taking the next logical step, Klaus Schwab and his followers wish to see government mandates transcend state borders, thereby transforming any business entity into an entirely dependent and controlled entity of the government. By design, such administrative units, commonly referred to as "modernized guilds," are not competing; competition is substituted with "cooperation," which is, of course, a weasel word for "central planning."

The absence of economic competition is just a corollary of a system where membership is compulsory, and only the government gives marching orders. The administrative units are granted (by the government's "licensing" or "chartering") monopoly status and, as such, a prearranged profit stream. Due to their unprecedented ability to concentrate resources, such systems may produce remarkable accomplishments, such as the Soviet space program or Germany's highway system, but these are exceptions. Once more, it should be repeated that under Fascism/Corporatism, the state controls and directs the economy from top to bottom without legally owning the businesses.

Following Mussolini's reforms, government-chartered syndicates covered Italy. These private-public hybrids became administrative state units and, at the same time, business units. For example, in 1933, the Mussolini government set up the Institute for Industrial Reconstruction (*Istituto per la Ricostruzione Industriale*, IRI). In 1988, Charles Delzell wrote, "The IRI holding company and other para-state corporations that Mussolini founded still exist today; they account for the most inefficient 20 percent of the nation's economy" (Delzell 1988, p. 134). The IRI was dismantled only in 2002. Since its inception, the government has appointed its Board of Directors, including the Chairman. Other similar Italian companies are ENI (*Ente Nazionale Idrocarburi*, 1953-present; Italy's government still holds over one-third stake) and EFIM (*Ente partecipazioni e Finanziamento Industrie Manifatturiere*, 1962-1992).

Under Italian Corporazione, the state apparatus was responsible for trains to arrive on time; consumer-driven competition was eradicated in all spheres of life. That is why Whitman defined Corporatism as "the delegation of powers that, in a given society, are generally considered *state* powers, to *private* organizations" (Whitman 1991, p. 752). Thus, Corporatism, in a strict sense, is not Fascism, but all societies that fully implemented Corporatism quickly evolved into Fascism, and vice versa. For example, Italy began with Fascism, and only after that introduced Corporatism; Germany began with Corporatism and morphed into Fascism. Lyttelton (2004) provides fascinating details of such transformations. The discourse of what is a feature of what (Fascism is a feature of Corporatism or Corporatism is a feature of Fascism) is a typical scholastic discourse, for it makes sense only for theoreticians. The thin veil that separated Fascism from Corporatism has been removed over the past century.

There is no doubt that Left Imperialists like the idyllic picture by Shaw: "In theory, capital and labor are hitched side by side to the Fascist chariot of state, while the dictator lashes both beasts impartially in his role of national charioteer. The private employer is retained, but he is stringently regulated by the state—to such a degree, indeed, that capitalistic *laissez-faire* of the old, familiar type practically disappears under state-planning" (Shaw 1934, p. 561). He continues, "Communism eliminates the private employer and profit-maker, but Fascism, at least in economic theory, retains him as a slave of the state" (Ibid.) In other words, rather than overthrowing capitalism, as Marxism prescribes, Corporatism, cherished by the old and modern Left, aims to bypass it.

To do so, they use numerous clever ways to control it, manage it, and get rich off it, hoping that Collectivist Utopia will somehow materialize at the end of the meritocide road. With the Left at the helm, of course.

In an effort to disentangle themselves from the past, modern corporatists have invented novel terms for Fascism, such as authoritarian Corporatism. Furthermore, "purified" capitalism has been given a new name—stakeholder capitalism. Unfortunately, as far as the identity of stakeholders is concerned, there is no consensus. The usual definition of stakeholders includes customers, employees, suppliers, governments, and communities, in addition to the rightful owners—shareholders. That is how the bait-and-switch works: the legal owners are forced to cede operational control over a business to somebody else. Then, after the project is complete, customers, workers, suppliers (some of whom may be foreign), and communities (read: local governments) determine prices, wages, personnel appointments, research, and development, among other things.

The government-imposed "downside protection" component of "stakeholder capitalism" is Left Imperialism's primary hidden and never-advertised weapon.

That rosy picture, however, comes with a disclaimer: all profits still belong to the legal owners (shareholders), while all losses are collectivized. That means customers, workers, suppliers, and communities will be forced to absorb the loss if something goes wrong. In conclusion, the government-imposed "downside protection" component of "stakeholder capitalism" is Left Imperialism's primary hidden and never-advertised weapon.

The stakeholder attitude is one of the methods most desirable to the Left of wrestling control by hybridization of Leftism and corporate financial power. It is a part of the modern movement that desisted from the idea of revolution at the beginning; now, it aims at the revolution at the end. Clearly, stakeholder capitalism is a Leftist undertaking dressed up as a campaign to protect the environment and human rights.

German physicist Walther Nernst, the author of the Third Law of Thermodynamics, was an enthusiastic farmer. When he bought a large farm estate in 1920, he sold all the cows and other livestock and stocked ponds with carp. Nernst said, "A thinking man...cultivates animals that are in thermodynamic equilibrium with their surroundings and does not waste his money in heating the universe" (Gratzer 2002, p. 25). That apocryphal scientific folklore illustrates the difference between old-fashioned shareholder capitalism and the "post-modern" stakeholder model. Namely, the latter model obligates a corporation to waste money on activities not essential to the business, like heating the Universe.

Milton Friedman offered the classical take on the issue. He wrote that "the businessmen believe that they are defending free enterprise when they declaim that business is not concerned 'merely' with profit but also with promoting desirable 'social' ends; that business has a 'social conscience' and takes seriously its responsibilities for providing employment, eliminating discrimination, avoiding pollution and whatever else may be the catchwords of the contemporary crop of reformers. In fact, they are—or would be if they or anyone else took them seriously—preaching pure and unadulterated socialism" (Friedman 1970).

By imposing the "social responsibilities" of a corporation on behalf of nebulous, self-proclaimed stakeholders, the corporate executive "becomes in effect a public employee, a civil servant, even though he remains in name an employee of a private enterprise" (Friedman 1970). "This is the basic reason why the doctrine

> **The Great Resetters offered their vision: "the business of Globalism is to take control over the business."**

of 'social responsibility' involves the acceptance of the socialist view that political mechanisms, not market mechanisms, are the appropriate way to determine the allocation of scarce resources to alternative uses" (Ibid.) The axiom commonly attributed to Milton Friedman is that "the business of business is business." In turn, the Great Resetters offered their vision: "the business of Globalism is to take control over the business." Make no mistake about them: they want to be in charge of spending somebody else's—shareholders'—money.

Empirical analysis by stakeholder-friendly researchers suggests that "acceptance of stakeholderism should not be expected to produce material benefits for stakeholders" (Bebchuk and Tallarita 2020, p. 92). Also, "analysis indicates that stakeholderism should be expected to produce only illusory benefits as well as seriously detrimental effects" (Ibid., pp. 95-96). The punchline of the study is that "[w]hile stakeholderism would not produce material benefits for stakeholders, it would introduce illusory hopes, misperceptions, and distractions that would have significant adverse effects on stakeholders" (Ibid., p. 96). That study demonstrates that stakeholderism makes "corporate leaders less accountable and more insulated from shareholder oversight, acceptance of stakeholderism would increase slack and hurt performance, reducing the economic pie available to shareholders and stakeholders" (Ibid., p. 92).

The Bebchuk and Tallarita article illustrates—well beyond any reasonable doubt—that "with corporate leaders having incentives not to benefit stakeholders at shareholders' expense, an attempt to benefit stakeholders by delegating the guardianship of their interests to corporate leaders would not be supported, but rather impeded, by the force of economic incentives" (Ibid., p. 100). Under "stakeholderism" authors understand "'stakeholder governance' or 'stakeholder capitalism' put forward an alternative approach that relies on and encourages corporate leaders to make choices that would on their own protect stakeholders" (Ibid., p. 94). They are against natural economic forces and offer the standard solution preferred by the modern Left—the government-based solution: "by adopting laws, regulations and government policies—such as labor-protecting laws, consumer-protecting regulations, and carbon-reducing taxes—aimed at protecting stakeholder groups. Such 'external' interventions would constrain and incentivize companies to act in ways that would improve the welfare of stakeholders" (Ibid., p. 94).

That is the same old precept: get control over business via some (entirely legal) "external interventions" and certain judicial tricks to "benefit stakeholders at shareholders' expense."

That is Obama's "spread the wealth around" slogan expressed via scholarly jargon. That is the "scientific" justification for Herculean efforts in the economic sphere by the previous generations of the promulgate-control-without-ownership cabal—from Richelieu to Mussolini, Hitler, Franco, Mao, Salazar, and Putin.

Bebchuk and Tallarita, like many other wannabe controllers, do not like that corporations can be formed "without previous authorization by the state" (Ibid., p. 103). Furthermore, they express general left-wing dissatisfaction that by the early 20th century in America, "corporate personhood was no longer a privilege individually received from the state but a form of business organization generally available to all enterprises" (Ibid.)

Numerous administratively and legally separate but ideologically linked entities promote Left Imperialism. If the WEF has its roots in the "engineering" side of the global dominance agenda, the "government" side is represented by the Business Roundtable, established a year after the WEF in 1972. By design, the Business Roundtable was an exclusive club of corporate CEOs. Initially, it lobbied in Washington, DC, on behalf of free-market ideas and thus was seen as being on the Right side of the ideological spectrum. However, in complete agreement with the Third Conquest Law,[59] the Business Roundtable slowly but surely moved to the Left. (Note the apparent correspondence with the application of Murphy's Law to politics: "Anything that can go Left will go Left.") "Doctors Without Borders" and "Journalists Without Borders" practiced medicine and investigative journalism before they morphed into left-wing outlets in accordance with the Third Conquest Law. Similarly, the Great Resetters should be named "Commissars Without Borders." For example, the United States would be promptly renamed *Reichskommissariat Amerikaland.*

Interestingly, the WEF did not follow the right-to-left dynamics of the Business Roundtable. That is because the WEF was Left from the outset. Needless to say, the brand-new Stakeholder *Über Alles* conception was cheered and applauded by left-wingers worldwide. Besides, it is no longer necessary to use the plural form of "stakeholders," for everyone understands who is the chosen one, the most equal amongst the stakeholders.

The noticeable leftward turn occurred in September 1997, when the Business Roundtable published its new corporate governance paper. The new declaration began with "[T]he Business Roundtable wishes to emphasize that the principal objective of a business enterprise is to generate economic returns to its owners" (Business Roundtable 1997, p. 1). Then, however, that classical corporate motto, brilliantly emphasized by Milton Friedman, followed by the tectonic shift: "To manage the corporation in the long-term interests of the stockholders, management and the board of directors must take into account the interests of the corporation's other stakeholders. Indeed, a number of states have enacted statutes that specifically authorize directors to take into

---

59. The Third Conquest Law states, "All organizations that are not actually right-wing will over time become left-wing." Unfortunately, as it frequently happens, what is currently known as the Third Conquest Law has nothing to do with the British Sovietologist Robert Conquest. It was proposed in 1989 by John O'Sullivan, an adviser to Margaret Thatcher (O'Sullivan 1989, p. 14).

account the interests of constituencies other than stockholders" (Business Roundtable 1997, p. 3). The "long-term interests" meant "interests of its present and future stockholders over the long-term" (Ibid.)

By 2010, Business Roundtable was pronounced by the Washington Post as President Barack Obama's "closest ally in the business community" (read: the Left's closest ally in the business community). In 2016, the Business Roundtable dropped the "economic returns to its owners" line. Instead, it proclaimed that a corporation "may consider the interests of all of the company's constituencies, including stakeholders such as employees, customers, suppliers and the community in which the company does business" (Business Roundtable 2016, p. 4).

Finally, in 2019, the Business Roundtable reworked the long-standing policy and elevated the combined stakeholders' interests above shareholders'. Captains of American industry bluntly stated that "each of our stakeholders is essential. We commit to deliver value to all of them, for the future success of our companies, our communities and our country" (Business Roundtable 2019, p. 1). That radical revision of the corporate principle and declaration of primacy of ambiguous stakeholders over rightful owners has finalized the formation of an alloy of government and business, which began four centuries earlier by European mercantilists and colonialists.

Of course, the Business Roundtable and other apologists of stakeholder capitalism do not unceremoniously cast aside shareholders—they bypass them instead. These self-imposed, unwanted, and unneeded "corporate constituencies" take control over industries using gentle, democratically elected, and law-abiding force while skillfully maintaining the fog of private ownership. Each country developed unique judicial mechanisms to deprive the rightful private owners of their rights. There are even different names for stakeholder capitalism in different countries and at various times. However, in essence, stakeholder capitalism is a form of state-managed mob rule on a larger, industrial scale.

ESG CONTROLS AND DICTATES

Left-wing ideology carries the potential for self-destruction and self-resuscitation, while conservatism has no similar intrinsic properties. External forces, such as the economic forces that drive capitalism's vitality, resurrect conservatism whenever it falls out of favor. This process never stops. After the Left got to power in the United States, in just a few short years, the "Woke" enterprises demonstrated their frailty by losing the competition to the pre-Woke mentality of doing business. Ultimately, these misguided businesses fail based on standard and accepted accounting measures. To counter that, the WEF introduced parallel, independent of traditional accounting measures of an enterprise's health. As a result, many previously near-bankrupt businesses are thriving in the new accounting universe known as ESG.

ESG is a textbook example of a creeping Global Reset scheme, which would be better assumed as a Global Redistribution scheme. It is, however, redistribution with a twist—no property changes hands, at least for the time being; instead, it is control over property that changes hands.

> **ESG is a textbook example of a creeping Global Reset scheme. It is redistribution with a twist—no property changes hands, at least for the time being; instead, it is control over property that changes hands.**

The history of ESG began not with the WEF but with the United Nations. The left-leaning UN Secretary-General Kofi Annan is commonly regarded as the founder of the modern "corporate sustainability movement." He spearheaded a UN initiative called "The Global Compact" in 1999 "with the primary goal of implementing universal principles in business" (The Global Compact 2004, p. vii). These "universal principles" originated from the "socially responsible investing" (SRI) idea, popular in the 1970s. Initially, the SRI was ideologically neutral; for example, it advocated divestment from businesses based on moral, religious, or other non-ideological arguments.

The lesson learned from SRI was nothing less than revolutionary. Suddenly, the Left spotted an ability to impose its vision of the future by managing the investing/divesting process. Working with the environmental movement (later wholly incorporated into the Left), new investment vehicles were proposed and implemented for the ecology-concerned population.[60]

---

60. Modern Leftists are trying to convince the rest of society that the primary goal must be protecting pregnant men from global warming.

Quite traditionally, the Left hijacked the novel idea, and the religion of the Assets Under Management was born. The Left capitalized on the existence of SRI, mutual funds, pension funds, and other institutional funds that manage trillions of dollars. By bringing financial managers to their side, the Left acquired the opportunity to decide what businesses would be provided financial support and which businesses would lose their competitive edge due to lack of financing. The only problem they encountered was the absence of commonly acceptable criteria to distinguish between "good" and "bad" companies (from the Left's delineation). The ESG ratings were devised to fill that vacuum.

ESG has standardized measurements of twenty-two specific metrics (34 in the expanded version). The ESG-conscious Assets Under Management are approaching one hundred trillion dollars, or about four times the United States Gross Domestic Product.

The Global Compact was, for sure, an UN-proposed dry run for the WEF-proposed Great Reset. ESG is a Leftist scorecard for corporations, a measure of the degree to which a state and a business are entangled. The Social Credit System is a complementary scorecard on the individual level, a degree of individual conformity to the Current Truth—as defined by the government. To conclude, the Left took the opportunity to play the role of Adam Smith's "invisible hand" of the free market, but, as mentioned before, the modern Left does everything in the open. Thus, the "invisible hand" is quite visible to everyone.

However, Globalists are aware of their limitations. Despite managing trillions of dollars, they realize that "only if all actors contribute to the integration of environmental, social and governance issues in investment decisions, can significant improvements in this field be achieved" (The Global Compact 2004, p. ii). Unfortunately, there is no other interpretation of "all actors" above than as a direct threat and negation of the free market.

In his "Davos Manifesto," Klaus Schwab explained, "A company is more than an economic unit generating wealth. It fulfills human and societal aspirations as part of the broader social system. Performance must be measured not only on the return to shareholders, but also on how it achieves its environmental, social and good governance objectives" (Schwab 2019). Curiously, Leftists always operate in triplets, and the Great Reset is no exception. The Resetters offer a new trinity: Environment, Social, and Governance. That

Pantheon of governments, corporations, and "independent," "voluntary" citizen organizations, like trade unions, emulates the religious trinity it is trying to dismantle and replace. However, the bottom line is that it is just a modern reincarnation of Corporatism/Fascism.

The obvious elephant in the room is that not all stakeholders are created equal. While the self-appointed company's constituency is deliberately vague, there will always be the ultimate and omnipotent stakeholder: government bureaucrats. From now on, the state's involvement in a business will extend beyond collecting taxes and enforcing contracts; it will be near-total control of an enterprise. Stakeholder capitalism means that the government would pretend it does not run a corporation while running it. Rephrasing Clausewitz, stakeholder capitalism is a collectivist revolution by other means. *Il Duce* and *Der Führer* adopted the same cynical interpretation in the 1930s.

Klaus Schwab complained at the G20 (B20) summit in 2022 in Indonesia that the multipolar world order is approaching, but, unfortunately, it may be coming at the expense of globalization. He warned that globalization could be over (which he, in that speech, equated with the old-fashioned American dominance), and the fragmentation ("localism") era is upon us. He emphasized the importance of public-private partnerships, claiming that society has to have "two co-pilots: business and governments" (Schwab 2022). Richelieu, Mussolini, Hitler, Lenin, Stalin, and Mao would be proud, because they knew for sure which co-pilot would be a captain.

IDEOLOGICAL COLONIZATION OF THE PLANET

Tyranny is a method of colonizing the autocrat's own country. Globalism, reformatted by the Left, is a method to colonize the only known inhabited planet. As Glenn Beck and Justin Haskins noted, "The Great Reset is a proposal that is breathtaking in its scope" (Beck 2022, ch.1). The Left Imperialists envision the total colonization of the planet—economic, financial, political, and ideological. The economic structure of Globalism is unmistakably socialist, for it will be based on worldwide, centrally planned looting by public-private partnerships and centrally planned distribution of crumbs to the government's supplicants. For sure, the terms "central government" and "world government" will be prohibited; the unwashed masses will be forced to use something different, like "World Economic Council" or simply "World

Politburo." Modern imperialists are descendants of murderous French Utopians, murderous Soviet Utopians, murderous Nazi Utopians, murderous Chinese Utopians, and other entrenched left-wing thugs.

The Left Imperialists' aspiration is toward subordinating national sovereignty to the International Socialist movement while utilizing the governing experience and modus operandi of the National Socialists. As Victor Davis Hanson put it, the Great Reset "offers us a global Fabian socialist future, repackaged as a European Union-like top-down diktat" (Hanson 2022). It could be described as a joint venture of well-educated have-nots and semi-educated haves. Unfortunately, if history is taken for guidance, such a political chimera will fail, and the first casualties will be well-educated have-nots.

Modern imperialists are descendants of murderous French Utopians, murderous Soviet Utopians, murderous Nazi Utopians, murderous Chinese Utopians, and other entrenched left-wing thugs.

The Nazi government mandated in April 1933—just a few months after coming to power in Germany—that, in solidarity with all other socialist parties in Europe, "the First of May be celebrated as the holiday of industrial labor" (The Farben Case 1949, p. 570). "May Day" has a long history in Socialist circles. Since 1889, it has been dedicated by the international socialist movement as a day of support for the proletariat and against capitalism.[61]

By 1933, only the Soviet Union had enacted the First of May as a state holiday; the Nazis joined by declaring "May Day" as the "Day of National Labor." During the festivities, Hitler did a standard Leftist trick: in his May Day speech, he redefined May Day from the symbol of class struggle into something entirely different. In front of a crowd of more than one million, he announced the termination of the class struggle in the Third Reich by saying, "The millions of people divided into professions, separated into artificial classes which, infested by the arrogance of rank and class madness, are no longer able to understand each other—they must find their way back together!"

---

61. In the United States, the socialist celebration occurs at the beginning of September, known as "Labor Day."

(Domarus 1990, p. 310). Furthermore, Hitler urged, "It is necessary to teach each rank and class the significance of the other ranks and classes. And therefore, we want to go forth into the cities to proclaim to them the necessity and the essentiality of the German peasant and go out into the country and to our thinkers and teach them the significance of the German working class" (Ibid., p. 312). If Hitler were alive today, he would sue Schwab for intellectual property infringement because the control mechanisms in the nominated "stakeholder capitalism" have many striking similarities to the corresponding mechanisms of the Third Reich.

In the same speech, Hitler tried to justify the recently introduced "compulsory labor service" in Germany by stating, "Mental and manual workers must never be allowed to be on opposite sides" (Ibid., p. 314). Even if Hitler made several unpleasant for Marxists passages in his speech, he borrowed the idea of "compulsory labor service" from fellow Leftist Leon Trotsky's idea of "labor armies," described in his 1920 seminal book *Terrorism and Communism*.

The Left tried "compulsory labor service" in the 20th century, but the results were unsatisfactory. So, the modern Left formulated the novel idea of "compulsory capital service" under the moniker of ESG metrics. The idea is to push the private sector to invest not where it can get the biggest returns but where governments can reap the most political rewards. ESG's set of twenty-two non-financial metrics and disclosures will demonstrate a company's business preferences—from serving customers to serving governments. The "old" capitalism always viewed politics through the lens of profits; the "Woke" capitalism drives corporations to consider politics a legitimate contributor to profits.

> **The Left tried "compulsory labor service" in the 20th century, but the results were unsatisfactory. So, the modern Left formulated the novel idea of "compulsory capital service."**

Currently, the WEF emphasizes that adopting ESG reporting by corporations is voluntary. However, they understand the powerful feedback loop that exists in every society. Therefore, they do not have to capture the entire business world ideologically. Instead, following Gramsci's plan, they hellbent on creating a "critical mass" of ESG-compliant businesses to push ESG to every corporation, large and small, via government interventions. They may succeed because corporations do not offer any resistance and have excellent reasons not to. In their calculations, the burden of ESG compliance is relatively tiny (note that ESG, like all other Leftist inventions, is infinitely malleable) and could be redefined as a business investment. Historically, ESG was developed in parallel with the Social Credit Score System for individuals. In practical terms, ESG is the Social Credit Score System for businesses.

Moreover, the return on invested capital offered by "shareholder capitalism" is tremendous because of the "guaranteed profits" promise. The Left is not without merit here. Leftists may maintain that promise for some time, but eventually, somebody else's (read: taxpayers') money will run out. That is why corporations worldwide are rushing toward ESG compliance. They know perfectly well that to survive under the newly developed global financial pyramid scheme, they must join it as close to its beginning as possible. Globalists are so obsessed with the grandiosity of their plans that they do not see that ESG-compliant corporations are ready to abandon the sinking Leftist ship at the first sign of diminishing profits.

Corporations will not tolerate wandering forty years into the land of promised profits. Corporations will relinquish their pristine score of the ratio of non-binary Asians to transgender Mohicans at the first hint that governments can no longer deliver profits. Nobody can forecast when it will happen. However, what can be predicted for sure is that de-transitioning back to a profit-based economy will be uglifying, painful, and prolonged because nobody will have the resources to afford something tantamount to the Marshall Plan.

In short, ESG is a mechanism to measure corporate aberration from Collectivist *raison d'être*. Under the ESG dictates, corporate success is no longer based on delivering profit to shareholders but on allegiance to the ruling political elite.

While ESG is propagandized as "voluntary," governments worldwide have found a way to force corporations to accept ESG metrics. Governments compile policies that "opting out of ESG is not an option. So, they force non-compliant businesses to conform to ESG by artificially creating real costs for not doing so. The conflation of money and power allows them to do this through litigation. They will sue companies—often with dubious or plainly meritless cases—to create litigation risk and costs. Even if the claims are meritless, businesses face real costs measured in lawyers' fees, litigation costs, and the risk—however small—of a monetary judgment" (Canaparo 2022). Lawfare does not aim to win lawsuits against adversaries per se but rather to cause the defendant to drown in legal debts. Thus, ESG is antithetical to the mission of the business enterprise.

In the era of classical capitalism, it was easy to pinpoint a class of haves and have-nots—just as Karl Marx did. As the name implies, the class division was based solely on property ownership. Under the post-Fascist Great Reset, the ownership demarcation will be blurred, and the delineation will be between cohorts of control and control-nots. The old wealth-based hierarchy will be replaced with a brand-new control-based hierarchy. An individual's distance from the top of the Globalist Olympus will be determined not by economic power, but by the level of adherence to ideological dogma (and corresponding Assets Under Management). Thus, segments of the population previously excluded from "high society" will be given a chance, but we are not talking about the unwashed masses here. Instead, the chance will be given to elected and unelected government bureaucrats and intellectuals who cannot acquire astronomical wealth in "old" capitalism due to the specifics of their profession: journalists, scientists, media personalities, and party functionaries. In a way, the Great Reset may be viewed as a non-traditional but clever and sneaky method of penetrating "high society" by redefining its meaning. However, the price to get there for society would be astronomical because it entails a transformation of the profit-driven economy into a conformism-driven economy.

> **Like imperialism of the past, Left Imperialism prefers not to ruin the institutions of the conquered. It prefers to keep them intact—at least as a façade—but repurpose them.**

The only way such an economy will survive is to be implemented everywhere and simultaneously outlaw competition on the planet. The international Left knows that if just a single—decadent—*laissez-faire* capitalist country is left intact, it will eventually out-produce and out-power the total sum of non-profit-driven countries. Thus, Trotsky's "permanent revolution" has morphed into "permanent imperialism" by his clever ideological successors.

Like imperialism of the past, Left Imperialism prefers not to ruin the institutions of the conquered. It prefers to keep them intact—at least as a *façade*—but repurpose them. This applies to both national and international organizations. In the era following the Great Reset, there will be room for the United Nations, the World Health Organization, the Vatican, and many others. All will play their designated role in the Utopian, "problem-free," "sustainable" superstate governed by the supranational Council of Syndicates. (Alternatively, it might be designated the Soviet of Syndicates, with the Politburo at the helm.)[62] The preceding remarks show that the Davos WEF meetings are nothing more than carving up god-like positions in the future Pantheon of the Left Olympus. In other words, the Davos meetings are Sisyphus races for a desirable position near the top of the serfdom pyramid. Finally, another possible illustration of The Great Reset would be substituting corporate raiders for political raiders.

The European Union (EU) is a microcosm of what Left Imperialism has in mind. It is probably the most anti-democratic institution in the West: its commissars are not elected and not subject to criticism. They meet in secrecy, keep their financial records secret, and are answerable only to the EU itself. As a result, they can control all aspects of the lives of ordinary Europeans.

MODERN MONETARY THUGS

If Maoism is an example of managing a capitalist economy with socialist methods, Modern Monetary Theory (MMT)—the financial engine behind the Left Imperialism—is an example of managing a capitalist economy with communist methods. Recall that under communism, scarcity no longer exists. It means that the money supply is unlimited. The corollary is that financial debt and fiscal deficits are illusory; they have no actual economic meaning because governments could easily overcome them by printing (or digitally issuing) more cash. Undoubtedly, unrestricted cash printing has a negative cash value, but financial Lysenkoism is extremely popular for every currency issuer worldwide.[63]

Left Imperialism has not only redefined the debt and deficits; they have also redefined and repurposed tax collection and processing. The amount

---

62. An authoritarian state is ruled by a dictator (autocrat). In contrast, a totalitarian state is ruled by ideology, not by individuals.

63. The cretinous idea of minting a one-trillion-dollar platinum coin to solve the debt crisis in the United States is well within MMT orthodoxy.

of tax collected no longer acts as a modulator of politicians' appetites; it has been ideologically weaponized. Under MMT, governments do not need tax revenues at all. Instead, taxes have morphed into a political tool for the punishment of the opposition and a reward for the party in power. From the individual-state paradigm, MMT tilts the balance of economic power from the governed to the government. No wonder Leftists worldwide are so enthusiastic about MMT: it paves the way for comprehensive population control. Note also that under MMT, the core export item of the United States became a federal fiscal deficit.

However, Modern Monetary Theory will not help Globalists, even if it insists that money is "a social construct." MMT may avoid the terrifying inflationary picture of people carrying a wheelbarrow load of money to buy a cup of ersatz coffee. After that, however, they will reach a point where existing computer hardware and software cannot handle financial transactions anymore. That is in a world where a cup of coffee costs one hundred trillion dollars in the morning and two hundred trillion dollars in the afternoon.

Contrary to what WEF wants people to believe the Great Reset does, it does not reset capitalism. Under the proposed "reset" capitalism, workforce and capital would still exist in their current forms, but with the crucial caveat: that existence would be under strict, even draconian, government control. Thus, the Great Reset resets the control part of society's equation; the key thing is that reset would be done synonymously with the "reset of control" by the previous generations of Italian, German, and Chinese Leftists. Note the absence of Soviet, Cuban, and North Korean Leftists on the list; they symbolize the unpractical—from the WEF point of view—"reset of ownership" path.

The modern Left Imperialists do not want bloody civil wars triggered by property confiscations and redistributions. Instead, they hyperbolize the "reset of control," assuming they can corral people into comfortable slavery without the bloody excesses of past attempts. Moreover, while the lure for capital into the newly developed system differs, the central theme has not changed since the 1920s. Namely, capitalists acquire rights to unalterable profits simply by joining the party and abdicating all macro-management and micro-management duties to government-approved bureaucrats. "Profits without headache" is a Siren song for capitalists under the Great Reset.

Many super-rich and super-powerful people swallowed the bait the Left Imperialists strategically placed. Innovations are no longer required. No competition ever materializes. No worrying about the tax burden because profit is arranged in advance no matter what. The threat of strikes and other unpleasant disruptions is vaporized. There are no investment risks whatsoever. It is a paradise on Earth for capitalists, complemented by a paradise for the sheeple, guaranteed by an omnipotent government Leviathan—or so they envision. The industrialists who sold their entrepreneurial soul to Globalists think they gained extraordinary influence over governments. Instead, governments have consolidated great control over businesses.

The post-Great-Reset world would be well under control; the Great Reset presumably eradicated any chaos in human civilization. It completely substitutes risk-aversion strategies for risk-taking ones. In a sense, The Great Reset represents society's total feminization (understood in a very narrow sense of risk disinclination) with the known price tag. Specifically, stagnation and inevitable decadence because social development requires risk-taking complemented by risk avoidance. In other words, the Great Reset is well-known and well-studied but rebranded and reformulated old-fashioned Leftist Utopia. Like previous Leftist Utopias, this one has one and only one answer to all society's ills: a government-owned, government-run, or government-managed solution.

WEAPONIZATION OF EVERYTHING

Today's Globalists differ considerably from many previous social movements that resulted in calamities for humanity. Unlike their ideological predecessors at the turn of the 19th and 20th centuries, Globalists of the 21st century are no longer an underground group of conspirators. Instead, they do their utmost to disseminate their ideas as widely as possible. Furthermore, they always strive to conduct themselves openly and, if possible, legally. President Obama did not lie when he said his administration would be "the most transparent administration in the history of the United States." Instead of what most people assumed, he understood the terms "transparency" and "openness" in his own Globalist vein.[64]

Collectivists cannot stand letting the electorate simply walk away and think independently; they are desperate to micromanage all aspects of a

---

64. As Gordon Anderson remarked, "What Obama wanted was people's transparency to the government, not the government's transparency to the people."

person's life. So, they utilize (read: weaponized) all technological achievements of "evil capitalists." Would cancel culture or Woke culture materialize without technological achievements that opened the door for Internet-based social networks?

The Left Imperialists' primary longing in the 21st century is not comprehensive control of wealth ownership—that will come later. Instead, they assert control over fear. Worldwide. Because fear, from their narrative, must be maintained at all times and controlled at any cost, individuals who develop symptoms of free will and independent thought must be eliminated from society long before the unreachable Utopia is reached. Subsequently, per the Left Imperialists, suppressing any dissent must occur during the initial "soft totalitarianism" phase; it makes the following "hard totalitarianism" phase more doable. Similar processes in the Soviet Union, the Third Reich, and Castro's Cuba were categorized as "weeding out the weak."

The recent political weaponization of the banking industry (i.e., using private financial records against opposing politicians) aligns with all the precursory weaponization projects. However, the weasels of Leftism are close to exhausting their weaponization abilities. Eventually, they will run out of things to weaponize.

There are countless examples of the political weaponization of all facets of human life, including private life.

There are countless examples of the political weaponization of all facets of human life, including private life.

Imagine yourself in the shoes of modern Leftist revolutionaries. The committed Leftist faces a challenging task in the absence of stalwart proletarians. What would one do if the crowd of disciples with blind devotion to the doctrine turned out to be virtually non-existent? Naturally, one would need to create such an electorate. Marxists developed their entire worldview around the contemporary "oppressed classes." The post-Marxists moved forward into the realm where "oppressed classes" do not even exist, so they must be invented.

Confidently, the Left has a well-defined internal structure and hierarchy despite its calls for "equality." The hierarchy—political hierarchy, that is—is not written in stone. Canonically, as Marx outlined it, the proletariat occupied the top rank of the revolutionary hierarchy. However, the hierarchical structure has undergone significant changes over time. An essential point to remember is that such a structure always exists.

Moreover, there is limited space at the top and almost infinite space at the bottom, as is the case in any hierarchy. The most notable trend in the 21st century is the ascent of illegal aliens—the substitute revolutionaries—from third-world countries to the top, above high-ranking dwellers of the past, such as women. The precise hierarchical structure reflects Leftist expectations of revolutionary drive on the part of a particular cohort. Similarly, blacks are now regarded as superior to women—in a revolutionary sense, of course.

Therefore, an illegal alien or a black man raping a white woman is no longer considered sufficiently outrageous by the Left to justify severe prosecution. Above all, such a rape constitutes an act of indecency against a hierarchically approved, relatively inferior person—a white woman. In contrast, if rape (or even alleged rape) occurs against any woman by a white male (white males are well below women in the revolutionary hierarchy), this would constitute despicable violence against a woman, the relatively revolutionary-superior individual. Most "#MeToo" cases involve non-black men or black men (in Wokespeak, "unvaginated individuals") who are classed as "not black enough." Additionally, the vast majority of Black Lives Matter (BLM) and Antifa thugs (who once occupied top positions in the revolutionary hierarchy) have been released following widespread pogroms in 2019 and 2020. Thus, Antifa and BLM thugs were more like a smoke screen for the Leftist's nobility-in-waiting.

The sex dichotomy (male-female) results from nature's self-organization triggered by dissipative conditions: death, violence, and illnesses. Without various forms of dissipation, life would be a paradise with an obvious consequence: the absence of harsh treatment inhibits evolution.

Eventually, Mother Nature settled into two sexes for the dominant creatures on the planet. Undoubtedly, all other combinations (single-sex or more than two sexes or no sex at all) have been tried before arriving at sexually dimorphic species. Nevertheless, as anybody can witness today, these attempts were not entirely successful. As a result, only double-sexed species made it to the top of the evolutionary pyramid.

The male-female distinction (based on, primarily but not exclusively, a combination of XX and XY chromosomes) is not strictly black-and-white. There is a negligible but non-zero number of genetic anomalies like hermaphrodites, but they never played any role in the political sphere. Their negligible small numbers prevented their incorporation into the Left political machine. However, another segment of anomalies—in this case, not biological, but psychological anomalies—was always present in society. Homosexuals have been known since pre-Biblical times and were mainly ignored by the general citizenry and corresponding governments because they were considered innocuous. Then, in the 1960s, the Left decided to militarize this population segment by elevating their "oppressed status."

Modern psychiatry still considers, quite a righty, homosexualism hurtless. However, homosexualism's weaponization by the Left led to a) the acquiring by homosexuals of an ideological component and, consequently, b) turning society against homosexuals. Joining forces with Leftist politics made homosexuals share the same unflattering epithets as dirty political operators. From the individual-state paradigm, homosexualism enlisted into the government coalition against the governed; it has self-redefined not as a "harmless anomaly" but as a destructive ideology carrying a solid negative cash value.

The story is as old as the world. As appointed cogs in the political, bureaucratic, and ideological machine, homosexuals have lost their true identity in the broad conglomerate of "oppressed victims." By trading their natural identity and linking with Leftists' messianic, post-Marxian Utopian schemes, homosexuals acquired a heightened ideological identity and institutionalized privileges. As a result, homosexuals, on the one hand, got codified recognition from the government but, on the other hand, strengthened the wall of prejudices against themselves from the general populace. Unfortunately, it certainly looks as though both "achievements" are here to stay.

At the beginning of the 20th century, left-wing feminists revealed their weapon of choice: the vagina. It was put into action initially for the genocide of blacks because one of the Left's icons, Margaret Sanger, was a follower of the racist pseudo-science of eugenics (just like her admirer and ideological colleague in Europe, Adolf Hitler). Even in the 21st century, the weaponized vagina is still in use. (Recall the Judge Kavanaugh drama and the anti-Trump "golden shower" hoax.)

Later, other private parts were weaponized, and the political movement LGBT was born. It largely succeeded in bringing down the Boy Scouts and normalizing actions sensed as abnormal (but innocuous in negligible doses) throughout human history. If they were confined to private bedrooms, such abnormalities were widely tolerated for millennia. However, political weaponization injected them into the public domain, including anti-parents LGBT brainwashing in public schools.

Society always considered gays and lesbians not just harmless but also, in low doses, beneficial to society because a same-sex relationship takes girly men and manly girls out of the evolutionary contest. From pre-biblical times, sodomy was tolerated by society, but only in extremely low doses. It is naïve to assume society would treat sodomy practiced by a minuscule minority in the same way if it were widely practiced. In high doses, same-sex lovemaking acts as a poison for society.

Gender dysphoria is a real medical condition; one remedy the affected individuals aim for is assigning additional identification to government records. Namely, they seek to include a category of "gender" alongside "sex." Most likely, if that were the case, nobody would seriously object. Unfortunately, the people with gender dysphoria also demanded something extra: a) not merely adding a "gender" attribute to government records but completely replacing the existing system with the new "gender" identity, and b) forcing society to accept their modified identity attributes. To add insult to injury, these people chose a judicial path to achieve their goals, bombarding courts with numerous lawsuits. It is an example of penetration across domains when government institutions are capitalized on to settle intra-society scores based on society's rejection of "gender identity."

Society stood idle when the trans activists forced the government's hand, but society rejected the idea of the full recognition of trans demands categorically.

Society stood idle when the trans activists forced the government's hand, but society rejected the idea of the full recognition of trans demands categorically. While Western societies let any member live their lives on their terms, society has no obligation to accept intrusion from the government domain. If a government accepts the existence of almost a hundred "genders," that is strictly government business. The people-to-people domain exists semi-independently of government and customarily ignores the government's back office. For example, the United States Federal government uses the metric system, while the rest of the country, including state governments, utilizes the imperial system. That fact should suggest that the full acceptance of multi-gendered individuals by society—if it is going to happen—will materialize long after accepting either metric or imperial units in the United States. Recognition from a government and recognition from society are two different things.

Besides, the colleagues of the non-binary folks inside the oppression pyramid are not allowing it to happen. They resist elevation to the top of the pyramid of white people because they suspect that these whites will utilize multi-genderism as just a trick to overcome competition inside the revolutionary hierarchy of "victims of capitalism." In other words, society tells trans people: "If you want your gender to be listed on your government-issued driver's license, that is fine with us. However, we will persist in treating human beings on the basis of their gametes: single-digit large, unmovable, or millions of tiny, highly mobile gametes."[65] Trans people may disregard their biology, but society will not accept such ignorance because, as we mentioned before, biological evolution is directionless.

Conversely, social evolution has a direction primarily argued and maintained by Conservatives. In the biological evolutionary race, Mother Nature has no idea where the finish line is or even whether there is a finish line. Still, in social evolution, the finish line is also unobservable, but there are many arguments for its existence. Biological evolution is a two-way street; conservatism makes social evolution a one-way street (with many potholes and bumps, of course).

The trans world is, in essence, a form of ideological barbarism, a pseudo-scientific justification that carries traces of Lysenkoism. In biological terms, the trans world is a chemical or surgical castration enclave, but the number of actually castrated victims is minimal. However, the number of non-biological victims is alarmingly large because the chemical castration is accompanied by a more severe syndrome—ideological castration, which looks at the moment to be irreversible, too. Ideological castration, like all other Leftist tools, is designed to convert people into heterogeneous and shapeless biomass, ideologically pure matter. Like a contagious virus, Leftism spread in

---

65. Note that algae and fungi have equal-size gametes; thus, Mother Nature produced unequal gametes sizes in mammals who eventually built civilization while algae are still algae.

human society and resulted in the total weaponization of everything. Being a totalitarian ideology, Leftism could not settle for anything less than total weaponization.

Likewise, the legalization of same-sex marriage by the government, while probably just, must be viewed through the lens of the individual-state paradigm. Namely, such a right exists only in due course of government-to-governed interactions; it has nothing to do with governed-to-governed business—i.e., the public. In other words, while society tolerates certain aspects of government business, normalizing same-sex marriage within the general public is out of the question because there are no effective legal or executive mechanisms to alter people's opinions.

While the government's decisions on some of society's ills are supported by both the Left and the Right, nobody should expect that the masses would soon overhaul their opinions on some subjects. The public's opinions are always based on a balance. For example, the average white opinion about blacks hangs on a balance of multiple examples. On the one side are BLM rioters and black perpetrators of Jewish pogroms in 2017-2020. On the other side, there is black (and possibly the greatest) American philosopher Thomas Sowell and (possible genius) black Supreme Court Justice Clarence Thomas. This balance, of course, cannot be quickly altered by any government decree or codified law.

Nevertheless, contrary to popular opinion, it was not precisely black men who ravaged American cities in the summer of 2019 after the death of carrier criminal George Floyd. It was an ideologically different human species—namely, black and white *Homo sovieticus*, who managed to live in the community largely unnoticed. These ultra-Sovietized thugs, as a rule, have no idea they are just marionettes in somebody else's grand scheme. Nevertheless, over the last decade or so, these poor thugs have grown increasingly hostile to any deviations from Leftist dogmas.

An overwhelmingly intolerant society could tolerate somebody else's business—including government business—but only under the condition that somebody else's business minds its own business and does not force it down the throat of the population at large. Society's drastic change of opinion might eventually materialize, but only if society recognizes its positive cash value through trial and error. Negative cash value guarantees the rejection of an idea regardless of its legal status; near-zero cash value ideas sometimes find an ideological or cultural niche and survive. For example, the Court of Public Opinion is still considering the long-term cash value of erasing traditional conceptions of marriage by the United States Supreme Court, independently from the government that issues marriage certificates to same-sex couples.

In summary, society accepts that the governing body will treat some people in a certain way. However, neither the government nor its proponents should expect widespread acceptance of it, at least in the near future. This applies to all cases where the Left has found "oppressed victims": same-sex marriage, abortion, "transgender rights," racism, and so on.

An intolerant society could tolerate somebody else's business but only under the condition that somebody else's business does not force itself down the throat of the population at large.

Maintaining a promiscuous mass of "victims" in the Left's pocket will inevitably lead to internal conflicts. It is well-known that there is tension between Leftist Jews and Leftist blacks. Recently, a heated conflict arose between lesbians and "women without a vagina"—"trans women." The Left positions its dogmas as infallible. Lesbians are forced to have sex with men who call themselves women since the latter are officially appointed "real" women, a practice which they (rightfully) reject as they avoid relationships with penis-equipped individuals (formerly known simply as "men") in the first place.

It is worth mentioning that women practically never participated in political life before the end of the 19th century. That is why they, like the Jews, were essentially a ready-to-go class of "oppressed victims" from the Leftists' point of view. As a result, Leftists throughout the 20th century successfully victimized women for political purposes. Thus, it should not come as a surprise to anyone that feminism (in contrast to the suffragist movement) is a purely Leftist movement. Indisputably, one of its founders was the racist Margaret Sanger.

The modern reincarnation of the status of women as victims is the infamous "War on Women," invented in the bowels of Leftist think tanks. As with deceived Jews, deceived women, brainwashed into believing they were victims, took to the streets dressed up in humiliating vagina costumes.

Leftists have divided America into primitive victim-oppressor groups; they claim to champion each victim group while, at the same time, fomenting them against each other. That sub-divided grouping offers Leftists a superior degree of control. Contrary to the adage that "diversity" is a euphemism for "quotas," "diversity" is a euphemism for "control." Collectivists declare diversity in how people look but mandate uniformity in how people think. On the contrary, Conservatives do not care how people look or think.

For Conservatives, race is immaterial, inconsequential, irrelevant, and unimportant. For the right-wingers, the issue of race does not need to be "settled" because their ideology does not allow such an issue to exist in the first place. "Race has no place in American life or law," President John F. Kennedy said. In 1961, he signed Executive Order 10925, which called for Federal government contractors to take "affirmative action" to curb discrimination against Americans because of their race, creed, color, or national origin. Since the late 1960s, dirty political operators have steadily weaponized Kennedy's "affirmative action." At the moment, it is leveraged not to prevent discrimination against blacks but to discriminate against other cohorts of Americans, like whites and Asian men. Many public institutions in the United States suffer not from "lack of diversity" and "systemic racism" but from systemic socialism. For Conservatives, the accident of birth that creates a certain level of melanin pigment (and gives skin its color) is beyond the ridiculous candidate selection method. Human civilization does not run on pigment. For millennia, society has run chiefly on physical abilities; today, it runs primarily on intellectual competitions. Less melanin is not inferior; more melanin is not superior. A focus exclusively on human melanin is, by definition, racist. All proponents of pigment-based selection criteria empower those who demand that a person's future be determined by a single criterion no human can alter, even theoretically. Human history is replete with many—mostly failed—examples of such thinking. For example, antisemitism focuses on a single criterion that no one can change because no one can choose their parents.

Rephrasing Lord Acton, diversity policies corrupt, and absolute diversity corrupts absolutely. The Diversity-Industrial Complex mandates that if a corporation cannot find enough women, indigenous natives, or any other exclusive group high enough in the Leftist diversity hierarchy, its contract with the Federal government should terminate. From simple supply-demand metrics, the explosion of transgenders, gays, lesbians, Native Americans, illegal aliens, and various never-heard-before genders and people of color represent the supply side. In contrast, the pro-Left government represents the demand side, offering protected cohort status. The "diversity" platitude does not lead to the most talented workforce possible; as such, the verdict is that the "diversity" idea has zero or even negative cash value.

ESG mandates that corporate management echoes local population demographics, but that mandate is not applicable outside the generic "West." For example, there are no calls to have a certain percentage of white men on the board of directors of any African or Asian company. There are no calls for black women on African corporate boards, either.

Thus, the point of "diversity" is control. Just as the point of "gun control" is control, the point of "climate change" is control, and the point of forced vaccination is control. Similarly, the point of abortion is control over women, the point of systemic white racism is control over blacks, and the point of inflation is population control. In other words, control tends to corrupt, and absolute control corrupts absolutely.

> **The point of "diversity" is control. Just as the point of "gun control" is control, the point of "climate change" is control, and the point of forced vaccination is control.**

A similar control-asserting trend is observable in the democratic political sphere, too. In the 21st century, the Left, as a rule, does not physically eliminate political opposition anymore; Leftists devise various methods to control it. Not only does the term "controlled opposition" exist in all countries—but the controlled opposition is widespread, too.

The Cult of Victimseekers

The modern Left is as eclectic as any ideology could be. They are seeking unsuspecting adherents from all segments of society. It has long been observed that the Leftist movement has transformed into a genre of a religious cult—the Cult of Victimseekers.

Like any cult, the Leftists have dogmas, worldviews, taboos, and idols. The list of "victims" of this cult is impressive. Well-known recent "victims" are nature (damaged by evil "old" capitalists), domestic animals (evil capitalists mock them), climate (the temperature of the air is warmed up by all the same evil capitalists), and sexual minorities.

Leftists always rummage around for an oppressive structure containing conflicting groups—real or fictitious. The noblest occupation for a Leftist is the search (or artificial creation) of another, hitherto unknown class of victims. It would seem that they have already tried everything possible, but the worldview of the Victimseekers is so comprehensive that it manifests itself in the most unexpected places. For example, the loss of the presidential election in 2016 and Trump's victory were taken by Leftists as yet more proof that they are victims—victims of the "collusion between Trump and Putin."

Here is a standard Left way to any right-wing challenges: offer a parade of horribles, find a new class of offended "victims," and propose the only solution they have—assign the problem to the government to fix, thus making it incrementally bigger and more powerful. So, Leftists are always in search of "victims." Immediately after being found, the "victims" will be assigned a fitting "ism." Of course, it will amount to another form of charlatanism. Leftists have escalated victim status to the level of the only virtue worth pursuing. The search for "victims" who will lead the Leftists to political power has become Leftism's means to an end. However, while searching for "victims," many Leftists have forgotten their Marxist roots. A superb illustration of this was the genuine indignation of then-Vice President Joe Biden when a journalist asked him whether he was a socialist.

The search for "victims" who will lead the Leftists to political power has become Leftism's means to an end.

As a result, modern Globalists in general (and the Democrat Party of the United States in particular) are not a monolithic movement. On the contrary, they represent the interests of various incoherent and often competing and warring classes of "oppressed victims," artificially united under the same roof by the Cult of Victimseekers.

One variant of Globalism is Muslim Socialism, which appears to be a form of Islamic expansionism in which Muslims are depicted as "victims." The doctrines of Islam certainly caused some followers suffering, especially compared with the West. Nonetheless, there are striking similarities between Leftists and jihadists. Namely, once something has been won (obtained, stolen, taken, granted, conquered, inherited, etc.), it is deemed sacred—and inviolable, and it belongs to them forever.

Brezhnev's well-known defense doctrine for socialist countries is also part of this series. According to Brezhnev's doctrine, the Soviet Union had the right to intervene in the internal affairs of other countries if they had already been establishing socialism or had expressed an interest in doing so. By applying this doctrine in practice, the Soviet Union aggressively interfered with the domestic affairs of many countries in Europe, Asia, Africa, and South America. In other words, the Cult of Victimseekers gives its followers a license to always be right. Marxism has no concept of failure: if a perpetrator kills someone for the "common good," it is glory as long as that target individual belongs to an "oppressive class." If the perpetrator dies for the "proletarian revolution" in the process, it is also glory. It applies to the umbrella ideology, Leftism, to some degree. Leftists never apologize for their deeds. Ever. The only exception is a sporadic apology for their "out-of-context words."

Another characteristic shared by jihad and all branches of Leftism is the animalistic hatred for the like-minded public from a neighboring clan. Shi'ite and Sunni Muslims engage in far more ferocious battles than wars with Jews, Christians, and other non-Muslims. Various estimates suggest that the number of Muslims slaughtered in intra-Muslim conflicts far exceeds the sum of Muslims killed by non-Muslims.

To illustrate, recall that the Stalinists-Leninists (later rebranded Communists) wasted Russia's Trotskyists and the Mensheviks. However, this did not prevent Communists and Social Democrats in the 1930s Germany from temporarily joining forces and engaging in bloody street fights with their peers, the National Socialists.

The modern terrorist organization Antifa, re-created by the Globalists, declares, like its predecessors of the early 1930s in Germany, that it is made up of anti-fascists. Despite this, Antifa members do not appear radically different from Fascists. However, their street battles often involve disputes between factions adhering to the same Leftist ideology. Today's decentralized Antifa consists of a bizarre mixture of close but not ideologically identical militants. While Antifa members wear clothes similar to Mussolini's Blackshirts, their behavior is reminiscent of the *Sturmabteilung* (SA) of the Nazis, also known as the "brownshirts" (*Braunhemden*).

As part of the SA, the SS had a special status from the very beginning—its members were militant brigades wholly owned not by a state (i.e., a government army), not by a wealthy individual (i.e., a private army), but by a political party. The army-like SS units were often termed the "Political Rapid Response Force" (*Politische Bereitschaft*).[66] BLM and Antifa follow that tradition to the penny—they obey only party orders.

The Left comprehended long ago that political exploitation of grievances does not even need actual grievances; artificial grievances will do. It was Adolf Hitler who pioneered this trend in socialism.

The slave-like dependence on government handouts yielded another type of "victim." That was undoubtedly the most outstanding achievement of the Left: instead of seeking "victims," the Left created them artificially. The Left comprehended long ago that political exploitation of grievances does not even need actual grievances; artificial grievances will do. It was Adolf Hitler who pioneered this trend in socialism.[67] It is widely accepted that if a society incentivizes victimization (the demand side), it will enter a dangerous spiral because the supply side will produce as many "victims" as needed.

Hitler theatrically created the "oppressed Aryan race." In America and Europe, the victim class manifested itself as welfare and corporate welfare, state-funded medical care, and widespread illegal immigration (known as "undocumented Democrats" in politically correct Newspeak). Comparatively, the "oppressed Palestinians" were artificially set up by the Soviet KGB after the Six-Day War in Israel in 1967.

---

66. The SS—the Nazi party military wing—were the first motorized military units in the history of Nazi Germany. The regular Army (*Wehrmacht*) still used mostly horsepower practically until the end of World War II.

67. Another contribution of Hitler to how political battles are fought today is using airplanes. That allowed him to participate in several political rallies per day, while his opponents were limited to just one event per day. In the United States, his fellow left-winger Huey Long pioneered using private planes for campaign purposes in the 1930s. He "revealed his sincere intention to become the first politician to stump the entire nation by air" (Snyder 1975, p. 142).

In America, "oppressed minorities" and "unprivileged classes" constitute about half the population. Moreover, the share of illegal immigrants who receive government benefits is approaching 50%, and each American taxpayer is forced to spend around $1,000 per year due to illegal immigration (FAIR Report, 2023). Leftists in the United States have thus orchestrated a grand strategy to divide the American population into two artificial classes—those who work and pay taxes and those who make a living off these taxes.

The modern Leftists are fighting so fiercely for the "rights of immigrants," not because the fate of illegal aliens worries them in any way. It is because Globalists anticipate illegal immigrants as the main "engine of the revolution," which must bring about socialist transformations and catapult the Globalists to power. Consequently, the greater the number of "engines" in a country, the happier the elite of the Globalist party will be. So, naturally, they call (irrationally and contrary to common sense) for opening the United States borders, dissolving the Border Patrol, and granting the right to vote to non-citizens. Basically, the American WEF coterie runs the program of de-nationization of the United States. The position of Globalists on this issue is ultra-uncompromising because, for them, illegal immigration is not a legal issue, but a political and close to an existential one.

Following Globalists, this is not a matter of violating the country's sovereign rights, but a matter of political survival. In the opinion of Globalists, illegal immigration encapsulates precisely that army of mere mortals stupefied by the propaganda of the masses. These mere mortals will be required to stand on the barricades in order to gain political power over every area of the planet for office philosophers. In essence, the idea might be expressed as follows: "If our citizens do not vote for us, we will import hordes that will."

Wealthy businessmen are also accounted as "victims." (Remember that victim status is often subjective and artificial, as is the case here.) Essentially, the current economic system of America and other developed countries conforms to classical *laissez-faire* capitalism only in the remotest sense. The vast majority of Americans, even the incredibly wealthy, are aware of their vulnerability to and almost complete dependence on Washington, DC bureaucrats, lobbyists, and politicians. So-called progressive policies dramatically turned at the end of the 20th century; they are no longer policies designed for the proletariat. Instead, they became the policies of multinational corporations.

Individuals who are proficient at milking the government are in high demand. Washington, DC, is not only the site of the most prominent political swamp in history. Moreover, the idea of "socialism for the rich" is at the nucleus of its existence, regardless of what other terms are used to describe how the rest of the country operates—capitalism or something else. The free-market or *laissez-faire* capitalism may stay outside Washington, DC borders, but the swamp-dwellers redefined the game long ago. Inside Washington, DC, the line between government and business is blurred to such a degree that Big Business becomes an extension of Big Government and vice versa. The conservative side of the individual-state paradigm indirectly forces a business to operate in a way that benefits corporations and, at the same time, society. 21st-century Washington, DC, operates under the opposing paradigm, limiting corporations' benefits and reassigning them to Washington, DC's political plankton.

The mosaic of heterogeneous groups under one Leftist umbrella has reached a critical mass. The more modifications and generalizations of the dogma are needed, and the more intense the internecine warfare is.

Treating a human being as an individual unites conservatives (add proper timeframe) and liberals (add proper timeframe because supertemporal comparison is impossible). Assigning copious characteristics of a group to a person is a clever method of human ideological control because the (artificial and spurious) borders separating groups are configured so that escape from the assigned plantation is impossible. Examples are skin color, the social status of parents, or other "accidents of birth"—all these characteristics cannot be "rolled back" or altered in any way.

The mosaic of heterogeneous groups under one Leftist umbrella has reached a critical mass. The farther society moves away from Marx's predictions, the more modifications and generalizations of the dogma are needed, and the more intense the internecine warfare is. Different cohorts of "oppressed victims of capitalism" cannot find common ground with other "oppressed victims" or a broad spectrum of abundant self-appointed victims. Anti-conservatism is the solitary umbilical cord that allows the modern Left to show at least an illusion of unity.

Numerous headhunters (or, rather, victimhunters) are plowing through the planet to find those who are not marginalized yet and who have the potential to become the next cannon fodder for revolution. Occasionally, Victimseekers stumble upon a goldmine. For example, Leftists did not need to persuade the Jews that they were victims. Antisemitism, for about two millennia, played a cruel joke on the Jews—they eagerly joined the first political movement that openly recognized the Jews as victims. Unfortunately, many Jews (to be more exact, those who consider themselves victims) are still committed to Leftist dogma. They refuse to recognize the obvious fact that the status of victims makes them cannon fodder for high-ranking Left ideologists. However, those Jews who do not consider themselves victims have long adhered to right-wing views.

As for the Jews associated with Leftism, it is always "Leftism *Über Alles.*" Since Napoleon Bonaparte closed Jewish ghettoes in occupied Italy and granted French Jews full civil rights, Jewish existence has been entangled with left-wingers. Metternich-Winneburg, the Austrian consul in Paris, wrote in 1806: "All Jews look upon Napoleon as their Messiah." Since then, many Jews have worshiped false gods, false prophets, and false Messiahs — as long as they exhibit a left-wing stance. However, many American Jews got red-pilled by the cauchemar of the 2023 Hamassacre, and widespread antisemitic atrocities, demonstrations, and threats decisively shifted them into the conservative column.

Jews in the diaspora were commonly treated as second-class citizens, so, being at the mercy of a state, they traditionally relied on local governments to protect them. On the contrary, Israeli Jews do not have that overwhelming dependency on the government. Thus, deprived (by the same local governments) of any means of protecting themselves, Jews in America and Europe tend to be aligned with political forces that favor powerful, illiberal governments—like the Leftist ones. The Leftist governments know that, so they never cease cultivating the status of Jews as "victims" to maintain the reliability of the Jewish voting bloc. One of the tools in their arsenal is administering a "proper dose" of antisemitism periodically. As a result, the watershed between left-aligned American Jews and right-aligned American and Israeli Jews is growing.

If more than 90% of American Jews were on the side of Leftists during the Bush presidency, his successor Obama had in his pocket about 80% of

Jews. (A fall of 10% was traceable to the openly anti-Israeli policy of Obama). With the advent of Trump, the tally of Leftist Jews dropped to about 70%. (Another 10% drop is ascribed to Trump's openly pro-Israeli policy).

This dynamic is analogously present in Israel. In 1948, socialists came to power in the newly reestablished Israel, and the opponents of socialism—the supporters of Vladimir Jabotinsky—were out of work. However, unlike in America, the Leftists in Israel were successfully outmaneuvered by the Conservatives.

This situation parallels the experience of the black population in America. Those who decided to escape from the Leftist political plantation have gained real freedom and ideological preferences of a conservative kind. The proportion of such a populace increased significantly under President Trump. Obviously, it coincided with the lowest amount of black unemployment in the history of America.

If someone decides an individual is a victim, the decision is final, and that person has no right to change it. Do not try to escape the plantation—the punishment will be quick and severe.

However, in being sanctioned "victims," many constituencies forget the reverse side of this coin. In the Left's eyes, if somebody is assigned the status of a victim, then this means that person must remain a victim until the very end. If someone decides an individual is a victim, the decision is final, and that person has no right to change or challenge it. Therefore, do not try to escape the plantation—the punishment will be quick and severe.

The amplitude of "victims" discovered by Globalists is growing. However, their quality and willingness to serve as cannon fodder for socialist transformations are falling. Of course, with time, these internal contradictions will blow up the Leftist movement of Globalists. It will happen when victimhood stops paying political dividends.

NATIONALISM AND GLOBALISM

The government—considered a frame of reference against which everybody is equal—is not the only such frame of reference. Indeed, it is not even the first.

Death is one such frame of reference against which everyone has equal standing; most likely, it is the very first. Unlike many other frames of reference, the death frame of reference is absolute, not relative; it is impossible to redefine the term "death" to bend it toward compliance with the political realities at hand.

"Death, therefore, the most awful of evils, is nothing to us, seeing that, when we are, death is not come, and, when death is come, we are not. It is nothing, then, either to the living or to the dead, for with the living it is not, and the dead exist no longer," said Epicurus in his "Letter to Menoeceus."[68] While Epicurus is undoubtedly relevant in the case of all forms of biological life, it never occurred to the hedonistic Epicureans that many humans have been thinking about, if not defeating, then outmaneuvering death. One such attempt is known as nationalism.

Death is a necessary condition for progress, prosperity, and pride. Without death, nationalism is impossible. Without death, self-organization is impossible. Even if there were creatures in the Universe that could live forever, they would always be in a miserable state. Without destruction, there is no self-structurization. There is no society to speak of, no science to speak of, and no evolution. Generally, there would be no progress despite some individuals' occasional "eureka moments."

Only death, the ultimate form of the necessary creative destruction mechanism of non-linear self-organization, gave rise to nations.

The necessary conditions for the self-organization of material systems in physics are well-known. They are a) the system must behave in a non-linear fashion, b) the system must be dissipative (i.e., energy loss, destruction, or death), and c) the existence of an overabundant external energy source. Humans possess all three necessary conditions; on the contrary, immortals would never be able to self-organize.

Humans realized long ago that we all die—death, at least material death, is undefeated. Thus, society has reoriented itself to deal with this inevitable reality. Millennia ago, the desire to endure eternity was cast off; the plan eventually emerged to develop a commodity that would endure forever. During the 18th century, French philosophers described it as a nation, and the term stuck.

---

68. As translated in Stoic and Epicurean (1910) by Robert Drew Hicks, p. 169.

Human societies self-organize, and as a result, countries are segregated by more than just geographical borders. Countries have distinctive differences stemming from their governments' relationships with those they govern. It is inconceivable that the natural process of co-evolution of humans and their self-organized creations would lead to establishing a single worldwide governing body. That implies not that the endeavors to bring about such a framework will not materialize but that such a structure will be an unattainable Utopia in the end. The probability of arriving at such a power structure is microscopic. The same microscopic probability shall be assigned to another extreme proposition—the absence of any countries whatsoever. Both of these cases indicate that any attempt to establish a World Government is likely to fail (recall numerous attempts by the Mongols, Alexander the Great, the Romans, and Communists). A similar attempt to knock down all nations and borders is doomed to failure.

In 1909, sociologist Georg Simmel, in his short but influential essay "Bridge and Door," proposed that "things must first be separated from one another in order to be together" (Simmel [1909] 1994, p. 5). That implies that humans must separate from one another in order to prosper together—a remarkable line of thinking that existed long before the term "self-organization" entered science and popular discourse. According to Simmel, separation and interconnectedness are integral features of the human experience. A human will always construct doors, bridges, walls, and gates. The absence of a door or a bridge will trigger a human reaction to correct (via a negative feedback loop) this deviation from the self-organizing trajectory. Consequently, Internet-based social networks are merely a means for men and women to distinguish themselves from their peers.

Humans must live separate lives in order to do tasks together. Similarly, each country must handle its own affairs before being involved in global issues.

Thus, humans must live separate lives in order to do tasks together. Similarly, each country must handle its own affairs before being involved in global issues. A similar conclusion can be drawn from Adam Smith's observation that pursuing self-interest is not incompatible with promoting the public interest.

What does nationalism mean? Nationalism is the proper term for the naturally occurring inclination of humans to organize themselves along certain transcendent lines. However, the exact demarcation lines have varied according to different epochs and territories, which led to the emergence of a number of definitions of nationalism in modern times. Such self-organization is not unique to humans; most living organisms tend to form colonies of the same species strictly delimited by territory. Countries in existence today (or, more precisely, the countries that have survived until the present) developed a clear sense of nationhood at one point in the past.

The story does not end here. Instead, the self-organizing phenomenon was isolated, reformulated, and elevated to political philosophy and ideology status. In a sense, the natural tendency of human societies to a statistical transformation from a certain magnitude of chaos to a certain range of order was weaponized for political purposes.

In short, nationalism is a human invention to assert power over the flow of time.

The term "nationalism" obscures two distinct forms of nationalism: the nationalism of the governed and that of the government. Since the government has become self-aware, government nationalism has played an increasingly prominent role in world affairs. In general, government nationalism reaches the stage of chauvinism significantly sooner than the nationalism of the governed. Another notable difference between the two types of nationalism is that only the nationalism of the governed is marked by a common attribute known as patriotism. On the other hand, government nationalism, especially exercised by a Leftist government, does not require patriotism. Instead, it consolidates the governed around specific transcendental issues and contradicts the primary objective of a self-aware government to keep the population disorganized and, therefore, more controllable and manageable.

Penetration of an alien political domain in the case of nationalism is similar to penetration in the case of free speech. To suppress unwanted speech by some of the governed, Leftists often appeal to the government and thus penetrate the government-to-governed domain instead of keeping it inside the society. In the case of nationalism, attempts to bring government nationalism into the governed society are well-known and usually are precursors to war. Such attempts are impossible without a powerful government-sponsored propaganda machine, proving that such penetration is a symptom of deep ideological divisions between the government and the population.

To reiterate, not only religion but nationalism must be separated from the state, along with the economy, science, and education.

Often, what is erroneously perceived as "nationalism" is, in reality, not nationalism, but rather racism, genocide, or ethnocide. However, these ideas are not looking into eternity; on the contrary, they are down-to-earth aggressive mechanisms of imperialism, colonialism, chauvinism, and revanchism. Moreover, these ideas arose on the level of international relations directly from the intra-society level; they are cultivated by centuries-old left-wing ideas of confiscating and redistributing a fellow neighbor's private property.

Beginning with Marx, Leftists despised nationalism; they intended to replace national solidarity with class solidarity. Not to mention, the strong negative connotation of nationalism on the Left could be attributed to the National Socialism of the Third Reich. However, it is just a dishonest linguistic shift. The negative connotation of the National Socialism of the Third Reich lies in its imperialism, not its nationalism. (As we mentioned earlier, the term "National Socialism" was stolen by German Fascists from the rightful owners, Italian Fascists. Also, Leftists have managed to assign a new meaning to nationalism—now it is somehow associated with racism.)

Liberals and nationalists, for some reason unexplained, believe they are on an eternal warpath. True, they are irreconcilable with each other, but for a simple reason: they apply to absolutely different domains. Both are natural results of humanity's self-organization, but classical liberalism (read conservatism) deals exclusively with internal social problems. Liberalism looks inward at society, while nationalism does not look inward or outward—it looks into eternity, and that distinction makes both of them valid but contactless.

Nationalism is a strictly single-level phenomenon; as soon as the self-organization is completed or nearly completed (i.e., a nation has been formed), no second-level (internal) self-divisions are encouraged. Therefore, nationalism as a phenomenon of top-level self-organization cannot be compatible with further self-separation and restructuring of society, such as separatism.

If there is no substantive activity on the dimension of self-organization below nationalism, it does not entail that nothing is above it. Imperialism can be viewed as a fine example of human self-organization that transcends nation-states. Typically, imperialism refers to a system of government that controls or owns other nation-states, either *de jure* or *de facto*.

Self-organization can be born only from chaos; well-organized structures cannot self-organize further. Another order of higher complexity cannot surpass the existing order. Recall the stock market adage, "The stock market trends up historically, but individual stocks fade to zero all the time." Rewording it, one could state that human civilization generally trends up, but individual countries fade into oblivion all the time.

Over time, all "weak" nation-states will disappear, and the world community will be represented only by those countries who survived evolutionary hammerings—the community of "strong" nation-states. These states are sufficiently "strong," meaning that none of them would tolerate a transnational governing body in any configuration that attenuates the state's sovereignty by an iota. It spells doom for all tryouts of the "World Government" or "World Court" or "World Bank." All such institutions may exist in the future, but they will play a purely ceremonial role, like the United Nations or Socintern. These international organizations may have some authority (and even carry some governing attributes), but only for "weak" states. That is why the modern Left is so obsessed with weakening all existing nation-states by using proven and tried mechanisms of panic, fear, and desperation. Realistically, Globalism without "global cooling," "global warming," a "global epidemic," or another global crisis of Biblical proportions is an oxymoron. "Ozone hole," "acid rains," "Bermuda Triangle," "planet Nibiru," and "disappearing polar bears" fit the picture perfectly. For the WEF, it is no longer a "climate crisis" but a "planetary crisis."

> **The WEF and Leftists— like Communists before them—aim toward the same objective. They plan to eradicate nation-states and substitute them with a constellation of unelected transnational global institutions.**

The WEF and Leftists—like Communists before them—aim toward the same objective. They plan to eradicate nation-states and substitute them with a constellation of unelected transnational global institutions. By the way, that is how Anarchists joined the Communists—they also wanted to eliminate the state, so Communists always determined Anarchists a good albeit temporary ideological companion.

As a part of the Leftist movement, Globalists had chosen a "peaceful," non-violent progression to building the empire after the successful military conquest. They utilized the clever methods of Romans, Windsors,[69] Habsburgs, Romanovs,[70] and Bourbons, expanding their influence while respecting local cultures and religions (to a certain degree). These masters of empire-building substantiated that both parties (the Metropole and the colony) made the most by joining the Empire—economically, culturally, and politically.

Ancient empires materialized when, through trial and error, conquerors learned that primitive expansionist warfare works better if the defeated are left to their own devices. That means local administration, ruling elites, and dominant religion are kept intact. Obviously, imperialism has more cash value than the brute occupation of somebody else's unwelcome land. Both nationalism and imperialism represent archetypical society's self-organization, but with a notable difference: nationalism operates in the transcendental domain, while imperialism is a down-to-earth phenomenon. That is why each one's development is quite the opposite of the other's. Moreover, imperialism retains a great deal of diversity amongst the underlying states, while nationalism aims toward the internal homogenization of their respective countries.

Another proper definition of imperial political structure would be an "involuntary federation." However, again, imperialism and nationalism are not mutually exclusive simply because they operate in different realms. Their driving forces represent different spheres, too: imperialism is motivated chiefly by the government, while nationalism is, by large, an area of the governed. In political terms, imperialism falls into the "foreign policy" category, while nationalism is rooted in internal affairs—that is, in theory. The reality, however, is much more complex. Confined to a country's borders, nationalism has a tremendous cash value. However, all attempts to cross the border directly diminish other nations' communication links between generations, and perpetrators must face the consequences.

"Climate change," once upon a time, settled as "global warming," which, in turn, previously reigned as "global cooling," is one of these global wealth

---

69. The House of Windsor is just a made-up name. That name was chosen in 1917 because of anti-German sentiment in Britain during World War I. The House of Windsor is really the German House of Saxe-Coburg and Gotha.

70. The Romanovs are, in fact, represent the German House of Holstein-Gottorp.

redistribution schemes. The climate-related terms must not confuse anyone; the financial redistribution mechanism has nothing to do with climate or Earth's air temperature. Extracting money from developed countries and transferring it to third-world countries has the same end for both sender and receiver: control the former and enslave the latter. Supposedly, money will not be "stolen" from developed countries; everything is planned to be done legally via voluntary international agreements touted as "Climate Accords."

Many consider high energy costs a failure of the "green energy" mantra favored by the modern Left. However, Globalists—often cloaked as environmental activists—have hailed the resulting energy crisis as a success because, in their view, any crisis benefits their cause. For example, in 2021, then-Prince Charles, a militant environmental activist, proposed a "military-style campaign to marshal the strength of the global private sector, with trillions at its disposal," to mitigate the effects of "climate change" (BBC 2021). In effect, Prince Charles considered somebody else's private wealth a legitimate reserve to tap into to achieve Utopian wishes. Per Klaus Schwab, "Rather than using these funds, as well as investments from private entities and pension funds, to fill cracks in the old system, we should use them to create a new one that is more resilient, equitable, and sustainable in the long run. This means, for example, building 'green' urban infrastructure and creating incentives for industries to improve their track record on environmental, social, and governance (ESG) metrics" (Schwab 2020).

Globalists—often cloaked as environmental activists—have hailed the resulting energy crisis as a success because, in their view, any crisis benefits their cause.

Even if it exists, anthropogenic global warming does not justify transferring money from the United States to third-world countries. However, from the Left's point of view, refusing to pay violates the "rights" of yet another "victim of capitalism." These freshly minted "victims" were carefully chosen and got themselves convinced that Western capitalism is the source of all their problems. They even brainwashed their citizens that most of their problems result from "climate change," and the United States is the primary culprit. So, it looks natural for the Left to demand the payment codified in the Paris Climate Accords. Nobody explained that a one-time payment of one trillion dollars (spread over ten years) will not fix "climate change." Nevertheless, the Left's brilliant voters think they can lower the temperature of planet Earth by simply wiring money from the United States Treasury to third-world countries.

The science behind anthropogenic climate change is feeble, but the associated PR campaign is brilliantly executed. Anthropogenic "global warming" is, most likely, non-existent—if one uses the ordinary meaning of words. For the Left, however, "global warming" is as real as it could be because Leftists have assigned a different meaning to the term. As such, it is a primary engine of the Left Imperialism expansion—using somebody else's money (mostly from American taxpayers) to bring on non-Western societies. Note the same setup here as in other modern Left endeavors: they do not own the money but appoint themselves to manage somebody else's money.

Consequently, under Globalism, elite status has changed its meaning too. In the past, "high society" status was determined exclusively by the assets owned, but the Great Resetters planned to redefine the elite status by the Assets Under Management. Under Globalists' schema, elite status no longer requires substantial material wealth; it requires absolute loyalty to party bosses and sincere belief in the Left pantheon of gods. However, adherence to the Leftist ideology does not mean "passive" compliance; being Leftist entails active—sometimes even aggressive—embracing of the Leftist dogma.

In addition, Globalism propels unelected bureaucrats into politically untouchable elites. By definition, the people who control the assets do not own them, so expect Margaret Thatcher's prophecy, "Socialist governments traditionally do make a financial mess. They always run out of other people's money," to materialize on a global scale (Thatcher 1976b). The day global Leftist Utopia is inaugurated will start a timer of its forthcoming downfall, because somebody else's money, measured in trillions of dollars, has the undisputable predisposition to return to its rightful owners.

It is still difficult to understand how the terms "nation" and "national," widely played on in the 19th century to symbolize German unification, have come to have such broad applicability. Moreover, it is unclear whether the term applies outside 19th-century Germany, which comprised about a hundred semi-independent principalities, large and small. Each of these micro-states had its own dialect of the German language and shared a common history and culture dating back a thousand years. So naturally, the movement was born to unify all these micro-princedoms to form a united German "nation." There are many historical causes for the German nationalism of the 19th century, but the main trigger was the Napoleonic dominance of the German lands. As a result, there are currently just four German-speaking countries: Germany, Austria, Luxembourg, and Liechtenstein. Also, some of Belgium and Switzerland are part of the German mosaic and speak German, too.

Right from the start, German politicians had never intended to create just one big, powerful state to confront Imperial France. Instead, Germans concluded that a predominant language, land, economy, and culture could form a state and an entirely distinct concept—a nation.

Initially, nationalism was part of the effort to overcome Napoleon's rule in Germany. So, it is no wonder it was equalized with liberalism at the time (albeit in a 19th-century context). Historically, the distinctions between a "state" and a "nation" were as murky as they are today. Extending the term "nation" into the past, one can easily see instances when a "state" was formed alongside a "nation," but on and off, they were separated over time.

A "nation" may exist without a "state" from time to time and vice versa. In this particular instance, the concept of a "nation" is separate from the concept of a "state." That was true for the fragmented German masses of the 19th century, and it remains true today. Analysis of such differences multiplied, and today, "nationalism," "rights of nations," and finally, the "United Nations" are standard terms. That is irrespective of whether the terms containing "nation" have any applicability outside the German unification struggle of the 19th century.

In the same way that a "state" is a form of self-organization of human society, a "nation" shall also be treated as a form of self-organization. These terms are nuancedly different, and Nicholas Berdyaev was the first to devise a formula to discern between them. His analysis proceeds from the application of the eschatological way of thinking. Berdyaev stated that humans are mortal; therefore, a state or government, as an example of human creation, is also mortal. "Nation" emerged when our ancestors realized the need to self-organize along transcendental lines rather than administrative ones. The newly created self-organized form was intended to achieve what was radically unachievable—immortality. Unlike all other animals, humans have always sought to transcend ordinary biological existence. Our predecessors figured that life is a process while death is an event and focused on life.

Per Berdyaev, "The manner of life of a nation is not to be defined nor explained, be it by race, nor by language, nor by religion, nor by territory, nor by state sovereignty, although all these signs more or less are extant for the national manner of life. And most correct are those who define the nation as an oneness of historical destiny. The awareness of this unity is also what comprises the national consciousness" (Berdyaev [1923] 2015, p. 86). Probably referring to Jews as an example,[71] Berdyaev states that "the nation is not liable to any sort of any rational definitions. No sort of rationally persuasive signs explain its manner of life. All ever farther and afar, into the mysteried irrational depth recedes the lifestyle of a nation in the measure of the application to it of rational psychological or sociological definitions" (Ibid., pp. 85-86). Finally, "[t]he nation is not merely the generation alive today, nor is it the sum of all the generations. A nation is not a mere composite accumulation; it is something primordial, an eternally alive subject within the historical process, it is there live and dwell all the past generations, no less so than the contemporary generations. Nation possesses an ontological core. The national manner of life conquers time. The spirit of the nation forestalls the devouring of the past by the present and the future. The nation is always striving towards imperishability, toward a victory over death, it cannot allow the exclusive triumph of the future over the past" (Ibid., p. 88).

A country is created when its boundaries are drawn, and its administration is set up. A nation is created when a communication link is up and running, connecting the past, present, and future.

Compare Berdyaev's proposition with Edmund Burke, who, in his "Reflections on the Revolution in France," described society as "a partnership not only between those who are living, but between those who are living, those who are dead, and those who are to be born" (Burke [1790] 1899, p. 82).

Berdyaev's nationalism concept casts the issue of mass illegal immigration in a very unusual light. Illegal aliens directly threaten the immortality facet of social self-organization because they alter and disturb—sometimes beyond repair—the communication mechanism connecting past, present, and future generations.

---

71. One of the notable differences between Jews and non-Jews is that Jewish nationalism got a separate name for itself—Zionism—while all other nationalisms are referred to simply as "German nationalism," or "British nationalism," or other "such-and-such nationalism."

Regarding the international Socialist movement, Berdyaev states: "Revolutionary internationalism destroys the past of nations and does not want to allow them to have their own future" (Berdyaev [1923] 2015, p. 90). Revolutionism (a term used by Berdyaev for Leftists) "sunders the bond of time, it annihilates the memory about the past, about ancestry, and it is deeply anti-national" (Ibid., p. 89). International revolutionaries represent a "religion of the all-devouring what is to come has no wish still to concern itself over any connection with ancestors, over the graveyards of their forefathers, over their imperishability and with what they have in common with them in life. The national consciousness is profoundly the oppose to this spirit" (Ibid., p. 89). A half-century later, Margaret Thatcher opined, "A man may climb Everest for himself, but at the summit, he plants his country's flag" (Thatcher 1988).

Berdyaev's theological argument is one of those rare contributions of divine inspiration to the field of *realpolitik*. The illustrated proposal clearly distinguishes between two items. The first is objective, material, measurable, and mortal—a country, its citizens, and its government. The second one is subjective, immeasurable, and immortal—a nation.

As a corollary, the terms "National Conservatism," "National Socialism," or "National Bolshevism" have no meaning as they pursue to unite ununitable mortal and immortal terms. However, as we know, these contradictory terms exist; therefore, we will also use them with a strong reasoning that they can be applied only to a particular historical period and place. That also applies to another commonly reputable term: "nation-state." The term "Christian Nationalism" is also an oxymoron as it unites ununitable items—relationship with God and relationship with time.

The intrinsic transnational feature of Leftism is well-known, but one commonly applied argument against it is based on National Socialism. However, National Socialism makes up an extraordinary case because it is, first, a case of stolen identity.[72] Second, the "National" in National Socialism has an entirely different meaning: it must be read as Aryan, not national. Socialists attack the "national" component of "National Socialism" because attacking the "socialism" part is strictly prohibited. In a sense, it is a method of pretending there

---

72. National Socialism in Germany could be described as the Aryan Brotherhood, a reference to the Muslim Brotherhood, another left-wing political group.

is no link between them. The race-based socialism of the Third Reich had nothing to do with nationalism, but it gave the word its awful reputation. The Third Reich was, in all of its intricacy, a creature of Race Socialism. That particular branch of socialism proved to be more revivable than many other Leftist peers, as the 21-century history of the United States demonstrates. The irrationality of National Socialism fundamentals was complemented by an entirely rational, pragmatic strategy for reaching the signaled principles. The modern Left operates under the same conditions: the irrationality of its ideologies and the rationality of its methods of pursuing Utopia. Note also that after World War II, National Socialism was transformed into Social Justice in the West and Arabic National Socialism in the East.

For the immortality of a nation to triumph, nationalism deploys incommensurable activities. It could be national culture, natural religion, national ideology, or something else "national." However, these attributes are secondary delineators and should be treated as such. That is why nationalism—at least theoretically—could be a feature of the Right or the Left.

Nationalism offered something utterly absent in all other living organisms—an ability to converse with the dead. Not directly, of course, but via intermediaries like the arts and science. That conversation in text form has been ongoing for over five thousand years; in the art form, it has been tens of thousands of years longer. Modern Leftism, like Marxism, rejects all bonds with the past—like nationalism—and considers any transcendental contacts irrelevant. Moreover, Marxists internalize their efforts, for they are convinced that any single country is too small for their grandiose Utopia. The Globalists made a logical step in the same direction by claiming the entire planet as the host of the future Collectivist paradise.

Anybody who declares war on nationalism declares war on Mother Nature. By way of illustration, as a result of natural self-structurization, the mathematical distribution function of urban centers and country population sizes follows an elementary (from a mathematical point of view) family of exponential probability distributions. The mathematical parameters of the distribution of city sizes in the United States and France are practically the same, pointing to the exact self-organization mechanism worldwide (Laherrère 1998). Likewise, country sizes follow the same probability distribution regardless of their continent. Doubtless, it would be Sisyphus's labor altering the result of the natural, multi-millennia evolution of human civilization.

Nationalism may be viewed as the desire to achieve immortality, but patriotism is the means to achieve it. Nationalism attempts to establish a superior, transcendent, eternal component of society. Patriotism is, by contrast, the achievement of an eternal nationalist end by mortals in transient, practical steps. As a set of present-day activities, at least theoretically, patriotism can be suppressed, while nationalism can be inhibited only with the total destruction of a nation. Modern Leftists resist all material efforts of society to pass immaterial treasures from generation to generation.

Stripping off a country's history and symbols does not kill a country; it kills a nation. A country's administration will undoubtedly be in the future in some shape or form after the turmoil, but a nation must rebuild from scratch.

Religion belongs to the same category as nationalism, meaning religion focuses on something immaterial that transcends inevitable mortality. The main difference is that written-in-stone dogmas accompany religions, while nationalism has no written (or even unwritten) rules. Both are products of human self-organization, and both have non-zero cash value, but nationalism, by definition, is open to experimentation and exponentially more flexible than any religion. Nationalism, like religion, proves that some intangible assets can have a measurable, positive cash value.

Another similarity between religion and nationalism is that their influence emanating from the transcendent realm could circle back into physical reality. In both cases, the danger lies in that such a feedback loop channels into society not directly but through the government and by the government. History knows many examples of when a government elevates some religion to a privileged status or amplifies nationalistic overtones. All known attempts spoiled all participating parties: society, government, religion, and nationalism.

Generally speaking, Western nationalism is neither on the decline nor growing. The reality is that the West has a sizable group of people with diminishing nationalism, which, in turn, is fully offset by a sizable group of citizens with increasing nationalism. It is evident that the Left demonstrates diminishing nationalism while the Right displays flourishing nationalism. Since the Left knows itself better than anyone else, it does not view itself in the future; therefore, Leftists do not require even the slightest metaphysical connection to eternity. The Left recognizes that the Utopia that motivates its desires is unachievable and, consequently, condemns itself to exile. Who can pinpoint the exact moment in time when Leftists, who were once deemed progressive, became regressive?

THE HEART AND BRAIN OF GLOBALISM

Colonialism represents the ultimate form of imperialism where one country (a Metropole) owns the other country (a colony) as a whole. In general, imperialism exists as a combination of ownership and control by a Metropole over a colony. Ownership may not be 100%, and control may not be 100%, but the combined effect of the two pillars of imperialism approaches 100%.

If the "old" imperialism preferred the ownership component, the modern Left Imperialism concentrates on the control part of imperialism's equation. Colonialism was never viewed in a negative light by the imperialists of the past. Instead, it was presented as a gift of modernity, civility, and order from a Metropole to a colony. Marx and Engels saw Europe's colonial wars as civilizing missions, too. The founders of Marxism considered white people as the representatives of a superior race and the best hope of bringing the inhabitants of faraway lands out of their barbarous state. Likewise, modern Left Imperialists view themselves as guardians of humanity, not as the planet-wide concentration camp guards they are.

As a result, it would be prudent to cease considering ownership and control of private property as separate entities. Just like electric and magnetic forces are mere manifestations of the fundamental electromagnetic force, ownership and control over private property are two representations of a more fundamental entity that (provisionally) could be denominated "imperodom" (from Latin *imperium*—control and *dominium*—ownership).

In terms of imperodom, the Right-Left discourse is just a tennis match between people and its creation, the state, where imperodom plays the role of the ball. Like an energy conservation law in physics, imperodom also conforms to a conservation law: the total amount of imperodom remains constant in a closed society. In such a society, the only transformation is between a portion of the imperodom allocated to the government and a portion allocated to the governed.

During the glory days of colonialism, "old" imperialism resorted to the divide-and-conquer strategy. Today, the Left uses the same method by theatrically dividing society into a variety of opposing cohorts. While the exact boundaries between these cohorts are arbitrary or non-existent, at any given time, there is a canonical list of "oppressors" and "oppressed."

In traditional Leftist thinking, imperialism embodies the highest stage of capitalism.[73] In their parlance, it means the last stage of capitalism, after which Socialist/Communist Utopia will magically materialize. However, existing data proves the opposite unequivocally: the current state of affairs indicates the final stages of the current incarnation of Leftism, not capitalism. The Left had morphed from the anti-imperialism of post-World War II into its own brand of imperialism. The appropriate generic term for such a stage of the Left's business is Globalism.

During the glory days of colonialism, "old" imperialism resorted to the divide-and-conquer strategy. Today, the Left uses the same method by theatrically dividing society into a variety of opposing cohorts.

In the opinion of some researchers, today's major difference in geopolitics is between globalism and nationalism. That may be true—everything depends on the frame of reference. However, the presented axiomatic political philosophy rejects such a simplification immediately. The dichotomy between "globalism" and "nationalism" is a false one—it exists only for those who have assigned a particular (and not shared by everyone else) meaning to the words "globalism" and "nationalism."

Some people believe that Globalization is a palatable mask that enables a small group of corrupt men to plunder the Western world. Nevertheless, reducing Globalism to a criminal enterprise is evidently simplistic and fails to address these evil men.

Inspired by the unprecedented growth of Islam over a millennium or so, the loose structure Globalists are using was thrown together to mimic Islam's loose, decentralized structure. First, there is no single-point authority worldwide; there are several respectable ideological centers instead. Second, there is no conspiracy; everything is done in the open. Moreover, Globalists want

---

73. Vladimir Lenin drafted his seminal book *Imperialism, the Highest Stage of Capitalism* in 1916. It was published in 1917. Shortly after World War II, the Left, archenemies of capitalism, began a process of rebranding imperialism and incorporating it, along with elements of capitalism, into mainstream Leftist thought.

everything they do to be broadcast as widely as possible. Third, all technological advances of capitalist society are cleverly deployed against the society that manufactured them. Finally, cadres of unfreedom are squeezing every bit of freedom and rights in the post-Enlightenment world to advance their quest.

In other words, modern collectivists run their ideological enterprise precisely like the Internet. Traditional imperialism was always centralized; modern Left Imperialism is deliberately decentralized. The Globalism business has no well-defined head of state, standing army, or borders.

There is no such entity as a "worldwide Leftist conspiracy" or "Globalist cabal." It is often characterized as a grand conspiracy by transnational armchair warriors. However, on the contrary, it is a genuine, open, and well-orchestrated effort that does not hide anything. All the moving parts of the Collectivist movement are scrupulously decentralized. Just as there is no "central computer" for the Internet, there is no "central Committee" of Globalists. All participants in Globalism are operating on autopilot, guided by distinctive but collinear strains of the same ideology. In a more or less uniform manner, local authorities—from the government to education to culture to the military—accept the "official party line" presented by international socialist organizations.

Thus, there is no such thing as a centralized command center for the Globalists. There is no unique location one can nuke to stop the Left's imperialist plans. Due to meticulous decentralization, there is no official "war room" where evil plots are concocted and controlled—and there are no "non-official war rooms" either.

Similar to the term Stochastic Terrorism, Stochastic Leftism uses mass communication to stir up random pre-brainwashed people (commonly known as "useful idiots") to carry out left-wing revolutionary acts. Unsurprisingly, these acts are statistically predictable but individually unforeseeable. The right-wingers employ Stochastic Conservatism, too, but with a caveat—it is seldom violent. Stochastic Leftism is the direct corollary of the decentralized structure of Left Imperialism.

UNRECOGNIZABLE MARXISM

As one of the most radical Leftist theories, Marxism has also been self-modifying. Over the 20th century, Marxism reluctantly renounced its revolutionary aim. Adherents of Marxism have gotten rid of proletarian dictatorship, the inevitability of workers' revolution, and the elimination of private property—all significant precepts of Marxism. While stripping off these secondary attributes—the process analogous to conservatism stripping off its secondary attributes—Marxism (or whatever is left of it) shows its ideological core. In terms of the individual-state paradigm, the epicenter of Marxism is the total dominance of the government over the governed. This core unites all Leftist political philosophies, which is the only thing that remains because the communist motto "Workers of all lands, unite!" has been disregarded, too.

Leftists surrendered the viewpoint of a revolutionary coup at the end of the turbulent but fruitless 1960s, along with Marxism's core clientele: the proletariat. The enslavement of the population via a quick proletarian revolution is no longer speculated as a viable option. Instead, the concerted commitment of modern Leftists became imposing gentle, incremental, practically invisible losses of freedom. They have neglected the idea of acquiring power via the redistribution of somebody else's property and are laser-focused on the issue of control.

In essence, Globalism is the bizarre idea that all humans everywhere should exist under the ideology of collectivist elites that populate the Acela corridor on the East Coast and Hollywood Hills on the West Coast.

Globalism, in other words, resembles alchemy running in parallel with chemistry. Globalists and alchemists use similar methods and share similar Utopian goals, and no one should expect any other end to it.

The Globalists' political weaponization of everything duplicates the old communist idea of militarizing everything. That is to say, Leftists prefer to call concentration camps "re-education camps." Communist Leon Trotsky introduced them to create "labor armies" to ascertain that socialism is more sapient than capitalism. It was intended to crush capitalism by overproducing and out-profiting it based on virtually no personnel expenses in hard labor camps. The National Socialists emphatically liked the concentration camps and stuck with calling them "re-education camps" once they gained power.

Total weaponization has reached science (recall the "global cooling"/"-global warming" hoax); media (recall the complete evolution of modern media into open propaganda outlets, where journalists act as ideological soldiers);

culture (an idea of "Cultural Marxism" by Antonio Gramsci); religion (recall Black Liberation Theology); sports; and many other endeavors.[74]

The election of socialist Barack Obama as President of the United States was the peak of Leftism. That peak was a once-in-a-Millennium event. It allowed for the weaponization of institutions—like the IRS and United States intelligence agencies (CIA, FBI, and others—probably all of them). In the same style, health care was weaponized (Obamacare) along with the United Nations. Trade unions were weaponized around the same time as genitalia and by the same perpetrators. Over and above, President Obama had elevated unions to the scale of political assault weapons (recall the General Motors saga).

> **The election of socialist Barack Obama as President allowed for the weaponization of institutions—like the IRS and United States intelligence agencies (CIA, FBI, and others— probably all of them).**

Of course, Obama inherited much neo-Marxist ammunition from his predecessors, like race. The "race card" is, in fact, one of the Leftists' unparalleled commonly exploited political assault weapons. However, they have practically run out of ammunition. The Democrats have kept the black population on the "Democrat plantation" for too long while conducting anti-black policies. The same applies to American Jews—they finally realized that Leftists used the Holocaust to keep the Jews in the Democrats' orbit while conducting anti-Israel policies. Democrats created the KKK and its modern version, Antifa, but these guys in black outfits suspiciously look like the reincarnation of Mussolini's Blackshirts, so, politically, that was a dead end. In short, the Left's strategic blunder is that it ran out of munitions before it ran out of the fight.

WHAT IS LEFT FOR THE LEFT?

Nothing left for the Left can conceivably be weaponized to satisfy Leftism's power-hungry totalitarian, racist, and antisemitic ideology. The transfer of Donald Trump's private financial records from banks and the IRS into the public domain is embarrassing but not deadly to Conservatism. However, it is

---

74. Black Liberation Theology (BLT) is cold-blooded fusion between pseudo-Christianity and militant Marxism.

deadly for those who still follow the despicable ideology of Leftism because it clearly shows that Leftists are forced to use their scant last reserves.

The ideological affinity of all Leftists means that all these Leftist movements pursue the same portions of the electorate. Perhaps that is why the Soviet Union fought on the side of the Third Reich for about one-third of the Second World War and two-thirds against it. (Compare with other allied countries that ideologically were on the opposite end of the political spectrum, both from the Soviet Union and the Third Reich.)

Collectivists of the 21st century are operating with the experience of Collectivists of the 20th century. Specifically, one of the lessons of the 20th century was the painful (for communists) realization that a well-educated population eventually erodes socialist ideas in a society. The Soviet communists pushed for 100% literacy, which was considered a necessary tool for societal control via indoctrination. However, to the dismay of communists worldwide, the well-educated population started thinking for themselves and pivoted away from Leftism. In a dramatic reversal from the Soviet era, modern Leftists adopted the opposite idea of the stultification of the masses. To put it another way, "cancel culture," the "Woke," and the bouquet of various "critical theories" should be reckoned as not separate, independent entities but elements of the national endarkenment plan. Contemplate, for example, that under Wokeism, new rules of personal hygiene, like the advice for women to check their testicles while in a shower, became commonplace.

> **Leftists have moved from the thesis of mass education to its antithesis of the population moronification. Globalists now consider it the essential element of population control.**

In the past, the Left had the temerity to offer 100% literacy. Today, as a jest about Gramsci's "Cultural Revolution," in a pure Hegelian manner, the post-socialist Leftists have moved from the thesis of mass education to its antithesis of the population moronification, which runs in parallel with the immiseration of the masses. Leftists implement a negative evolutionary feedback loop: when education is substituted with indoctrination, it produces less capable future teachers who, in turn, produce even more incapable teachers and nescience. Globalists, in a funny, absurd, and grotesque form, emulate the attributes of the Third Reich. Globalists' anti-fascist plan is to fight Fascism with re-education (including re-education camps), concentration camps, and total censorship, but the irony of the situation never comes to them. This exercise in pretzel logic is the quintessence of the course toward the deculturation of society. Their thinly veiled game is to plunge the population into an ideologically induced coma. Global mental darkness was not easy to come up with, but the Globalists now consider it the essential element of population control.

At a certain point in their development, all governments-by-coercion began developing novel methods of population control and enslavement. One of these methods is "percussive sublimation" of new, previously unheard "human rights."[75] Recall LGBT "rights," the "right to health," the right to be protected from "microaggressions," and the right to be addressed by "proper pronouns." Note that all these newly discovered "rights" mandate the expansion of state apparatus to maintain and enforce. Offering the population novel "rights" that do not require government expansion is taboo.

The transformation of Leftist thought from intellectual freedom to intellectual GULAG is modern political philosophy's most considerable, unusual, and under-researched evolution. It seems the laurels of the GULAG haunt the Leftists; the number of attempts to reincarnate a mental GULAG under differing names is self-evident. No surprise here: mindlessly following Hegel's dialectics, the Leftists spent the entire 20th century under anti-imperialism flags before self-synthesizing into dedicated imperialists. All the bogeymen that the Leftists used to blame as evil are now on their side—the CIA, the FBI, the Army, the Navy, oligarchs, and an intoxicating social media industry.

Meanwhile, avoiding a decisive ideological battle—discourse on the primary issue within the individual-state paradigm—is a well-established Leftist position. Since the Fabian Society of the 19th century, Leftists have tended to wage ideological battles on secondary attributes. Typically, these attributes are chosen from the bank of commonly disgusting things, like totalitarianism, antisemitism, racism, or the non-ideological sphere, like abortion or environmental pollution. Thus, the modus operandi of Leftists is pretty straightforward. A despicable secondary attribute is forcibly assigned to the Right side;

---

75. The term "percussive sublimation" was coined by Laurence J. Peter and Raymond Hull (Peter and Hull 1969, p. 33).

thus, the discussion instantly ends with fanfare and a victory lap (accompanied, as a rule, by tenure, a think tank, or a TV contributor position).

NEW WORLD ORDER AND PERMANENT CLASS CONFLICT

By now, Marxism, in its entirety, has been refuted. Modern communists and their allies are fighting a battle they have already lost. Over the years, the Marxist electorate has dwindled and gotten older, but it has not gone. However, Marxism's ever-morphing—albeit dogmatic—nature allowed its devotees to hide behind a smokescreen of myriad separate names. While using various camouflaging names, modern Marxists still believe quasi-religiously in the historically transient nature of capitalism. However, the pin is always near the propaganda bubble for ideologies with zero or negative cash value. In other words, such ideologies have little room to maneuver; they are constantly threatened to become extinct. That threat forces adherents of such ideologies to be highly creative in hiding, concealing, and mimicking, and modern Leftists are not an exemption.

Post-Marxism creates an atmosphere of permanent class conflict, where "class" is generalized as a token of race, sex, sexual preferences, nationality, immigration status, and, of course, the dogmatic class itself. Admittedly, Marx's "class" of the 19th century means, today, whatever the current demand of the divide-and-conquer strategy is.

The secret of a Polichinelle is that the Davos-promoted New World Order is just old-fashioned Left Imperialism, and the Great Reset is just an old-fashioned Leftist pre-revolution. The danger of the Great Reset is that it aims to restructure people's lives while leaving the *façade* of government-to-governed relations intact. Harmony of "equity, inclusion, and diversity" is possible, but only within a forced-labor camp whose habitability is wholly dependent on the outside world. However, in the case of the final destination advocated by the Left Imperialism, there will be no "outside world." Instead, the barbed wire will be everywhere, but mostly unseen, to pressure the inhabitants to "own nothing and be happy."

The "own nothing and be happy" catchphrase originated in Danish politician Ida Auken's 2016 article titled "Welcome to 2030: I Own Nothing, Have No Privacy, and Life Has Never Been Better" (Auken 2016). First, it was reprinted on the WEF website; subsequently, the WEF produced a short

90-second video clip containing the phrase "you will own nothing, and you will be happy." However, it is just one of two legs the Great Reset stands on. The second leg (and true objective) is "You will be owned. And you will be happy."

One of the most deranged things about the Globalists is that the general channel of attack, oddly enough, is directed against not a minority, but the majority of the population. The standard political warfare line of assault, which has been tried with unquestionable success many times in history, is an attack against a minority. Yet, for the first time in the history of the West, the country's majority—the white population—is under attack, but it is not the minority that waged the attack. That is another paradoxical sign of our time, especially in the United States, where the white majority is well-armed.

In that case, if neither the majority nor the minority wages the attack, who does?

The perpetrators are from the outside. They utilize an army of useful idiots inside the country to carry out the program of socialist evolution toward the socialist revolution. (Note that such an army, conveniently, was assembled by earlier generations of Leftists.) Thus, the force of the current gamble on revolution is not internal; it is external. However, there is no invading army with a charismatic leader at the helm. Instead, an army of dogmatic keyboard warriors plans a decentralized ideological raid on traditional Western institutions.

In the United States, the self-brainwashed, unarmed, and loosely organized adherents of an evil cult are attempting to attack the well-armed majority of the country. In the past, merely a few such coup businesses were successful—in Russia (but it became a "success" only after a bloody civil war, in which most of the population was disarmed) and in Germany. So how did the Bolsheviks and Nazis manage to pay for their success? They sold the confiscated property. In Russia, the property was confiscated (officially: "nationalized") from the wealthy; in Germany, the property was confiscated from European Jews.

Imperialism and anti-colonialism used to be two opposing forces in the 20th century. First, after World War I, elements of imperialism were incorporated into Left anti-colonialism. Second, the anti-colonialism component of Leftism gradually faded after World War II. Third, Leftists rebranded imperialism. Finally, in the 21st century, the former anti-colonialist forces have joined forces with reformulated imperialism. The pendulum has swung.

All instances of Fascism (in Italy, Germany, Spain, and the Soviet Union) had adopted, at least in part, the ideas of Left Imperialism. Note that post-World War II decolonization was promoted by the Soviet Union exclusively for its imperial aspirations. As we witnessed numerous times, the Left had weaponized decolonization to expand its influence and enslave other countries.

On the surface, the immigration policies of Leftists look like replacing whites with non-whites to improve their vote tallies. However, it is not the whole idea but a side effect. Instead, as stipulated by the Cloward-Piven strategy, the drive is to create multidimensional chaos in Western democracies to pave the road for The Revolution (cultural disintegration, political disintegration, racial disintegration, and national disintegration in general). Thus, with all due sympathies to folks from third-world countries who endure horrific suffering under various inhumane regimes (add authoritarian stereotypes here at will), they are used and abused as unwitting accomplices for the Left Imperialists.

Mancur Olson insisted that "the 'Marxian' revolutions that have taken place have been brought about by small conspiratorial elites that took advantage of weak governments during periods of social disorganization. Not Marx, but Lenin and Trotsky provided the theory for this sort of revolution. See Lenin's *What Is to Be Done* for an account of the communist's need to rely on a committed, self-sacrificing, and disciplined minority, rather than on the common interests of the mass of the proletariat" (Olson 1971, p. 106).

Davosists consider themselves part of that exclusive club of the "committed, self-sacrificing, and disciplined minority."

WHENCE WOKEISM?

Why did the explosion of "Woke" ideas happen in the 21st century, even though the Leftists three or four generations ago—in the Third Reich—already embraced similar "Woke" tendencies? The Nazi slogan *Deutschland Erwache* (literally "Woke Germany") was popular in the Third Reich. It was commonly depicted on banners below the swastika. A simple Internet search produces numerous results on the subject. Most likely, modern "woke" activists have no idea where the term originated from. Why did the "Woke" lie dormant for so long? To answer this question, one must ask yet another guiding question: "What comes first—Globalization or 'Woke'?"

Once it is put in these terms, it should be clear that the "Woke" came well after the Left took the helm of economic globalization, thus creating political Globalization with a capital G. The direct material beneficiaries of Left Imperialism are the same personages who promote the "Woke" ideological dogmas. They are the new elite (or at least they think about themselves as such), the new ruling class, and the self-anointed emissaries of the future global Utopia.

> **The "Woke" came well after the Left took the helm of economic globalization, thus creating political Globalization with a capital G.**

The ascendancy of the religion of Wokeism requires that the opposing forces—conservatism—were practically dormant. In contrast, conservatism had played an active, corrective role in the wake of the Soviet-inspired pre-revolution in Paris in 1968. It highlights a feature of conservatism—acting as part of an ideological negative feedback loop that dampens wild swings deviating from the main path of social development. Note that no complex system is stable without some negative feedback that would hold runaway events at bay.

One of the modern reincarnations of Leftism—"Wokeism"—is thriving because it exemplifies a cult within a cult. So, the only (rhetorical) question still up for debate is this: Is Leftism a Cult of Victimseekers within a cargo cult, or does it represent a cargo cult within the Cult of Victimseekers?

The "Woke" promised a lot to many cohorts of "victims." Each cohort of freshly minted revolutionaries got the exact promises its members wanted to hear, while the Left is meandering from one failure to the next. Left-wing ideas tend to reincarnate under different labels; thus, the permanent class struggle morphed into the idea of permanent revolution. Nowadays, it has been customarily reintroduced as permanent victimhood. It seems that Wokeism was born in the so-called first world with only one aim: transforming it into the third world. However, the problem is not Wokeism per se but the attempt to oblige it as the compulsory state ideology.

The natural progression of every form of Leftism—regardless of the starting point—ultimately sets globalist aspirations and ideology in motion. On that path, the existence of independent thinking and independent choice must be erased, for it is mandatory to implement a bee-hive mentality. Globalism cannot survive without a single ideology ruthlessly enforced by various structures within the human hive. They envision a society with a clearly defined hierarchical structure under an ideological monopoly, with "Woke" patricians at the top. The heads of nation-states (Presidents, Kings, Prime Ministers, etc.) would be collectively renamed Gauleiters of the Global Reich. In other words, the old Marxist slogan "Workers of all lands, unite!" got reestablished by Globalist promoters of the Global Nanny State into "Commissars of all lands, unite!"

The Great Reset aims toward nothing less than a revolution because it drastically alters elite status, like any other Leftist revolution. Upon completion, commissars will be taking shots instead of "greedy capitalists." Furthermore, the Left commissars intend to steward somebody else's private property to the degree that would mold them utterly indistinguishable from the legal owners.

"Save the planet" means commissars. "Use proper pronouns" means commissars. "Men can menstruate" means commissars. "Diversity" and "equity" mean commissars.

It took the Leftists three generations since the Communist Manifesto to successfully try the newly formalized socialist game plan. Multiple failed installations followed that initial experiment by the Russian Bolsheviks for another five generations. During that time, the intergenerational discussions within all strains of Collectivism were enduring and, as one can attest, not fruitless, eminently on the cultural and educational fronts.

The Left Imperialism is the latest and paramount achievement in the Left's philosophical toolbox. Globalism is the culmination of two centuries of left-wing thought. Inarguably, the modern Left has learned the lessons of all hitherto failed proceedings to reach the Socialist Utopia and betrayed one of the primary tenets of Socialism—forced redistribution of wealth from the wealthy to the poor. The track record of doing just that is well-known: every time such redistribution was tried, it led to massive terror and/or civil war. Instead, the Left has climbed to the next stage of abstraction, where compulsory wealth redistribution is applied not between individuals but between countries.

Followers of Marx claim that the essence of capitalism is the exploitation of workers by other people designated as exploiters. However, the modern

Left has a different modus operandi; to use Marxist language, they aim to exploit exploiters.

Of course, the Left Imperialists reject the notion that they are imperialists. They do not think of themselves as power usurpers or property pillagers but are, for all intents and purposes, pillagers pretending to be a Collective Emperor. However, unbeknown to these wannabe Emperors-Commissars, they will eventually not survive contact with reality by worshipping the half-baked version of Marxism. So instead, they erected an over-hyped ideological colossus that children, brainwashed by postmodernism and intellectually mal-adjusted, constructed.

Because the Great Reset argues for corporations established and managed by governments, it should come as no surprise that these administrative-business units receive protection from governments, including various tax and monetary stimuli and financial bailouts. Such bailouts—straight from the Fascist playbook—have become the norm since the second half of the 20th century. One of the consequences of the Great Reset would be the complete insulation of politicians and corporate leaders from constituents (read: second-class stakeholders).

Fascism was Leftism with a bonus: imperialism. Likewise, the National Socialism of the Third Reich was Leftism with a bonus: racism. Soviet (International) Socialism had offered the Left two bonuses: imperialism and anti-colonialism. No, it was not the cognitive dissonance of the Soviet Politburo. Soviet leaders utilized decolonization rhetoric only to mask their imperialist ambitions. Soviet anti-colonialism was monodirectional; the targets were strictly "capitalistic regimes." Countries that announced a socialistic development path were summarily turned into *de facto* Soviet colonies, and Soviet imperialists strictly prohibited anti-colonial movements in such countries. This monodirectional, cynical stratagem was spotted by Herbert Marcuse, who generalized and propagandized it in his best-known paper, "Repressive Tolerance."

Finally, Globalism represents a strain of Leftism on steroids with a bonus: imperialism on steroids. The Globalist's plot is to amass a transcontinental empire unheard of before—a Leftist decentralized Leviathan on a global scale, where every country on Earth will have colony status. Globalism is likely the logical endpoint of Leftism—at least for the 21st century.

The proposed so-called "Great Reset" structure is unique. So, when

Leftists claim that Socialism in the such-and-such country has failed because "it was not true Socialism," it must not be rejected outright. What they are trying to bring to fruition has genuinely never been tried. It was a long and painful learning curve for the Left. By now, they have given up on a) the idea of permanent revolution, b) the idea of a single worldwide country ruled by a single government (read: United Nations), c) the idea of National Socialism, d) the idea of International Socialism, e) the idea of bankrupting the rich, f) the idea of enriching the poor, and, finally, g) the idea of Socialism as a transitional phase and springboard to Communism. Moreover, the Great Reset has junior partners—Chinese communists, Socintern-affiliated progressives, Trotsky's Fourth International,[76] and post-Soviet pro-Soviet followers in Africa and Latin America—who are not sitting idle in the inter-Left race to worldwide leadership.

The latest cadres of the wannabe global dictators—Left Imperialists—were always searching for the smallest administrative unit's optimal (from the management standpoint) size. After the League of Nations failed, the United Nations was born; however, it was built on the same foundation: its smallest administrative unit is a nation-state. Today, the United Nations is the place where the *brüderschaft* ritual is practiced between different strains of Leftism.

Then, the idea of a "multipolar world" came to the front pages. It promoted the establishment of "regional blocks" of countries as the smallest administrative unit of global governance. The Davosians went even further by implicitly recanting sovereignty altogether, for their *idée fixe* of the primary administrative unit is a transnational private-public partnership. Thus, instead of contesting the existing borders, the Left Imperialists decided to circumvent them by forming a transnational control structure. The WEF aims to erode national sovereignty without altering any existing borders. Globalists are trying to centralize political power in an openly decentralized way. In other words, the "multipolar world" is a euphemism for the Globalists' unorthodox planet-wide administration. In this, the modern Left follows The Communist Manifesto: "the Communists are further reproached with desiring to abolish countries and nationality" and "the working men have no country."

The United Nations seems to have brought to an end its aspirations

---

76. Fourth International, a revolutionary socialist international organization, was founded by Leon Trotsky in 1938, in opposition to Stalin-controlled Third (Communist) International, and still exists.

for establishing a World Government. Thus, the Socialist International (Socintern) has failed to establish a World Government through the United Nations. That New York-based bastion of Socintern has lost its evolutionary race and abdicated in favor of another Leftist institution—the World Economic Forum. Many other previously influential people and institutions have folded under the WEF's weight. In a sense, the WEF is not a self-appointed leader of the global Left. On the contrary, it is a more or less legitimate umbrella organization that managed to unite many formerly incoherent branches of Leftism.

The Left Imperialism produced a sophisticated, well-discoursed scheme of permanent Socialism. *De jure*, nations will be allowed, albeit headed by marionette governments. However, *de facto*, the New World Government will be at the helm, controlling all aspects of each country's economic, cultural, religious, and political life. Unquestionably, the Left wants to convert every country into a wholly owned and fully dependent subsidiary (read: colony) of the New World Government. The dogmatic creed of Marxism will be abstained from, for economic relationships within the confines of the colonies will no longer be tethered to classical capitalism or classical socialism. (Note that they will retract the old Marxism with a straight face, claiming that it was insufficiently nuanced.) The exact ratio of public-private partnerships will be monitored, and the desired value of "equity" will be strictly enforced by the New World Government. (In this, it looks like the Globalists adopted a significant part of the Chinese communists' economic model.) The Left has not directly left the "old" Marxism in the cold. Instead, the Left offered the generalization of Marxism, the generalization on a radically different, higher, and never-targeted planetary scale. The term "post-Marxism" seems assuredly proper here, but "trans-Marxism" would do, too.

> **The Left wants to convert every country into a wholly owned and fully dependent subsidiary (read: colony) of the New World Government.**

According to Margaret Thatcher, "Personal freedom and economic freedom are indivisible. You cannot have one without the other. You cannot lose one without losing the other" (Thatcher 1976a). So, inhabitants of the Left Imperialist colonies would lose their economic freedom, and personal freedom would follow. With Globalists, master-slave economic relationships will be elevated to the level of Metropole-colony economic relationships.

Customarily, the Left's solution to a problem is to do more of the same thing that created that problem in the first place. With Globalism, the Left offered something original. Nevertheless, even the newly hatched imperialism is still Leftist in nature, albeit more rigorously vetted and researched. Unfortunately for Utopia, even the generalization of Marxism is destined to fail for the same reason classical Marxism and the Left, in general, failed everywhere.

As maintained by Collectivists, blatant confiscation (read: stealing) of the fruits of people's labor was supposed to bring about unending prosperity. Pumping out wealth from one subset of citizens and dumping it on another subset of citizens was always considered by Collectivists as the greatest invention of all time, a Perpetuum Mobile, a permanent wealth-equalizing machine. Nobody told the Social Justice Warriors that such a confiscatory machine could exist for a limited time; its existence is limited by the ratio of targeted wealth to the velocity of pumping it out.[77] This limitation is unique because it applies across all confiscatory scales—individual, societal, and global.

TOTAL CONTROL AND PERMANENT REVOLUTION

In retrospect, the evolution of Leftist thought was pretty straightforward. Collectivists started from "oppressed individuals," after moving to "oppressed classes," and afterward arrived at the "oppressed nations." The social experiment with the "oppressed nations" (in Mussolini's Italy and the Third Reich) had failed, so the Left instinctively fell back to the proven strategy—the current grandiose expansion of "oppressed classes" is at the top. If the original "oppressed class" included just workers, now it includes women, minorities, racial minorities, sexual minorities, and many others. As for the failed Fascist experiment, the Left analyzed it and concluded that total wealth redistribution—singularly forced redistribution—is not a winning strategy. So, the Left intellectual cadre decided to drop this requirement until better days. Markedly, they, *à la* Third Reich, picked up the mantra of "control" as the

---

77. The popular anecdote in the last years of the Soviet Union was "Russian tsars over 300 years accumulated wealth that lasted for only 70 years."

panacea for the unreachable Utopia.[78]

One of the arguments in favor of describing Left Imperialism as the natural, predetermined next step in the left-wing thought process is based on analysis of the final destination, the cherished Utopia. The end state of society—a stateless society—is characterized by absolute material equality. Most Leftist thinkers have concluded that absolute material equality, if reachable, will lead to a stagnant state of affairs due to the absence of any incentives. The resulting Utopian society will eventually weaken and could be easily conquered by neighboring capitalist countries. Comrade Trotsky pioneered such a line of thought. As a practical matter, it means that the Left paradise on Earth, to survive, must be established in all countries almost simultaneously (in a historical timeframe). As it is known, Trotsky reused and generalized (and redefined) the long-existing Marxist term "permanent revolution" to describe it. Currently, the concept is fully integrated into Globalism.

In the introduction to the first edition of his book in 1931, Trotsky wrote, "The socialist revolution begins on national foundations—but it cannot be completed within these foundations" (Trotsky [1931] 2010, p. 146).

Trotsky continued, "The maintenance of the proletarian revolution within a national framework can only be a provisional state of affairs, even though, as the experience of the Soviet Union shows, one of long duration. In an isolated proletarian dictatorship, the internal and external contradictions grow inevitably along with the successes achieved. If it remains isolated, the proletarian state must finally fall victim to these contradictions. The way out for it lies only in the victory of the proletariat of the advanced countries. Viewed from this standpoint, a national revolution is not a self-contained whole; it is only a link in the international chain. The international revolution constitutes a permanent process, despite temporary declines and ebbs" (Ibid.)

In essence, Trotsky's thought was based on the fact that the economy is not isolated inside a country; it has a global nature. When the Left successfully hijacked Americanism, they sought a system that would—finally!—deliver the linking of all countries into Trotsky's "international chain." The detailed argument about the "economic and political untenability of national

---

78. Schwab's book *Shareholder Capitalism* is The Control Manifesto by modern Leftists.

socialism" (Trotsky [1931] 2010, p. 148) was published by Trotsky three years earlier, in 1928 (Trotsky [1928] 1957). By all means, the internalization of revolutionary movements was just one aspect of Trotsky's multifaceted methodology. The others—like the transformation of the bourgeois revolution into a socialistic one—are mostly irrelevant to the current state of affairs.

Note that Trotsky applied the term "national socialism," referring to Stalin's tactic of building socialism in one country; his viewpoint on the term has nothing to do with another branch of socialism, German "National Socialism." Nevertheless, these terms did coexist back in the 1920s, which was the cause of many misunderstandings that still exist and are not thoroughly clarified.

Trotsky's argument against the Utopian idea of establishing a socialist economy in a single country is pretty straightforward: "Marxism takes its point of departure from world economy, not as a sum of national parts but as a mighty and independent reality that has been created by the international division of labor and the world market, and that in our epoch imperiously dominates the national markets. The productive forces of capitalist society have long ago outgrown the national boundaries. The imperialist war (of 1914-1918) was one of the expressions of this fact. In respect of the technique of production socialist society must represent a stage higher than capitalism. To aim at building a nationally isolated socialist society means, in spite of all passing successes, to pull the productive forces backward even as compared with capitalism" (Trotsky [1931] 2010, p. 160).

Trotsky stressed the "supra-national character of modern productive forces" (Ibid., p. 167). He asserted that "productive forces created by capitalism are not adapted to national markets, and can be socialistically coordinated and harmonized only on an international scale" (Ibid., p. 169).

"The seizure of power by the international proletariat cannot be a single, simultaneous act" (Ibid., p. 170), and the world socialistic revolution "unavoidably extends over decades" (Ibid.) Over a century ago, Trotsky ridiculed any country's attempts to gain independence from the world markets—even in the case of the isolated Soviet economy.

Trotsky characterized Stalin's program as "ideological garbage, an official manual of narrow-mindedness, an anthology of enumerated banalities" (Ibid., p. 178). Stalin's answer was a pickaxe in the hands of Spanish communist Ramon Mercader, who worked for Stalin's secret police, the NKVD.[79] Modern Leftists are desperately trying to avoid being blamed for producing an "anthology of enumerated banalities." Their answer has been crystallized after a lengthy learning curve, after several preliminary attempts like the United Nations, the Socialist International, Soviet Imperialism, the Club of Rome, and so on. They vested their latest hope in the World Economic Forum.

Meanwhile, control by itself never led to the desired result. On the contrary, control over people, industries, or even countries added not an iota to the radical Left plans. So, the convergence of Fascists' total control idea and Trotsky's permanent revolution idea was practically inevitable.

Enthralled by the Siren call, billionaires voluntarily sell their souls to Collectivist gods, guaranteeing their lives will be profit-rich and problem-free (or so they think).

Modern Leftists no longer practice left-wing economics; their economic foundations have little to do with 20th-century planned, socialist economics, where private property is outlawed. The World Economic Forum is a Siren that removes probably the worst headache for billionaires—the delivery of corporate profit. The ideological justification behind the World Economic Forum scenario guarantees a certain degree of profit. Enthralled by the Siren call, billionaires voluntarily sell their souls to Collectivist gods, guaranteeing their lives will be profit-rich and problem-free (or so they think). The WEF is just another grandiose Leftist project to dominate the world. Before WEF, there were Socintern, Comintern, Nazi, Socintern again in the form of the UN, the Club of Rome, and Bilderberg—the list demonstrates the highly competitive field. WEF, the Club of Rome (currently a shell of its former glory), and Bilderberg (which also seems to have gone by the wayside) represent attempts to analogize the Soviet Politburo. The Soviet Politburo was a gerontologic structure with absolute power over the vast Soviet Empire spanning Europe, Asia, Africa,

---

79. Mercader was sentenced and served all 20 years in a Mexican prison. Upon his release in 1960, he moved to Moscow, where he received the highest Soviet decoration—the Hero of the Soviet Union Award—almost a decade after Stalin himself was murdered by poisoning.

and Latin America. The Soviet-inspired Left Internationalism (implemented via Socintern and Comintern) was a primitive form of Globalism. However, nobody officially used the term "Soviet Empire"—it was an imperial entity without a name. The WEF aims for a similar nameless setup.

Enter the Total Ideological War.

The French journalist Leon Daudet introduced the term "total war" on February 9, 1916, at the peak of World War I, after the first major aerial bombardment of Paris (from a dirigible), in which twenty-six people died.[80] German General Erich Ludendorff popularized Daudet's *La Guerre Totale* in his 1935 book *Der Totale Krieg*. General Ludendorff (who gambled on sending Lenin into Russia in 1917 with millions in hard currency to trigger a revolution to make peace with Russia and succeeded) also coined the term "*Ueberstaatliche Maechte*" (Supranational Powers). Ludendorff assumed that such powers were held by Jews, Masons, Marxists, and Catholics. In other words, he was a Nazi long before the Nazis came into existence. In contrast to Clausewitz's adage that war is a continuation of politics by other means, Ludendorff was a follower of a Darwinian vision of international politics. As such, he considered war the fundamental principle of international relations.

Total ideological war pits the political energies of opposing segments of society against each other, so any opposition member—individual, corporate, or institutional—is classified as a legitimate target. It is an all-out ideological conflict, and the Left is proficient in waging it. The essence of Ludendorff's total war concept is that modern warfare is not a war of professional armies but a war of nations. Likewise, a total ideological war is a battle not between professional politicians but between opposing political machines. Therefore, everyone participates in the total ideological war in one way or another, and everyone—from children to retirees—is a valid target.

The remarkable parallel between total war and total ideological war is that before World War II, the term "total war" and its meaning were known only to a limited circle of military strategists. Likewise, the term "total ideological war" did not exist. However, immediately after World War II, military and ideological approaches took off dramatically.

---

80. Leon Daudet was son of Alphonse Daudet, the author of *Tartarin of Tarascon*.

The Left's total ideological war demands that all entities—government institutions, media, universities, artists, librarians, sexual perverts, teachers, doctors, the entire demographic mass, everything, and anything—must be placed at the disposal of political leaders and ideological activists. "The end justified the means" is not just a pop slogan, but an operational manual for the Left.

Paraphrasing William Gibson, one can conclude beyond reasonable doubt that Left Imperialism, as a worldwide phenomenon, is already here—it is just not evenly distributed. British politician William Harcourt famously remarked in the House of Commons in 1894, "We are all socialists now." In the 21st century, quite accurately, John Lukacs despairingly observed, "Considering the ubiquity of the welfare state—we are, at least in one sense, all national socialists now" (Lukacs 2005, pp. 40-41). Modern Collectivists are not the ingenious political operatives of the 20th century who built the Leftist machinery under the guidance and support of the Soviet Union. At the helm of Leftism in the 21st century are their offspring—Globalists. Drunk on entitlement, they keep the pedal to the floor while racing to the cliff of the ideological abyss.

Leftists will continue to cannibalize their elements. However, that process is not endless—it will stop when their collective fantasy runs out of victims' categories.

In the near future, Leftists will continue to cannibalize their elements. However, that process is not endless—it will stop when their collective fantasy runs out of victims' categories. The asymmetrical nature of society's development (provided, in part, by conservatives) guarantees that Leftist ideas eventually will occupy the place in the ideological sphere currently populated by many other old ideas without positive cash value. No, it is not a graveyard—we are destined to live with such ideas forever—but their influence will be as harmless as "knock on wood" or "Friday the 13th" ideas.

LEFT IMPERIALISM

Geoeconomics is in an intricate relationship with geopolitics. Sometimes, they are synchronized and sometimes out of step because there is no effective negative (corrective) feedback mechanism in international relations. The chances that such a mechanism would magically appear are slim, which returns us to the alternative idea of geoconservatism. That idea would make all governments too weak to even think about aggressive or unfriendly moves against their citizens or neighbors. That is Utopian, of course, but only to a degree, because such a power structure worldwide would constitute a desired negative feedback mechanism. The existence of sufficiently small-scale governments that would barely deal with issues of garbage, crime, and highways is on a collision course with the One World Government under Globalism.

Bolsheviks have worried about a socialist economy surrounded by a free-market economy since taking power in Russia in 1917. Likewise, free-market economies must worry about socialist economies because, as Trotsky assuredly showed, no country can be completely insulated from the outside world. That means non-free-market economies can impose policies that directly or indirectly affect free-market economies by utilizing the state's power. Weaponized domestic economic policy can produce a range of disastrous outcomes in the international arena—from a mere distortion of free-market mechanisms to outright enslavement of foreign economic sectors. Unfortunately, the Chinese communists are doing just that.

The prolonged coexistence of two different economic schools disproportionally damages the free-market ones because they, by definition, do not have the same powerful ally as the state. Foreign government intervention in their economy influences all other economies in the interconnected world. Protectionism may help control foreign adversaries' predatory practices in the short term, but it certainly hurts in the long run.

The only feasible solution to the problem is the original American political-economic model: a protective external shell and soft internal (economic) tissue. A conservative state must act in the international arena as ruthlessly as socialist ones and, at the same time, protect its domestic prosperity. In addition to a limited number of internal regulations, an enormous number of external regulations must be enacted. These international regulations must be strictly enforced. No one country can achieve that alone; geoconservatism assumes all free-market economies must establish a joint front against non-free-market ones.

Modern Leftists (American Democrats, for example) are more truthful than their predecessors. They do not hide their ultimate (Utopian) pernicious agenda and work tirelessly on the intermediate—and reasonably achievable—ambition of setting up the behemoth government, the unprecedented tyranny of the state Leviathan. Here lies one of Leftism's most noticeable logical fallacies—the apparent disconnect between the ultimate idea of a stateless society (communism) and the intermediate mark of an all-powerful and all-knowing state apparatus. Are Leftists that stupid? Most likely, the answer is no. The most obvious answer would be that modern Leftists would stop after establishing government tyranny in a limited set of countries and then enforce tyrannies upon the rest. For them, there is nothing to pursue after establishing the worldwide *GULAG* and pole-to-pole *Gestapo*.

To conclude, there are two ideological Utopias (recall that "utopia" in Greek means "nowhere"). Both the Right and the Left camps claim that their Utopia would maintain peace among nations. However, these camps talk about different visions of peace. The left-wing Utopia is a peaceful transcontinental *Konzentrationslager* where nation-states may exist but play only a ritual role. The right-wing Utopia is a harmonious brotherhood of countries with so emasculated government apparatus that they constantly struggle to allocate resources for picking up garbage. However, while living in the right-wing Utopia is flourishing, it is inherently unstable. The moment one—even a tiny country—starts military aggression, there is nobody (unless they adopt the American model of having a hard external shell and internal soft tissue) to stop it. On the contrary—and that is the main danger of the Great Reset master plan—the left-wing Utopia is an exemplary island of stability and corresponding shared misery.

The two centuries of formalized Leftism have no parallels in human history. However, history rhymes, and in this case, it rhymes with the fate of famous 1930s German car racer Manfred von Brauchitsch. Born to a wealthy Prussian family, he won several prestigious races, but from 1934 to 1939, he won only three out of forty-five races. Still, it is pertinent to note how exactly he lost these races. In most of the races, von Brauchitsch led the pack, speeding to inevitable victory, and then, close to the finish line, something always happened. Either a tire blew up, he got outmaneuvered on the last lap, blinded by the Sun, or something else. For being "chronically second," he got the nickname "*die Pechvogel*"—the unlucky bird. Likewise, Leftism had its glory days, but it is an unlucky bird now. Leftism celebrates victories less often, even if the cacophony of Leftist commentariat dominates the mass media and trumpets that Leftism is on the verge of winning. That triumph, always "at spitting distance," proves to be elusive because people refuse to embrace dystopian, revolutionary insanity.

Globalism is a revolution of the governing elites, by the governing elites, and for the governing elites. Globalism is a top-down phenomenon; it differs from all previous left-wing revolutions, which were driven in the opposite direction, albeit with the same vision. That is why the order of events is different, too: under the Left Imperialism, tyranny comes first, and the actual revolutionary coup may come second. On the contrary, all previous attempts to reach Leftist Utopia began with a revolutionary coup and ended with tyranny.

> **Globalism is a revolution of the governing elites, by the governing elites, and for the governing elites.**

The Left Imperialism is a textbook example of government elites crossing the government-to-governed boundary and penetrating the intra-society domain. That is a monumental task because society is bound by volumes of unwritten rules and traditions, some of which could be easily traced to the cavemen epoch. It explains why modern Leftists meticulously follow Gramsci's "Cultural Marxism" recipe: to "soften the target."[81]

However, the penetration of Leftism into more and more institutions of society has some unexpected consequences: the Left huddles itself into a self-imposed ideological ghetto. Over the last two centuries, the Left has withdrawn any reference to political philosophies and economic systems that history seems to have discredited. That is why no elite Davosians who practice nihilistic self-worship promote communism or even socialism. Marxism, Communism, and Socialism are eponymous words for misery and the absence of toilet paper. These terms are anathema to the modern Left playbook. Nobody in his mind on the Left would promote Fascism or National Socialism by their actual names. They learned their lesson. They invented a universe of obscure smokescreen terms, like "shareholder capitalism." Only

---

81. Christopher Rufo (2023) created a comprehensive compendium of radical Left activities in the United States on the Cultural Marxism front.

conservatism and capitalism do not have the urge to hide behind a veil. The global Collectivist movement thinks they have found a way to enslave the world population for the last time. They are no longer rooting for a bottom-up revolution. Instead, they unequivocally identified the Achilles heel of conservatism: national borders.

For those familiar with the largest segment of the United States federal budget—entitlements—the Great Reset will appear as a pretty familiar albeit exceedingly grandiose schema involving not only individuals, but corporations and governments as recipients. In other words, the Great Reset could be renamed the Great Redistribution, practiced and tested by Leftists worldwide. Meanwhile, Globalists plan debt, borders, elections, taxes, wages, sovereignty, and free-thinking irrelevant by resetting their meanings. That is why it is called the Great Reset.

The Right Utopia is attainable but unstable. The Left Utopia is unreachable but theoretically stable.

While the ground zero of both the Left and the Right ideologies are Utopian, there is a noticeable difference. Namely, the Right Utopia is attainable but unstable. However, along the path to the final destination, the Right society is more or less stable and burgeoning (but does not guarantee a crisis-free or worry-free existence). Alternatively, the monoideological Left Utopia is unreachable but theoretically stable. It plausibly looks like the modern Left has chosen not a Utopia but a movement toward Utopia as an end in itself. The final destination for the Left is an ossified, worry-free, and crisis-free society; life in such a society resembles a concentration camp from which there is no escape because the camp covers the entire planet. The left-wing endeavors are endless, fruitless prologues toward tyrannical paradise. Interestingly, prison guards are prisoners in such a society, too, because the Left is trying to build an artificial black hole that offers humans no escape.

They plan to build a worldwide Panopticon, an ideal prison for the non-ideal, non-ideologically compliant public. However, the compliant ones, along with the watchful wardens, will be in adjacent cells. So, everybody will be happy, controls and control-nots.

The Left's focus on the movement toward Utopia instead of the Utopia itself has a long history. For example, in a January 1889 article for the official organ of German Socialists, *Die Neue Zeit*, prominent socialist Eduard Bernstein wrote probably his most memorable meme, "I frankly admit that I have extraordinarily little feeling for, or interest in, what is usually termed 'the final goal of socialism.' This goal, whatever it may be, is nothing to me, the movement is everything" (Bernstein [1899] 1993, p. xxviii).

After the predictable furor, later in 1899, Bernstein noted that "My proposition 'that what is usually termed the final goal of socialism is nothing to me, the movement is everything' has often been seen as a rejection of every definite goal of the socialist movement, and Mr. George Plekhanov has even discovered that I have quoted this 'famous sentence' from the book Towards Social Peace by Gerhard von Schulze-Gavemitz." In the words of Raymond Aron, Marxism is ambiguous and inexhaustible; likewise, the attempts to reach the Left Utopia are inexhaustible—just because "the movement is everything."

The conflict between the Right and the Left is not the struggle between the right and the wrong because a) the terms are shifting, and b) the definitions of the terms are evolving. One can easily find examples when the Right and Left parties borrowed the positions of their foes. Generally speaking, the Right and the Left, from a historical position, frequently fought non-overlapping political battles. Under the individual-state paradigm, the Right and the Left have achieved clear antagonistic and dialectical status. From Heraclitus's "unity of opposites" perspective, they are just two antipodean forces behind the evolution of freedom. Quintessentially, the Left is not intrinsically Evil per se; it is rather self-euthanizing and self-resurrecting. The Left could be compared with Goethe's words about Mephistopheles in "Faust" as "part of that force that always wills the Evil and always produces the Good."

Collectivism capitulates to freedom—promoted by Conservatism—not because Good always triumphs over Evil but because collective psychosis and stupidity inevitably yield to reason.

The common opinion is that Nazis radicalized Marxism. In reality, Nazism is a predictable, legitimate, and logical development of the general Leftist ideas, floating around for just enough time that somebody would dare to implement them. However, modern Collectivists mask their Fascist essence with anti-fascist rhetoric.

Moreover, the main totalitarian versions of Leftism, like Fascism, National Socialism, and Stalinism, are considered aberrations from mainstream

Marxism. However, 21st-century events suggest that Marxism itself was instead an aberration, a heretical branch of mainstream Leftism, not the other way around. For example, many modern Marxists dropped Marxism's well-known and cherished maxims, like the proletarian revolution, the abolition of private property, and other labor-related demands. Moreover, Marxism is just one of the numerous derivatives of Leftism popularized by tyrannical Soviet Union leaders. When Marxism lost its dominance, the world realized that Fascism, Communism/Marxism, National Socialism, Statism, and many others were sub-ideologies that branched off from a common ideological ancestor, Leftism. Note that Leftism, contrary to some of its spinoffs, like Fascism, is a perennial doctrine.

All offshoots of Leftism are just degenerate versions of the same ideology. Leftism is a genus of many species (read: specific ideologies). After World War II, many new species entered the world: Critical Theory, Woke, Postmodernism, Queer Theory, Post Colonial Theory, and countless others. Some of them are Marxian, but some are not. Nuanced differences exist between the natural offspring, but all worship the state in their quest for raw power. In the grand scheme of things, every modern Leftist has been a Nazi in ideological embryo. Marxism, Fascism, Progressivism, Statism, Wokeism, etc., are simply marketing campaigns for Leftism, different avenues in pursuit of the same goal.

As it happened, Collectivists transformed the postulate of the dictatorship of the proletariat into the dictatorship in the name of the proletariat. (Note that humans are preconditioned to believe that a dictatorship is a one-man show. However, modern Collectivists have altered that notion: the proposed supranational dictatorship is planned to be a collective dictatorship.) They understand that dictatorship is "natural" in the sense that it is a confirmed "path of least resistance." Free societies are not "free," for they require a constant influx of energy to overcome their inherent instability. Dictatorship offers stability—the stability of a penal colony. The distance from the Nanny State to the Warden State is lengthy but straightforward.

The class-oriented (read: labor-oriented) strains of Leftism were dominant in the 20th century but now are leaving the political arena. Some Marxists worldwide still adhere to this 19th-century orthodoxy, but the majority accept the hard truth—for the labor movement to survive, labor demands must be dropped. Unfortunately, that leaves them with mainstream Leftism—a totalitarian ideology of enslavement.

The individual-state paradigm brings so much clarity to here, and to other century-old questions. At the moment, the survival of orthodox Marxism (with or without the "neo" prefix) has never looked more precarious. The fundamental reassessment of Victorian Marxism is long overdue.[82] Only unorthodox, deproletarized Marxism—emasculated from the proletarians-related issues and slogans—has a chance of survival. However, in such a form, it will not be different from mainstream Leftism: the illiberal and misanthropic ideology. Despite the palpable lack of achievements, apparent setbacks, sufferings, and chaos instigated by the Globalists, the situation is somewhat rational because modern Globalism is Leftism pushed to its logical limits.

The rise and fall of the Soviet Union marked the beginning and the end of Marxism's appeal and popularity worldwide. However, faded Marxism does not mean disappearing Leftism. Dilapidated Victorian Marxism is no longer a force to be concerned about, but modern Leftists are out of the ideological asylum. The anti-globalization (anti-Americanization) Left circa 2000 is no more. They no longer promote outdated, unpractical, and ramshackle Marxist dogmas regarding the inevitability of workers' revolution and proletarian dictatorship—they

Leftism activates the downfall of every culture it penetrates because the Left oversupplies mediocrity while the Right oversupplies meritocracy.

decided to proceed straight to dictatorship. Globalism (modern Leftism) is an incoherent and fluid synthesis of classical Marxism, remnants of racial Socialism, and globalist elements of Trotskyism.

Contrary to Conservatism, Leftism is known for denying the power of law and affirming the law of power. As a result, Leftism activates the downfall of every culture it penetrates because the Left oversupplies mediocrity while the Right oversupplies meritocracy. It is no longer feasible to hypothesize that Leftism is a positive cash value ideology; it has been empirically proven that

---

82. James Lindsay has a fascinating theory that Victorian Marxism and some non-Marxian versions of Leftism are strongly influenced by Gnosticism, the secret parasitic religion (or rather a cult). However, a big difference exists between worshipping an essentially non-material deity and worshipping an explicitly material state. Thus, Leftism is only tangentially connected to Gnosticism.

Leftism offers only negative cash value for any society but presents a clear path to self-aggrandizement for wannabe *Führers*.

For everyone who at least somehow knows how to add up cause-and-effect relationships, it becomes apparent that historically, Leftism has been wholly debunked. Leftism could be compared to a piece of donkey droppings (at least from the American frame of mind) on humanity's Road to Freedom. It is stuck on the wheel of history and periodically reaches the top of it. While on top, the Left wrests the wheel of history and turns toward the road of illiberal fundamentalism by demanding total control of every aspect of human lives. In the process, they bulldoze to prove that they are the ones who do the turning. Unfortunately for them, however, the wheel keeps turning without paying much attention to a granule of somebody's ideological excrement. Every time Leftists come to power, it sparks a noticeable devolution of society. As a result, the smelly substance—commonly known as the Marxian "specter of communism"—will unavoidably hit the ground repeatedly.

However, instead of a movement on a wheel of history, the Leftist worldview could be better observed as a movement on the Möbius strip: while it moves, evolves, and produces many offspring, it is inherently one-sided. Like the unorientable Möbius strip, Leftism cannot be reoriented: no reforms, discussions, or setbacks can alter its primary objective of enslaving the people or catalyze its eventual exposé. That is why all Leftist strains ultimately culminate in a coercive government, either authoritative or tyrannical.

In a sense, a Collectivist monoideological paradise is a ghost of Schrödinger's cat: while the box is closed, it is not there at all; when the box is open, it is dead on arrival. Thus, the Great Reset is not what the Collectivists think it will be. Instead, long before a worldwide Utopia is uttered, Big Government will be reset, along with public education, public health, and law enforcement. Top-down management will end. Citizens will take back power. Leftism will experience widespread revulsion; it will be reset (and collectively perceived) to its primordial condition as the ideology of tyrants. Ultimately, everybody will see Globalists as erudite, charming, and murderous commissars. De-Nazification following World War II was the right step. A massive de-Globalization is required to confront the Nazi's distant relatives, the Globalists. However, please be advised that, like 20th-century Marxists, 21st-century Leftists cannot be bribed, cajoled, or persuaded to nullify their aggressive imperialistic resolve.

Please make no mistake: the WEF's open non-conspiracy is real. Regrettably, it is often compared to Ian Fleming's fictitious SPECTRE, with the Evil mastermind Ernst Stavro Blofeld (or his parody supervillain, Dr. Evil) at the helm. However, the entire SPECTRE enterprise would be just a single line in the enormous WEF project plan for the unobtainable total victory. Ultimately, the current incarnation of Left Imperialism will fail because it has nothing to offer—not in the long run or the short term. Unfortunately, that spectacular failure will mark the beginning of the new cycle of the battle between Good and Evil that surprisingly always produces Good.

Like Kipling's Mowgli, the Left Imperialists are screaming the Master Words—"We be of one blood, you and I," but there is no answer from the bygone Fascists. There is something grimly comic that the Left counter-Enlightenment agenda has devoured them all.

Chapter
4

Summa Ideologicae

This chapter is devoted to definitions. Readers who have read previous chapters may find the following definitions somewhat banal. Even so, they still have the advantage of generally being true, especially when it comes to ideologies we keep learning from at an ever-expanding pace, even though they are long gone.

This chapter was originally intended to be short, containing only one-sentence definitions of various ideologies. However, while compiling the definitions, certain exceptions were discovered that required a lengthy explanation. It is imperative to mention that these exceptions are dual in nature. First, they may be a direct consequence of the Gödel incompleteness theorem inherent in axiomatic theories. Second, some ideologies are incoherent and self-contradictory. Socialism, for example, has a solid core, while its principles and methods of forced egalitarianism are fluid. In general, the nobility of Leftist rhetoric cannot be reconciled with the despotic systems they created.

Liberalism was an ideology that advocated the primacy of people's wealth over government wealth.

Conservatism is an ideology that advocates the primacy of people's wealth over government wealth.

These two definitions are practically the same—intentionally—but their equivalence corresponds to a limited set of space-time points. It should be noted, again, that such equivalency exists solely within the one-dimensional individual-state paradigm.

Leftism is an ideology that advocates the primacy of government wealth over people's wealth.

Capitalism is a state of society where most wealth, both *de jure* and *de facto*, belongs to its people.

Socialism is a state of society where most wealth, either *de jure* or *de facto*, belongs to a government.

Fascism is a form of Socialism where most wealth *de facto* but not *de jure* belongs to a government.

Communism (*Marxism*) is a Utopian form of Socialism where the entire wealth, *de jure* and *de facto*, belongs to a non-existing government.

Globalism is a Utopian form of Socialism, where most wealth in most countries *de jure* belongs to their respective oligarchs, but the supranational body *de facto* rules over the countries.

Feudalism is a state of society where most wealth, both *de jure* and *de facto*, belongs to a small exclusive group titled noblemen, which *de jure* governs a country.

Oligarchic capitalism is a state of society where most wealth, both *de jure* and *de facto*, belongs to a small exclusive group called oligarchs, which *de facto* governs a country.

Maoism is a form of Socialism where wealth allocation between people and government is under stringent government control.

Bolshevism is a method of mostly *de facto* massive wealth confiscation and redistribution.

Menshevism is a method of mostly *de jure* massive wealth confiscation and redistribution.

Leninism (*Stalinism*) is a method of preserving Socialism by terror.

Trotskyism is a method of preserving Socialism by exporting it from one country to another.

It should be noted that these definitions are direct corollaries of the individual-state paradigm, and readers who have already read the preceding chapters do not need any additional explanations. Moreover, these definitions are atemporal, meaning they are valid regardless of the evolutionary perturbations and modifications.

Still, some readers may consider the definition above surprising. That is because they are pre-conditioned to evaluate some ideologies—like Fascism, for example—by their tactics or Auschwitz-Birkenau Museum instead of their ideology. The individual-state paradigm provides certainty regarding the differences between Conservatives and Liberals, the Right and the Left. However, just like Communism, Anarchism must be evaluated somewhat differently. It must be examined on two levels: based on its heralded dogmas and the basis of its actual practices. They have hardly any or no relation to each other, but that is a symptom of all Utopian schemes.

In terms of history, Anarchism has always been an extraordinary phenomenon. Is it possible to provide a rigorous definition of a subject that is inherently (and in many cases deliberately) vague and contradictory? Is it possible to rationalize the irrational? Anarchists have attempted to reverse the clock since the 19th century by denying the outcomes of human self-organization. Although moving from a well-organized to an unorganized society requires relatively little energy, Anarchism will remain a Utopian concept.

Anarchists need to plan their actions based on the political reality that exists on the ground, as it is for all Leftists. However, their Utopian worldview is constantly at odds with the realities of life. In most cases, it even contradicts the dominant narrative. Many countries' existence and distinct hopes in the international arena united Communists and Anarchists at the beginning of the 20th century. Moreover, Utopian egalitarianism still unites anarchists and Globalists in their political quest.

In general, anarchists oppose the natural self-organization of humans, known as "government." They view the government as the ultimate oppressor, regardless of the form in which it is instituted. However, to be fair to Anarchism, most of human history has been characterized by oppressive forms of government. The Anarchist philosophy assumes that there will be no non-coercive governments as a matter of principle, since it accepts the coercive nature of the state as a given. Compare the anarchists' logic with Marxism. In line with Marx's logic, if private property is outlawed and eventually disappears, then the primary responsibility of government, the protection of private property, ceases to exist. Therefore, Marxists have consistently regarded anarchists as junior partners rather than equal partners; they knew that private property and an evaporated government could not coexist.

From the anarchists' point of view, "when government is abolished, wage slavery and capitalism must also go with it, because they cannot exist without the support and protection of government" (Berkman 1929, p. 185). The question of private wealth for anarchists has a simple solution: "Such a condition of things where there would be liberty instead of government would be Anarchy. And where equality of use would take the place of private ownership, would be Communism. It would be Communist Anarchism" (Ibid). Next, under Anarchism, "no one will be permitted to monopolize the land or the machinery of production. It means that private ownership of the *sources of life* will not be tolerated" (Ibid., p. 184). As direct proof that Anarchism is just another collectivization scheme, Berkman stated that the "meaning of Communist Anarchism is this: the abolition of government, of coercive authority and all its agencies, and joint ownership—which means free and equal participation in the general work and welfare" (Ibid., p. 196). Of course, the "equal pay" will go along with "joint ownership," because "labor is social, it stands to reason that the results of it, the wealth produced, must also be social, belong to the collectivity" (Ibid.)

Customary to the Leftists, anarchists offer smashing observations of political currents and society's evolution. For example, French philosopher Pierre-Joseph Proudhon (who coined the expression, "Property is theft!") wrote in 1849 in a short-lived newspaper *La Voix du Peuple* (notice the 19th-century political vocabulary):

"The Church said in times past, speaking like a tender mother: 'All for the people, but all by the priests.'

The Monarchy came after the Church: 'All for the people, but all by the Prince.'

The Doctrinaires: 'All for the people, but all by the Bourgeoisie.'

The Radicals changed the formula, but failed to change the principle: 'All for the people, but all by the State.'

It is always the same governmentalism, the same communism.

Who then is going to finally conclude: 'All for the people, all by the people, including the government'?"

A passage such as the one above illustrates why the Anarchist/Communist Sirens are widespread today despite quite a troubling past implementing it. A well-known example of anarchist societies can be found in some parts of South Ukraine in the aftermath of the post-communist revolution's bloody civil war between 1917 and 1922. Several prominent anarchists set up states (sorry, "communities") there, containing many farm families interacting loosely with each other and the outside world. There was no doubt that wealth belonged to the people, but their lives resembled self-imprisonment behind the walls of their farmhouses. The formal government, law, and order were absent, but the conceptualization of freedom, as understood under the individual-state paradigm, was absent, too. All these Anarchist communes were short-lived, for they became attractive takeover targets for neighboring states, primarily Communist Russia.

However, rejecting a naturally occurring government leaves people at the mercy of an infinitely intolerant mob. One of the guiding principles of the directionless mob is that there are no principles at all. The nullification of self-structurization does not beget people "free." Instead, it makes them as unfree as one can imagine. As long as the mob "rules," there are no minorities since they cannot and do not exist in the mob's jargon. Only one freedom is honored in anarchy: the right to die if one dares to stand up to the mob. As a result of Anarchism, everyone must obey "the current thing" as dictated by the fickle mob rather than the "freedom to do as one pleases."

As soon as the government is removed from the picture, the only thing left is ochlocracy ("mob rule"). In the absence of a government, the "rule of the masses" replaces the "rule of the law" (even if there are well-established laws that govern mob behavior). In the view of anarchists, the abolition of government is a prelude to absolute freedom. The result is that men are disengaged from the government-established level of unfreedom and are delivered into the realm of the mob's absolute unfreedom. In addition to abolishing the government, Communists and German National Socialists acknowledged that the ochlocracy posed a significant danger to society, too. That is why they invariably complement it with a program aimed at "creating new men."

As in physics, if a political philosophy disregards one particular frame of reference, an infinite number of alternative frames can be used as a benchmark. Followers of such an ideology are forced to invent something artificial, such as the existence of freedom within the mob camp. They must use pretzel logic to convince all others that dropping one particular frame of reference was the right decision. In point of fact, it appears quite strange to physicists.

They know many suitable frames of reference exist, but merely a few make logical sense. For example, it is logical to describe the movement of a car against a frame of reference called "Earth" in preference to a frame of reference anchored at the center of the Milky Way galaxy. Continuing the analogy, Anarchism is a political philosophy that situates itself at the center of its own frame of reference.

As with all left-wing theories, Anarchism asserts that government is based solely on coercion instead of consent. However, the consent part was the cornerstone of the Enlightenment and should be viewed as one of the critical turning points between the Left and the Right. Due to this, anarchists, like libertarians, artificially overemphasize freedom, although they misunderstand and misinterpret it.

Anarchism belongs to the category of resolutions described by Mencken: "[T]here is always a well-known solution to every human problem—neat, plausible, and wrong" (Mencken 1920, p. 158). Anarchists placed the coercive, authoritarian state on the pedestal of absolute Evil; thus, getting rid of a state became an *idée fixe* for them, regardless of its practicality. Such ideas have microscopic cash value, and human history is proof of it. However, Anarchists offered something beneficial—a well-reasoned critique of Marxism, especially the idea of proletarian dictatorship.

Throughout the 19th century, Marx's leading ideological rival was Russian revolutionary socialist Mikhail Bakunin ("revolutionary socialist" was the 19th-century common moniker for anarchists). For example, he highlighted the apparent differences between Marx and Bismarck but also spotted something that unites them against anarchism: "It is the out and out cult of the State" (Bakunin [1867] 2010, p. 21).[83]

Anarchism, per Bakunin, is against liberty that is "licensed, measured, and regulated by the State" (Bakunin [1867] 2010, p. 12). He argues—in a classical left-wing manner—that "liberty must establish itself in the world by the spontaneous organization of labor and of collective ownership by productive associations freely organized and federalized in districts and by the equally spontaneous federation of districts, but not by the supreme and tutelary action of the State" (Ibid., p. 13). Confronting Marx in 1867, Bakunin,

---

83. Bakunin had something in common with Marx—both were ardent antisemites.

the founder of Anarcho-Collectivism, stressed that "[t]he Communists believe they must organize the workers' forces to take possession of the political power of the State. The Revolutionary Socialists organize with a view to the destruction, or if you prefer a politer word, the liquidation of the State" (Ibid., p. 13-14). For Communists, "[t]he State having become sole proprietor...the State will be also the only Capitalist, banker; money-lender, organizer, director of all national labor and distributor of its products. Such is the ideal, the fundamental principle of modern Communism" (Ibid., p. 19).

Anarchism claims to provide maximum freedom but should be treated with caution. As seen from the perspective of the individual-state paradigm, the vision of "freedom" is simply a term within the umbrella of government-to-governed transactions. In the absence of government, society is categorically unfree. The critical point is that the absence of government does not equal zero government. It is similar to the situation in physics, particularly when measuring the temperature of outer space. Temperature measurement requires interaction between two physical bodies (one of which is a thermometer). Due to the almost vacuum situation, there is no thermodynamic interaction; consequently, there is no "temperature" to speak of.

As nature abhors a vacuum, so does politics abhor a vacuum of power. The claimed non-governed states could not survive any dedicated aggressor, and both anarchists and communists who call for the dissolution of the government are aware of this fact. While Communism and Anarchism are Utopian, dead-end branches of Leftism, Globalism could be viewed as a more or less rationally expected, natural outcome of Leftist theories. Starting with Trotsky, the idea is a) to dissolve national governments (this is the part anarchists and communists agree on) and b) to set up a supranational state. Local administrations would remain in a conventional form for some time. However, a complete structure would feature a decentralized worldwide governing body for over two hundred or so satellite colonies (sorry, "states"). The relationship between the worldwide governing body and satellite "states" would be a pattern of the relationship between a Metropole and its colonies, equating such a global structure with reformulated imperialism. Thus, Leftists in the 21st century are carriers of the imperial mentality inherited from Soviet and Fascist imperialism of the 20th century. There is no room for anarchists in the Globalists' worldview.

Anarchists are unmistaken that governments and society exert pressure on individuals. Additionally, they recognize that society's pressure cannot be eliminated in principle, so they concentrate all their efforts on eliminating the government. However, they fail to realize that society has a non-linear character. Thus, even if the government part of the "oppression" is suddenly removed, the societal part will rise to replace it. Typically, this occurs in the form of mob rule. Anarchists believe that the stateless "community" is capable of governing itself. However, as reality sets in, it resembles the jungle rule as a substitute for the rule of law.

In truth, the structure based on the formal rules of government and the informal rules of society has proven to be an evolutionary winner. The symbiotic relationship between society and the state, one of its self-organizing masterpieces, provides an excellent example of synergy when the resulting structure is more robust than the sum of its parts. Removing a critical pillar of human civilization leaves society at the mercy of the herd, which is why Anarchism is usually associated with chaos. However, the theory of Anarchism does not advocate chaos. Chaos is one of those unexpected consequences that are regularly present in all Utopian schemes. Moreover, modern anarchists openly "admit that Anarchism is entirely impractical" (Sartwell 2008, p. 6).

There is a problem with correctly attributing Anarchism to the Right or Left ideologies. A proper answer to such a classification must address the incoherence and contradictions inherent in Anarchism. For example, according to one of Anarchism's theoretical foundations, this philosophy might appear to be in the Right column since it presumably nullifies government and government wealth as well. However, Anarchism also nullifies private property along with government property, making it a solid Leftist ideology. There is no reason to consider such contradictions as cognitive dissonance since they arise directly from Anarchism's conflicting foundations, not from the individual-state paradigm.

The nuances between Communism and Anarchism were brilliantly highlighted by a prominent Anarchism theoretician, Alexander Berkman, in 1929. Per Berkman, Communists (Bolsheviks) "want a powerful government or State, while Anarchism means doing away with the State or government altogether...[T]hey want their dictatorship, their government, to compel people to live in Communism. Anarchist Communism, on the contrary, means voluntary Communism, Communism from free choice" (Berkman 1929, p. 185).

Essentially, Communism and Anarchism are two Leftist Utopian schemes with a fundamental difference: Communism emphasizes forced equality, while Anarchism emphasizes unenforced equality. However, the "equality" category only emerges in the context of government interaction. Therefore, it opens up to the inevitable conclusion that Communism and Anarchism are unworkable. Quixotic attempts to prove otherwise are naïve, just like the anarchists' notion that crime will wither away along with the state.

Nobody knows Leftists better than their peers. As such, Bakunin offered a sober warning to the left-wing revolutionaries: "After a brief moment of liberty or revolutionary orgy, citizens of a new State, they will awake to find themselves slaves, playthings and victims of new power-lusters" (Bakunin [1867] 2010, p. 45). The countless number of left-wing coups worldwide meticulously followed the startling prophecy.

Finally, in Anarchism, two main factions exist; the difference between them is the same as that between the rest of the Leftist movement: revolutionaries and evolutionists. The revolutionary movement insists the government must be abolished through a social revolution. For example, "We think that the necessarily revolutionary policy of the proletariat must have for its immediate and only object the destruction of States" (Bakunin [1867] 2010, p. 33). In contrast, evolutionists prefer a "natural" path to eliminate government (Proudhon). Nevertheless, this is beyond the scope of this book.

Anarchism is a Utopian form of Socialism where a non-existent government exists.

AFTERWORD

Who is John Galt? You are.

BIBLIOGRAPHY

Addicott, David A. C. 2017. "The Rise and Fall of the Zaibatsu: Japan's Industrial and Economic Modernization." *Global Tides* (Pepperdine University) 11.

Allitt, Patrick. 2009. *The Conservatives: Ideas, Personalities Throughout American History.* New Haven: Yale University Press.

Auken, Ida. 2016. "Welcome To 2030: I Own Nothing, Have No Privacy And Life Has Never Been Better." *Forbes.* https://www.forbes.com/sites/worldeconomicforum/2016/11/10/shopping-i-cant-really-remember-what-that-is-or-how-differently-well-live-in-2030/?sh=558a7ca01735).

Bakunin, Mikhail. [1867] 2010. *Marxism, Freedom And The State.* Translated by K. J. Kenafick. Whitefish: Kessinger Publishing.

Ball, Terence. 1995. *Reappraising Political Theory: Revisionist Studies in the History of Political Thought.* Oxford: Clarendon Press.

Bastiat, Frederick. [1850] 1998. *The Law.* Irvington-on-Hudson: Foundation for Economic Education.

Bazhanov, Boris. [1930] 1990. *Bazhanov and the Damnation of Stalin.* Translated by David W. Doyle. Ohio University Press.

BBC. 2021. *Charles to say 'war-like footing' needed.* November 1. https://www.bbc.com/news/uk-59115203.

Beck, Glenn, and Haskins, Justin Trask. 2022. *The Great Reset: Joe Biden and the Rise of Twenty-First-Century Fascism.* Kindle. Brentwood: Forefront Books.

Beevor, Antony. 2006. *The Battle for Spain: The Spanish Civil War 1936-1939.* New York: Penguin Books.

Berdyaev, Nicolas. [1923] 2015. *The Philosophy of Inequality: Letters to my Contemners, Concerning Social Philosophy.* Translated by Fr. S. Janos. frsj Publications.

Bergh, Andreas and Henrekson, Magnus. 2011. "Government Size and Growth: A Survey and Interpretation of the Evidence." *Journal of Economic Surveys* 25 (5): 872-897.

Berkman, Alexander. 1929. *Now and After. The ABC of Communist Anarchism.* New York: Vanguard Press.

Berle, Adolf A., and Gardiner C. Means. [1932] 1999. *The Modern Corporation and Private Property.* New Brunswick: Transaction Publishers.

Bernstein, Eduard. [1899] 1993. *The Preconditions for Socialism.* Translated by Henry Tudor. Cambridge: Cambridge University Press.

Black, Conrad. 2022. "The War on Capitalism." In *Against the Great Reset: Eighteen Theses Contra the New World Order*, edited by Michael Walsh. Bombardier Books.

Bosworth, R.J.B. 2006. *Mussolini's Italy. Life under the Fascist Dictatorship*. New York: Penguin Books.

Bruner, Seamus. 2023. *Controligarchs: Exposing the Billionaire Class, their Secret Deals, and the Globalist Plot to Dominate Your Life*. New York: Sentinel.

Burke, Edmund. [1790] 2003. *Reflections on the Revolution in France*. Edited by Frank M. Turner. New Heaven: Yale University Press.

Business Roundtable. 2016. "Principles of Corporate Governance."

Business Roundtable. 1997. "Statement on Corporate Governance."

Business Roundtable. 2019. "Statement on the Purpose of a Corporation."

Canaparo, GianCarlo. 2022. *Why Corporate Environmental, Social, and Governance Enforcement Is Self-Reinforcing Scam*. June 9. https://www.heritage.org/progressivism/commentary/why-corporate-environmental-social-and-governance-enforcement-self.

Chaitin, Gregory J. 1999. *The Unknowable*. Springer.

Chomsky, Noam. 1988. *Language and Politics*. Edited by C.P. Otero. Montreal, New York: Black Rose Books.

Corcoran, Terence. 2021. *The murky rise of Klaus Schwab's stakeholder 'capitalism' and the WEF's Davos corporate plan*. January 22. https://financialpost.com/opinion/terence-corcoran-the-murky-rise-of-stakeholder-capitalism.

Cruz, Ted. 2023. *Unwoke: How to Defeat Cultural Marxism in America*. Washington, DC: Regnery Publishing.

Curry, Robert. 2023. *UnLocke-ing the American Founders*. February 2. https://www.americanthinker.com/articles/2023/02/unlockeing_the_american_founders.html.

David Chambers, Carsten Burhop, and Brian Cheffins. 2016. *The Rise and Fall of the German Stock Market, 1870-1938*. Department of Economic and Social History at the University of Cambridge, University of Cambridge.

Delzell, Charles F. 1988. "Remembering Mussolini." *The Wilson Quarterly* 12 (2): 118-135.

Domarus, Max. 1990. *Hitler. Speeches and Proclamations 1932–1945*. Translated by Wolfgang Domarus. Wauconda: Bolchazy-Carducci Publishers.

D'Souza, Dinesh. 2017. *The Big Lie: Exposing the Nazi Roots of the American Left*. Washington, D.C.: Regnery Publishing.

Dunn, Charles W., Woodward, David J. 2000. *The Conservative Tradition in America.* Rowman & Littlefield Publishers.

Durant, Will. [1926] 1962. *The story of philosophy: the lives and opinions of the great philosophers of the Western world.* New York: Simon & Schuster.

Epstein, Mikhail. 2021. *Ideas Against Ideocracy: Non-Marxist Thought of the Late Soviet Period (1953–1991).* New York: Bloomsbury Academic.

FAIR Report. 2023. "The Fiscal Burden of Illegal Immigration on United States Taxpayers ." Federation for American Immigration Reform, Washington. https://www.fairus.org/sites/default/files/2023-03/Fiscal Burden of Illegal Immigration on American Taxpayers 2023 WEB_1.pdf.

Feynman, Richard. 1974. "Cargo Cult Science." *Engineering and Science* 37.

Fohlin, Caroline. 2007. "The History of Corporate Ownership and Control in Germany." In *A History of Corporate Governance around the World*, edited by Randall K. Morck, 223-281. Chicago: The University of Chicago Press.

Freeden, Michael, Mark Stears, and Lyman Sargent. 2013. *The Oxford Handbook of Political Ideologies.* Oxford: Oxford University Press.

Freeman, R. Edward. 1984. *Strategic Management: A Stakeholder Approach.* Marshfield: Pitman Publishing.

Friedman, Milton. 1982. *Capitalism and Freedom.* Chicago: The University of Chicago Press.

——. 1970. "The Social Responsibility of Business is to Increase its Profits." *The New York Times Magazine.*

Gauchet, Marcel. 1996. "Right and Left." In *Realms of Memory: Rethinking the French Past, Vol. 1*, edited by Pierre Nora, 241-300. New York: Columbia University Press.

Gindler, Gary. 2020. *Dynamics of Meaning.* December 21. https://arxiv.org/abs/2108.09179.

——. 2019. *Introduction to Politiphysics.* https://osf.io/preprints/socarxiv/xacpn/.

Goldberg, Johah. 2008. *Liberal Fascism: The Secret History of the American Left, From Mussolini to the Politics of Meaning.* New York: Doubleday.

Goodchild, Peter. 2004. *Edward Teller, the Real Dr. Strangelove.* Harvard University Press.

Google Ngram. 2019. *Conservative/Liberal.* https://books.google.com/ngrams/graph?content=conservative%2Cliberal&year_start=1789&year_end=2000&corpus=en-2012&smoothing=0&case_insensitive=true.

——. 2019. *Right-wing/Left-wing.* https://books.google.com/ngrams/graph?content=left-wing%2Cright-wing&year_start=1789&year_end=2000&corpus=en-2012&smoothing=0&case_insensitive=true.

Gratzer, Walter. 2002. *Eurekas and Euphorias.* Oxford: Oxford University Press.

Greene, Russell. 2022. *What Are the Aims of Business?* December 6. https://lawliberty.org/forum/what-are-the-aims-of-business/.

Gregg, Samuel. 2022. *The Next American Economy: Nation, State, and Markets in an Uncertain World.* EPUB. New York: Encounter Books.

Gurfinkiel, Michel. 2015. *Jewish Conservatism: The Moment is Ripe.* June 4. https://www.meforum.org/5298/jewish-conservatism.

Hanson, Victor Davis. 2022. "The Great Regression." In *Against The Great Reset.* New York: Bombardier Books.

Hazony, Yoram. 2022. *Conservatism: A Rediscovery.* EPUB. Washington, DC: Regnery Gateway.

Henry, Robert Selph. 1999. *The Story of the Confederacy.* Old Saybrook: Konecky & Konecky.

Hessen, Robert. n.d. *In Defense of the Corporation.* 1979: Hoover Institution Press.

Hull, Raymond and Laurence J. Peter. 1969. *The Peter Principle.* London: Pan Books.

Hülsmann, Jörg Guido. 2007. *Mises: The Last Knight Of Liberalism.* Auburn: Ludwig von Mises Institute.

Jaffa, Harry V. 2009. *Crisis of the House Divided: An Interpretation of the Issues in the Lincoln-Douglas Debates.* Chicago and London: The University of Chicago Press.

James, William. 1898. "Philosophical Conceptions and Practical Results." *University Chronicle* 1 (4).

Jeffreys, Diarmuid. 2008. *Hell's cartel: IG Farben and the making of Hitler's war machine.* EPUB. New York: Metropolitan Books.

Kessler, William Conrad. 1938. "The German Corporation Law of 1937." *American Economic Review* (American Economic Association) 28 (4): 653-662.

Kirk, Russell. 2001. *The conservative mind: from Burke to Eliot.* Washington, DC: Regnery Publishing.

Kolakowski, Leszek. 1983. *Totalitarianism & the Lie.* May. https://www.commentary.org/articles/leszek-kolakowski/totalitarianism-the-lie/.

Krauthammer, Charles. 2013. *Things That Matter.* New York: Random House.

Kuntz, Thilo. 2018. "German corporate law in the 20th century." In *Research Handbook on the History of Corporate and Company Law.* Cheltenham: Edward Elgar Publishing.

Laherrère, J., Sornette, D. 1998. "Stretched exponential distributions in nature and economy: "fat tails" with characteristic scales." *Eur. Phys. J. B* 2: 525–539.

Lenin, Vladimir. [1899] 1964. *A Retrograde Trend in Russian Social-Democracy.* Vol. 4, in *Collected Works*, 255-285. Moscow: Progress Publishers.

Levin, Mark R. 2021. *American Marxism.* New York: Threshold Editions.

Lukacs, John. 2005. *Democracy and Populism.* New Haven: Yale University Press.

Lyttelton, Adrian. 2004. *The Seizure of Power: Fascism in Italy, 1919-1929.* New York: Routledge.

Magness, Phillip W., and Michael Makovi. 2022. *Das Karl Marx Problem.* November 16. https://www.aier.org/article/das-karl-marx-problem/.

Manchester, William. 2017. *The Arms of Krupp.* EPUB. New York: Little, Brown and Company.

Mann, Robert. 2019. *Becoming Ronald Reagan: The Rise of a Conservative Icon.* Lincoln: Potomac Books.

Marx, Karl and Engels, Friedrich. [1861] 1975. *Marx-Engels Collected Works.* Vol. 41. Moscow: Progress Publishers.

Marx, Karl. [1852] 2010. "Letter to Joseph Weydemeyer in New York, 5 March 1852." In *Marx & Engels Collected Works Vol.39* . Lawrence & Wishart.

——. [1844] 1988. *The Economic and Philosophic Manuscripts of 1844.* Prometheus Books.

Marx, Karl, and Engels, Frederick. [1862] 1984. *Marx & Engels Collected Works.* Vol. 19. Lawrence & Wishart.

Masters, Roger D. 1983. "The Biological Nature of the State." *World Politics* (The Johns Hopkins University Press) 35 (2): 161-193.

Mencken, Henry Louis. 1920. *Prejudices: Second Series.* Vol. 2. New York: Alfred A. Knopf.

Nader, Ralph and Mark Green. 1975. "Reforming The Corporate Economy: The Case For Federal Charters." In *Hearings, Reports and Prints of the Joint Economic Committee, Parts 1-5. 94th Congress*, 1310-1316. US Government Printing Office.

Nader, Ralph, Green, Mark, and Seligman, Joel. 1976. *Taming the Giant Corporation.* New York: W.W. Norton and Company.

Nash, George H. 2006. *The Conservative Intellectual Movement in America Since 1945.* EPUB. Wilmington: ISI Books.

O'Sullivan, John. 1989. "O'Sullivan's First Law." *National Review* 14.

O'Sullivan, Noel. 2023. *Postface. Has Conservatism a Future?* February 3. http://journals.openedition.org/rfcb/10633.

Olson, Mancur. 1971. *The Logic of Collective Action: Public Goods and the Theory of Groups.* Cambridge: Harvard University Press.

Orwell, George. 2013. *George Orwell: A Life in Letters*. Edited by Peter Davison. New York: Liveright.

———. 1968. "The Collected Essays, Journalism and Letters of George Orwell, Vol. III. As I Please: 1943–1945."

———. 1944. "Grounds for Dismay." *The Observer*, April 9: 3.

———. 1944. "What is Fascism?" *Tribune*, March 24.

Palm, Franklin Charles. 1920. *The Economic Policies of Richelieu*. University of Illinois.

Podritske, Marlene and Peter Schwartz, ed. 2009. *Objectively Speaking: Ayn Rand Interviewed*. Lexington Books.

Ramus, Petrus. [1569] 2006. May 9. https://plato.stanford.edu/entries/ramus/.

Ray, John. 2004. "Explaining The Left/Right Divide." *Society* 70-78.

Revel, Jean-Francois. 2009. *Last Exit to Utopia*. New York: Encounter Books.

Röpke, Wilhelm. 1935. "Fascist Economics." *Economica* 2 (5): 85-100.

Rorty, Richard. 1987. "Thugs and Theorists: A Reply to Bernstein." *Political Theory* (Sage Publications, Inc.) 15 (4): 564-580.

Rossiter, Clinton. 1982. *Conservatism in America*. Cambridge: Harvard University Press.

Rufo, Christopher F. 2023. *America's Cultural Revolution: How the Radical Left Conquered Everything*. New York: Broadside Books.

Saad, Gad. 2021. *The Parasitic Mind: How Infectious Ideas Are Killing Common Sense*. Washington: Regnery Publishing.

Sartwell, Crispin. 2008. *Against the state: an introduction to anarchist political theory*. Albany: State University of New York Press.

Schuman, Frederick L. 1934. "The Political Theory of German Fascism." *The American Political Science Review* 28 (2): 210-232.

Schwab, Klaus. 2019. *Davos Manifesto 2020: The Universal Purpose of a Company in the Fourth Industrial Revolution*. December 2. https://www.weforum.org/agenda/2019/12/davos-manifesto-2020-the-universal-purpose-of-a-company-in-the-fourth-industrial-revolution.

———. 2022. *Full Speech at G20 / B20 Indonesia*. https://www.youtube.com/watch?v=u_vvq84X_rI).

———. 2020. *Now Is the Time for a 'Great Reset'*. June 3. https://www.weforum.org/agenda/2020/06/now-is-the-time-for-a-great-reset.

———. 2020. *Now is the time for a 'great reset'*. June 2. https://www.weforum.org/agenda/2020/06/now-is-the-time-for-a-great-reset/.

——. 2021. *Stakeholder Capitalism*. Hoboken: Willey.

Scruton, Roger. 2011. *Speaking Neatly*. July 27. https://spectator.org/speaking-neatly/.

——. 1984. *The Meaning of Conservatism*. London: MacMillan.

——. 2009. *Totalitarian Sentimentality*. December 9. https://spectator.org/40477_totalitarian-sentimentality/.

——. 2014. *What do Conservatives believe?* January 6. https://www.conservativehome.com/platform/2014/01/roger-scruton-what-do-conservatives-believe.html.

Shaw, Roger. 1934. "Fascism and the New Deal." *The North American Review* 238 (6): 559-564.

Simmel, George. [1909] 1994. "Bridge and Door." *Theory, Culture & Society* 11 (1): 5-10.

Snyder, Robert. 1975. "Huey Long and the Presidential Election of 1936." *Louisiana History: The Journal of the Louisiana Historical Association* 16: 117-143.

Sowell, Thomas. 1993. *Is reality Optional?* Stanford: Hoover Institution Press.

——. 1985. *Marxism: Philosophy and Economics*. George Allen & Unwin.

——. 2013. *The Left's Central Delusion*. July 5. https://www.nationalreview.com/2013/07/lefts-central-delusion-thomas-sowell/.

Stabile, Don R. 1987. "Veblen and the Political Economy of Technocracy: The Herald of Technological Revolution Developed an Ideology of 'Scientific' Collectivism." *The American Journal of Economics and Sociology* 46 (1): 35-48.

Sundance. 2023. *Ronna McDaniel Reveals the 2024 Secret Weapon the RNC Constructed to Defeat the Ballot Harvesting Process*. April 26. https://theconservativetreehouse.com/blog/2023/04/26/ronna-mcdaniel-reveals-the-2024-secret-weapon-the-rnc-constructed-to-defeat-the-ballot-harvesting-process/.

Tallarita, Roberto and Lucian A. Bebchuk. 2020. "The Illusory Promise of Stakeholder Governance." *Cornell Law Review* 106: 91-178.

Thatcher, Margaret. 1991. *Speech at Hoover Institution*. March 8. https://www.margaretthatcher.org/document/108264.

——. 1975. *Speech to Christian Democratic Union Conference*. May 25. https://www.margaretthatcher.org/document/103034.

——. 1978. *Speech to Conservative Central Council*. April 8. https://www.margaretthatcher.org/document/103651.

——. 1976. *Speech to Conservative Central Council*. March 20. https://www.margaretthatcher.org/document/102990.

——. 1988. *Speech to Conservative Party Conference*. October 14. https://www.margaretthatcher.org/document/107352.

———. 2003. *Speech to the Atlantic Bridge.* May 14. https://www.margaretthatcher.org/document/111266.

———. 2002. *Statecraft: strategies for a changing world.* London: Harper Collins Publishers.

———. 1976. *TV Interview for Thames TV "This Week".* February 5. https://www.margaretthatcher.org/document/102953.

The Farben Case. 1949. https://phdn.org/archives/www.mazal.org/archive/nmt/07/NMT07-T0558.htm.

The Global Compact. 2004. "Who Cares Wins—Connecting Financial Markets to a Changing World." June. https://www.ifc.org/wps/wcm/connect/topics_ext_content/ifc_external_corporate_site/sustainability-at-ifc/publications/publications_report_whocareswins__wci__1319579355342.

Thompson, C. Bradley. 2019. *America's Revolutionary Mind: A Moral History of the American Revolution and the Declaration That Defined It.* New York: Encounter Books.

Thorne, M.J. 1990. *American Conservative Thought Since World War II: The Core Ideas.* New York: Greenwood Press.

Trotsky, Leon. [1931] 2010. *The Permanent Revolution & results and prospects.* Translated by John G. Wright and Brian Pearce. Seatle: Red Letter Press.

———. [1928] 1957. *The Third International after Lenin.* Translated by John G. Wright. New York: Pioneer Publishers.

Veblen, Thorstein. [1921] 2001. *The Engineers and the Price System.* Batoche Books.

Vermeule, Adrian. 2021. *Catholic Constitutionalism: A Primer.* November 8. https://iusetiustitium.com/catholic-constitutionalism-a-primer/.

Watson, George. 2010. *The Lost Literature of Socialism.* Cambridge: The Lutterworth Press.

WEF. 2020. *The Great Reset: A Unique Twin Summit to Begin 2021.* June 3. https://www.weforum.org/press/2020/06/the-great-reset-a-unique-twin-summit-to-begin-2021/.

Whitman, James Q. 1991. "Of Corporatism, Fascism, and the First New Deal." *The American Journal of Comparative Law* 39: 747-778.

Index

ABOUT THE AUTHOR

DR. GARY GINDLER is an accomplished American columnist and distinguished political scientist, focusing primarily on anti-leftism and anti-communism.

Born in Ukraine to a military officer father and pediatric nurse mother, Dr. Gindler's upbringing required adherence to various military orders, leading the family to reside in multiple regions of the Soviet Union. He earned a Ph.D. in Theoretical Physics from the USSR Academy of Sciences, specializing in mathematical aspects of wave propagation in random media. In addition, he was one of Russia's Internet pioneers alongside colleagues from the Kurchatov Institute of Atomic Energy during the 1980s.

Having relocated to the United States in 1995, Dr. Gindler resides in New Jersey. His prolific writings have been featured in esteemed publications such as American Thinker, Frontpage Magazine, Human Events, New Right Network, and The Gateway Pundit, among others. A sought-after expert, he frequently participates in political talk shows in New York, Chicago, Israel, and Canada.

In 2019, Dr. Gindler introduced the groundbreaking science of Politiphysics, applying methods of mathematical physics to political economy. His notable achievements include providing a theoretical foundation for the Laffer Curve and presenting a mathematical definition of freedom.

Active on Twitter/X, Dr. Gindler predominantly shares his work through the Gary Gindler Chronicles website. Fluent in English, Russian, and Ukrainian, his lifelong hobby is Ham Radio, which he has cultivated since early childhood.